Settlements and Divisions
Ireland 1870-1922

PAURIC TRAVERS

First published 1988

Helicon Limited
Ballymount Road
Walkinstown
Dublin 12

Distributed by
The Educational Company of Ireland Limited
Ballymount Road, Walkinstown, Dublin 12

© Pauric Travers 1988

Cover: *Going to the Levee, Dublin Castle*
By Rose Barton, 1856-1929.
Courtesy of National Gallery of Ireland

Disk conversion: Softrans International Ltd.

Printed in the Republic of Ireland by
Criterion Press Limited, Dublin

CONTENTS

*For my mother and in memory of
my father, Henry John Travers*

Foreword

The growing interest in the history of Ireland in recent decades has led to a substantial increase in the number of scholars engaged in research and study. Old and cherished interpretations have been questioned, as historians discover new sources or ask new questions of the old. Much of this new thinking is, however, hidden from the public in learned journals, which are not easily accessible. The aim of this series of nine volumes is to make available to a wider readership the fruits of the most recent researches. Each volume is self-contained, and each author, a specialist in the field, has been free to put forward his own analysis of the period with which he deals. Taken together they form a lucid and stimulating account of Ireland's history from the earliest times.

Art Cosgrove,
Elma Collins,
General Editors

Preface

Inevitably in an undertaking such as this, one incurs considerable debts which are only partly repaid by public acknowledgement. My most immediate debts are to the joint editors of this series, Art Cosgrove and Elma Collins, and to my publishers who have been supportive, patient and helpful. Likewise I am indebted to my colleagues in the History Department at St Patrick's College, Drumcondra, Dr Paddy O'Donoghue and Dr Jimmy Kelly, for their comments on the text and for their general support and advice. I would also like to thank Éamon and Michael Travers for their comments on my typescript.

I am grateful to the staff of the various Archives and Libraries in which I worked. In addition, I should also thank the authors of the many specialist works on the period without which a general history such as this could not be written. Much of what I have written is based on my own original research but I have also consciously tried to adhere to the brief of the series by distilling the fruits of specialist scholarship for a more general audience.

Finally, and above all, I thank Mary Moore for her encouragement and understanding.

St Patrick's College,   *Pauric Travers*
Drumcondra
Dublin

Ireland: around 1870

Introduction

This book, as the title suggests, is primarily concerned with politics and political issues. In Ireland, the period 1870-1922 was one of settlements, attempted settlements and divisions. In particular, the upsurge of nationalism which occurred from the 1870s onwards dictated the political agenda and ultimately reshaped both the balance of power and the constitution. The land settlement of the late nineteenth and early twentieth century, which transferred the ownership of land from landlord to tenant, signalled the economic decline of the protestant ascendancy. The political settlement of 1920-22 which repealed the union with Britain and gave twenty-six counties dominion status, marked the victory of the nationalist movement outside the north-east of Ireland and at the same time enshrined partition. The major focus of this book is on this transformation.

Under the leadership of Isaac Butt, the early Home Rule movement of the 1870s was a modest affair with modest aims. Butt sought to reconcile his nationalism and his protestantism. His failure and the advent of Charles Stewart Parnell saw the adoption of a more aggressive approach in which the powerful appeal of the land question was used to further the Home Rule cause. The attribution of endemic agrarian problems to English rule fuelled both an insistent land agitation and the nationalist movement itself. Not that Parnell was a social revolutionary. His vision of a Home Rule Ireland was one in which the Anglo-Irish country gentleman retained his importance. Others of Parnell's class were less willing to flirt with nationalism but they did see the value of a constructive social and economic policy which would draw the teeth of nationalist discontent. The hiatus which followed the death of Parnell in 1891 gave the constructive unionist movement a valuable opportunity to prove the merits of *their* alternative policies. Their failure to win over moderate nationalist opinion sealed the fate of the Anglo-Irish and left the opposition to nationalism in the hands of a much more vociferous form of unionism. The shifting balance of power within Irish unionism, from south to north, which was finally accomplished during the Home Rule crisis of 1912-14, paved the way for partition.

If constructive unionism represented the last throw of the dice by the Anglo-Irish, the third Home Rule bill of 1912 represented the last realistic attempt by the constitutional movement to achieve victory before it was swept away by a new, more aggressive generation of nationalists. In the same way as Butt's followers were swept aside by Parnell, Parnell's successors were rendered increasingly peripheral by the emergence of the new nationalism, which combined the cultural interests of Young Ireland with the Fenian commitment to physical force. In the words of Nicholas Mansergh, compromise was driven out of Irish politics. Not until 1920-22, did Irish or British attention turn seriously to the negotiation of a political settlement.

These are the major themes of this book but before elaborating on them it is necessary to look in more general terms at Ireland in the period and to identify those factors which helped to set the context not just of political debate but of social life. That is the purpose of Chapter I. Amongst the most significant of these factors, apart from the Act of Union, were the nature of the administrative system, the rural nature of the society and its underdevelopment, lack of industrialisation, the prevalence of emigration and religious differences. These factors *inter alia* provide some clues to the failure of the Irish labour movement to emerge as a significant alternative to nationalism and unionism. That failure and the reasons for it will also be considered.

1　Government and Society 1870 - 1922

A healthy nation is as unconscious of its nationality as a healthy man of his bones...everything is in abeyance in Ireland pending Home Rule. The great movements of the human spirit which sweep in waves over Europe are stopped on the Irish coast by the English guns of the Pigeon House Fort. Only a quaint little offshoot of English pre-Raphaelitism called the Gaelic movement has got a footing by using nationalism as a stalking-horse, and popularising itself as an attack on the native language of the Irish people, which is most fortunately also the language of half the world, including England. Every election is fought on nationalist or anti-nationalist grounds; every appointment is made on nationalist grounds; every judge is a partisan in the nationalist conflict; every speech is a dreary recapitulation of nationalist twaddle; every lecture is a corruption of history to flatter nationalism or defame it; every school is a recruiting station; every church is a barrack; and every Irishman is unspeakably tired of the whole miserable business, which nevertheless is, and perforce must remain his first business until Home Rule makes an end of it, and sweeps the nationalist and the garrison hack into the dustbin.

Shaw: The curse of nationalism

G M Trevelyan's definition of social history as the history of a people with the politics left out has long been criticised for its under-estimation of the relationship between social life and politics.[1] Nowhere more than in Ireland is the close connection between the two so evident. And, in no period more than 1870-1922, is a historian more likely to be influenced by Shaw's adage that in Ireland everything is political. The adage might better read that in Ireland everything is politicised. No doubt, Shaw's comments which are marked by his usual overstatement were coloured by the fact that they were made at the height of the Home Rule crisis. Yet, always the 'friendly enemy' of Irish nationalism, he does identify one of the predominant characteristics of political discourse in the period 1870-1922. The gradual democratisation which that period witnessed, at least in the sense of wider participation in the political process, was accompanied by an increasing obsession with the 'national question'. The achievement of a measure of self-government, however limited, was not only the main aim of the nationalist movement and the defence of the Union the main priority of unionists: all other issues, political, social or economic, were approached with these yardsticks in mind.

The administration of Ireland

The preeminence of the 'national question' was not simply the product of the nationalist ideology which developed with such force in this period. Most of the major institutions of Irish life, administrative, social and political, had long since been shaped by similar considerations. The very administration of the country with its unusual centralisation, lack of local contribution and semi-colonial nature is the most obvious example. Despite the Act of Union of 1800 and the attendance of Irish MPs at Westminster, Ireland was not closely integrated with the rest of the United Kingdom. The continued existence of a separate Irish executive based in Dublin Castle acted as a barrier to closer union and sometimes promoted greater diversity. Political exigencies shaped administrative policy and the administrative structure was an equally important factor in shaping Irish politics. In the first half century or so after the union, administrative policy moved slowly towards closer integration of Britain and Ireland with such developments as the union of the two exchequers in 1817 and the gradual equalisation of taxation, especially in the 1850s, by Gladstone. However, in the next half century, many developments such as the establishment of the Congested Districts Board and the department of agriculture with their peculiar structure, and the land purchase policy itself, tended to lead in the opposite direction.

It was tacitly accepted, even by opponents of nationalism, that Ireland was indeed different and needed to be treated differently. Thus, for example, the police force was not controlled by the localities, nor was education. Ireland was claimed as an integral part of the kingdom but in practice was kept at arm's length. This was if anything entrenched by the expensive land purchase policy and by the advent of welfare legislation particularly after 1906. The financial cost of Irish government was proportionately double that of Britain but Irish revenue from direct and indirect taxation was generally more than sufficient to cover that. However, the combination of constructive unionist policies in Ireland and Liberal welfare legislation such as the provision of old age pensions meant that by 1910 Ireland was a net beneficiary from the central exchequer. In other words, Ireland was being subsidised and the large ageing population and other widespread social and economic problems meant that this was likely to increase. This fact was not lost on key administrators in the British treasury who, as a result, began to look much more favourably on nationalist demands for self-government.[2]

At the head of the Irish administration was the Irish executive consisting of the lord lieutenant, the chief secretary and the under-secretary. The lord lieutenant was the representative of the crown but, although he was originally the senior political officer, as the period progressed more and more of the responsibility devolved on the chief secretary. The lord lieutenant was expected to play a ceremonial role and required a sizeable independent income. From the 1880s onwards, such was the intensity of political passions that a lord lieutenant appointed by the Liberals might expect to have his social functions shunned by unionists and vice versa. Not surprisingly it became more and more difficult to find a suitable peer who was willing to undertake the task. The chief secretaryship was an even more thankless position which involved constant travel between London and Dublin. Few ministers were exposed to such hostility and scrutiny in parliament. He was responsible for such a diverse range of matters that one commentator compared him to Pooh-Bah, Lord High-Everything-Else of the Mikado of Japan.[3] The post was shunned by many because Ireland was seen as the graveyard of reputations. The under-secretary was, in effect, the senior civil servant in Ireland although with some notable exceptions he was more a routine clerk than a principal permanent adviser. This was of some significance as his senior colleagues generally had little direct knowledge of Ireland at the time of their appointment.

The Irish executive had the reputation of being the Irish government but its freedom of action could be limited. On one side it was answerable to cabinet and parliament and on the other much of the actual administration was carried out by a congeries of semi-autonomous boards and departments, some of which were responsible to the chief secretary's office, directly or indirectly, and some of which were responsible to the treasury or to other British departments. In all there were by the turn of the century almost fifty such boards operating in Ireland, ranging from the inspectorate of lunatics to the inspectorate of mines which was attached to the Manchester district. Their functions were often poorly defined and overlapped, with, for instance, the Estates Commissioners, Congested Districts Board and department of agriculture sharing many functions. The absence of an effective centripetal force allowed these boards to assume considerable power. [4]

This lack of coherence was exacerbated by the changes which were taking place in local government. The reform of local government which had taken place in England slowly but inevitably led to similar reform in Ireland. The grand juries which were monopolised by local landowners gave way to more democratic county, urban and rural district councils in 1898. Democratisation gave to nationalists in the south greater access to power at a local level and this created further problems for central government.

The Irish administrative system was 'chaotic and effete'. The most significant point about the finding of the royal commission on the rebellion in 1916, that the administrative structure was 'anomalous in quiet times and almost unworkable in times of crisis', was the general agreement with which it was greeted. Unionists and nationalists had been saying the same thing for at least thirty years. However, despite this consensus, successive governments proved unwilling or unable to introduce significant reform, largely because it was seen to touch on the central political issue. The result was that the government found itself facing first an agrarian war and later a nationalist revolt with an administrative structure which was inefficient and inflexible. Therein lies the explanation for the seeming incoherence of much British policy in Ireland in these years.

The provision for insanity and the insane provides as good an illustration as any of the vagaries of Irish government and indeed of Irish society. Segregation of the insane was still relatively new in 1870, as was provision for their welfare on a national basis. Yet both were surprisingly well developed in Ireland at this time. There had been the basis of a national system of care and control in existence since 1817, whereas the English system dated from 1845 and the French from 1871.[5] The early provision in Ireland was partly a response to the English movement for reform in this area but, significantly, it also sprang from Irish circumstances such as the absence of a poor law at that time and the extremely centralised nature of Irish government. Between 1814, when the Richmond asylum was built, and 1869, when the Monaghan asylum was built, 22 asylums were built in Ireland, providing over 7,500 beds at a total cost approaching £3 million.[6] Organised on a district basis, each was controlled from the 1840s by medical superintendents under the supervision locally of boards of governors and nationally of inspectors responsible to the chief secretary's office, Dublin Castle. The system was financed partly from local rates and partly by the treasury.

Such an early and elaborate provision for the insane might suggest a widespread concern for one group at the margins of society and may seem to indicate an appetite for innovation. However, whatever about the pre-1870 period, this would certainly not be true thereafter. The system, once in place, rapidly stagnated. The major preoccupation became cost rather than service, and, if anything, this trend became more marked after the democratisation of local government in 1898. Insofar as the concerns of the new nationalist-controlled local bodies went beyond the question of who was to pay for asylums and how much, insanity was seen as part of the national question. Social reform, it was argued, would have to wait resolution of the national question. Indeed, the crowded asylums were seen as a product of the degeneration and dispiriting of Ireland by the famine and ultimately by England. Nationalists could hardly encourage the process by supporting dependence. The responsibility lay with central government which should alleviate the burden on the ratepayers of the localities. Thus the new nationalist controlled authorities proved themselves more protective of the ratepayer and no more interested in the welfare of the needy than their predecessors.

Emigration

Ireland was a predominantly rural country linked to a well developed industrial one. This simple fact was at the root of many of the fundamental conflicts of the period. In 1891 45 per cent of the working population was employed directly in agriculture as opposed to only 17 per cent in England and Wales.[7] The particular problems of rural Ireland are examined below (pp14-32). However, one which requires consideration here is that of emigration. There was no more profound influence on Irish society in the period 1870-1922 than emigration. Emigration was not, of course, new. It had been a feature of Irish life since at least the late eighteenth century. What had then been a small but steady stream became a flood in the decades spanning and immediately after the famine. However, it might have been expected that as the immediate crisis passed and with the restoration of stability if not economic growth, emigration would return to its previous proportions. This was not to be the case. The Irish were arguably an emigrant people even before the famine but emigration then took place in the context of a growing population. The continuance of steady emigration after the famine was made more significant because of the continuing drop in population of which it was the major cause.

Two statistics help to put the trend into perspective. Total population in 1870 was approximately 5·5 million. Between the beginning of 1870 and the end of 1920 almost 2·4 million emigrated. While there was a steady exodus throughout the period, there was considerable fluctuation in the rate of emigration from decade to decade and, indeed, within decades. In the 1870s for instance, the total number of emigrants per thousand population fell from a high of 16·9 in 1873 to a low of 7·1 in 1876. In the 1880s the level of emigration increased dramatically partly because of the agricultural depression. In 1883, 108,724 people (or 21·6 per 1,000 population) emigrated. This was the highest figure for a single year since the early 1850s and it has not since been surpassed. In no year in the 1880s did the rate of emigration fall below 12·6 per thousand population. Thereafter the rate did begin to fall. It reached its lowest point during the first world war when emigration almost dried up. In 1918, for example, less than 1,000 people emigrated.[8]

Emigration 1870-1920[9]

Decade	Total	Total per 1,000 pop
1870s	603,271	11·3
1880s	804,910	16·1
1890s	449,551	9·8
1900s	358,855	8·1
1910s	167,682	3·8

Table 1

The reasons for the continuance of large-scale emigration are not as clear-cut as might be expected. During and immediately after the famine emigration was a sheer economic necessity. Thereafter that was sometimes but not always the case. At times of agricultural depression such as the late 1870s and early 1880s there was an upsurge in emigration. However, it needs to be remembered that the period overall witnessed an improvement in social conditions and living standards. Such improvements were, of course, relative but they do suggest that the rate of emigration was related to rising expectations as well as to poverty. That view would seem to be borne out by the way in which emigration responded to economic conditions in North America. The low rate of emigration in the late 1870s is directly attributable to the economic depression in the United States. When that depression eased in the 1880s the rate increased. So the exodus in the 1880s is not simply a product of Irish conditions. Some of those who went then might have gone earlier had there not been a depression in the United States. Emigration was a product both of 'push' and 'pull' factors.

The 'push' factors which led people to emigrate were by no means always the same and they did not apply equally in all areas. Eviction was a relatively rare reason for emigration. Popular folklore suggests it was the bullock which drove the people from the land i.e. that the shift from tillage to grazing displaced the population. Karl Marx supported this view when he wrote in *Das Kapital* that 'the Irishman, banished by sheep and ox, reappears on the other side of the ocean as a Fenian'.[10] A cursory examination of trends may seem to bear out this view. For example, between 1881 and 1911 rural population declined by 25 per cent while the number of cattle increased by 21 per cent and the acreage under tillage declined by 26 per cent. However, emigration was high both in areas which underwent a move to tillage and those which did not. Neither was emigration something which was experienced solely by the western seaboard counties as is often assumed. It is clear that different factors operated in different areas. The move to tillage was important in the south and midlands. In the west, the obliteration of the cottier class begun by the famine was continued so that by 1900 that class had virtually disappeared. Farm labourers were outnumbered by farmers. In the north east, economic recession in Ulster's traditional industries played a part. Irish society was not homogeneous, and neither was its emigration.[11]

Emigration had enormous positive and negative effects. Irish emigrants, like others, brought with them their culture and traditions which helped shape their new homelands. The new Irish communities in the United States, Australia and elsewhere also retained their ties with Ireland and from a distance looked sympathetically on the movements within Ireland which courted their favour and funds. However, the psychological impact of such large-scale emigration can only be guessed at. Certainly national degeneration caused by emigration was repeatedly cited by nationalist commentators as proof of the ill effects caused by the Act of Union.

Social change

It has been said that Ireland after the union was a land which most people wanted to leave.[12] Whatever the literal truth of this assertion, it suggests an unduly bleak state of Ireland in the latter part of the period. Those who remained at home enjoyed a modest but definite improvement in living standards in both rural and urban areas. Modernising influences came slowly but they did come. Improved educational opportunity was a passport to social mobility. There was some relative growth in the towns and in cities. In 1871 urban population was 22·2 per cent of the total, whereas by 1911 it was 33·5.[13] However, outside of Dublin, Belfast and Cork, the towns were predominantly centres of trade rather than of industry. The growth of trade made this the golden age of the shopkeeper, a development with political as well as economic repercussions.

The growth of regulation and control bore fruit in better sanitary conditions. Many visitors commented on the visible improvement in Irish towns.[14] Urban architecture improved and sea-side resorts flourished. Hotels, theatres and cinemas sprouted. Victorian novels were read widely. The suburbs of Dublin and of the major cities spread and necessitated the provision of services and the further development of municipal authorities. Trams and bicycles came into their own. Likewise the literary renaissance in the period was a reaction against the permeation of Victorian culture. Ireland, or at least urban Ireland, was coming more and more under the influence of the mores and customs of Victorian England. Even the Gaelic Athletic Association, on one level so distinctively Irish a phenomenon, was at the same time part and parcel of a world-wide sports revolution which was servicing the needs of modern society by providing organised spectator sports. The GAA grew partly from the same ethic and necessity which produced the Irish Rugby Football Union in 1874 and the Irish Football Association in 1880. Like Irish society as a whole it was subject to a range of influences local and international which sometimes pulled in different directions.[15] The best testimony to the impact of external influences is the nationalist movement itself which drew so much of its motivation from what it saw as creeping anglicisation.

The period witnessed a significant improvement in education and literacy which had social implications particularly for the catholic middle class. The establishment of the national school system in 1831 was not followed by similar innovation in the secondary system and the limited access to third level education for catholics continued to be a matter of grievance until 1908. However, there was slow progress in these areas. Until 1878, there was no state funding of secondary education. The Intermediate Education Act of that year introduced a system of indirect funding under which grants were made to schools on the basis of the performance of the pupils in public examinations. Secondary education remained largely the preserve of those who could pay but there was a gradual opening of access for lower middle class catholics, not least because of the spread of christian brothers' schools. This contributed to greater representation of catholics in the professions, civil service and elsewhere. The new generation of educated catholics from a lower middle class background was to play a major role in the political upheavals of the later part of the period.[16]

Religion and politics

The educational system was essentially denominational, a reflection of the fact that religion remained one of the predominant influences. In 1871, 76·69 per cent of the population was catholic, 12·34 per cent church of Ireland, 9·20 presbyterian and less than 1 per cent methodist.[17] Post-famine Ireland witnessed an upsurge in religious practice affecting all denominations. It was also a time of upheaval. The disestablishment of the church of Ireland in 1869 marked the beginning of a period of uncertainty for that church which was heightened by the wider social and political changes which took place in the next fifty years.

The position of the catholic church was changing too and at least some of its prelates saw its power as being under threat from modernising influences. However, its main challenge was to come to terms with the emergence of the nationalist movement. With the growth of nationalist organisation, the catholic church surrendered much of the direct political role which it had exercised earlier in the century, but it remained a powerful social and political influence. Perhaps the greatest mistake of government policy in the nineteenth century was its failure to forge an effective alliance with the catholic bishops. Had catholic interests been protected the identification of catholicism and nationalism might have been less strong. After all, in equally catholic countries in Europe catholicism and nationalism were at loggerheads and the church was a bastion of the *status quo*. The persistence of the government in seeing the Irish catholic church as closely controlled by Rome and subject to manipulation by the papacy against British interests contributed to the continuance of the church's role as the most important counter-balance to state power.

The period of intense organisation and romanisation which had been inaugurated by Archbishop Cullen in the 1860s gave way to a period of consolidation. The major concerns of the church in the period were the spiritual and moral welfare of its flock. For that reason, it exercised a keen interest in educational issues. It was more hesitant to venture into overtly political issues, particularly after the fall of Parnell. It was broadly supportive of the constitutional nationalist movement and suspicious of secret societies and the physical force movement. However, it largely adopted a watching brief. Even the 1916 rising produced remarkably little reaction. Of the thirty-one catholic bishops in Ireland, only nine commented publicly on the rising. Of these, seven emphatically condemned it, one hesitantly condemned it and one condoned it.[18] Thereafter opinion, particularly among the lower ranks of the clergy, radicalised in tune with society as a whole. The one great example of clerical involvement in the later part of the period was the conscription crisis of 1918 when the hierarchy endorsed and actively assisted the anti-conscription movement. This produced the ritual cries of 'no popery' in the tory press and the assertion by Lloyd George that the bishops had declared war on the king's government. Again, however, this missed the point. The catholic hierarchy was not a monolithic body: some bishops were Sinn Féiners, some were not. Their decisive stand against conscription was designed to prevent disorder and violence, not to create it. They feared chaos more than anything and with the Irish Volunteers committed to resist conscription by force if necessary, the bishops intervened to assert their control.[19]

The labour movement

The catholic bishops were suspicious of social change and not surprisingly looked with unease on some of the possible side-effects of urban development. In particular the rise of the labour movement gave cause for concern. The predominance of the national question also hindered the development of the labour movement in Ireland and militated against the emergence of a party system based on class divisions such as was developing in Britain and most continental European countries. The response of nationalism to labour demands was that sectional grievances must wait and while an alliance between labour and nationalism emerged outside of the north east, it was a relationship in which the former was always the weaker partner. In Ulster, where a large proportion of industrial workers were based, unionist politicians offered precisely the same arguments to persuade protestant workers that class differences should be shelved because of the nationalist threat.

There were of course other reasons for the weakness of the Irish labour movement. Ireland was a predominantly rural society dominated by conservative rural values. While there was a tradition of agrarian radicalism, its main demand was land ownership. Once a peasant proprietorship was established by government legislation the limits of that radicalism became more evident. The attachment to land-holding and tradition was entrenched by the church. While individual priests might be sympathetic to labour organisations, the church as a whole was suspicious of anything which smacked of socialism. The Irish catholic ethos, like the nationalist ethos, was essentially rural and overtly suspicious of urbanisation and industrialisation, characteristics which were associated with materialism, anglicisation and even protestantism.

For instance in 1902, Bishop Hoare of Ardagh and Clonmacnoise rejected industrialisation as a solution to Ireland's problems:

> People thought if they had big factories like Belfast and Birmingham they would have plenty of employment and no need for emigration. Well, there were some drawbacks to that system too. It is a well known fact that the taking of people from their rural districts into the large towns and cities has led to physical decadence. If they could get honest work and an honest wage for the poor people in their cottage homes, it would, in his opinion, be much better than those hives of industry, as they are usually called, but he would call them huge destroyers of the morals of the people.[20]

The lack of industrialisation outside the east coast limited the potential breeding ground for social radicalism. Furthermore, the prevalence of emigration removed from Ireland many of those who through dissatisfaction with the *status quo* might have turned to radical alternatives, and ironically in the process fuelled the developing labour movements in other countries, notably in Britain and Australia.

Nonetheless, a labour movement did emerge and played an important part in Irish affairs particularly after the turn of the century. Trade unions had developed in the nineteenth century but, like their British counterparts, they were essentially a conservative force aimed primarily at defending the relatively privileged position of skilled workers in traditional industries. Otherwise their function has been described as being 'to support the men when sick and bury them when dead'.[21] Most of the unions were British based. They were affiliated with the British Trade Union Congress, established in 1868, until the establishment of an Irish equivalent in 1894. This development did not presage a new radical emphasis. The aims of the Irish TUC were defined as being to 'promote better relations between the employer and employee' and its motto was cited as 'defence not defiance'. In 1895, a motion calling for the nationalisation of the means of production, distribution and exchange was decisively rejected by the TUC. William Field, a nationalist MP, told the delegates that 'socialism was all right if they had to deal with angels and not with human nature.'[22]

A similar conservatism characterised the attitude of labour organisations to politics. For example, James Connolly's Irish Socialist Republican Party attracted virtually no support from the Irish working class. By the turn of the century the nationalist *Leader* could write that there were no native born socialists in Ireland and that 'the third rate hangers-on to the skirts of some cheap school of Socialism that may exist here and there are at bottom only victims of anglicisation'.[23] There was little support for the establishment of a separate labour party. It was argued that the nationalist Irish party adequately represented the interests of labour. There was also a desire not to alienate the Ulster protestant workers who formed such a large proportion of the labour constituency. Only gradually was the reticence about political organisation broken down. The Local Government Act of 1898 stimulated involvement in local politics. The success of the British labour party at the 1906 general election provided a further stimulus. Finally the approach of Home Rule, which it was thought would at last remove the national question, led to the establishment of a labour party by the TUC between 1912 and 1914.

While the mainstream labour movement remained largely docile, the five years 1907-12 did see the advent of a more aggressive and militant wing. This was born partly out of the appalling slum conditions of Dublin but even more it was the product of the charisma and organising genius of James Larkin. Born in Liverpool, of Irish parents, Larkin came to Ireland in 1907 as an organiser of the British National Union of Dock Labourers and quickly organised a dock strike in Belfast. He then established the Irish Transport and General Workers' Union which was a new departure in Irish trade unionism as it was radical, politically orientated and aimed at unskilled workers. Larkin's syndicalist ideas were given a forum by the establishment of the *Irish Worker* and his new union spread rapidly, particularly in Dublin. Labour candidates, including Larkin himself, were conspicuously successful in the 1912 corporation elections. More significantly, industrial relations deteriorated rapidly. An employers federation was established in Dublin to counter union militancy. A series of strikes in 1911-12 culminated in the 1913 'lock-out' when William Martin Murphy, owner of the Dublin Tramway Company and proprietor of the *Irish Independent*, led an attempt to break the power of the transport union. The struggle was long and bitter and ended in defeat for Larkin but it did become a *cause célèbre* and a useful symbol of struggle and hardship for the growing labour movement such as the Peterloo massacre had been for the British labour movement a century earlier.

With the departure of Larkin for America, labour found itself once again occupying a subservient role to nationalism. The relationship was sealed by the 1916 rising in which Connolly and the Irish Citizen Army, a product of Larkin's earlier struggle, participated. The rising and the executions had mixed results for labour. It gained respectability among nationalists and the ITGWU experienced a major upsurge outside Dublin, almost doubling its membership and recruiting especially among town and farm labourers. On the other side of the coin, the death of Connolly and the absence of Larkin meant that in a formative period the labour movement lacked strong leadership. Between 1916 and 1921, the movement was to an extent an adjunct of the nationalist movement, as the decision to withdraw from the 1918 general election under pressure from Sinn Féin shows. It has been argued that by abstaining at this election when a new generation of voters were voting for the first time, labour missed a golden opportunity. However, when labour did finally put forward candidates, in 1922, it won 17 seats, which is hardly less than it could have expected to win in 1918. The truth is that labour subservience had been long since established.

The experience of the labour movement is the best illustration of the predominace of narrower political issues over social and economic ones in the period under consideration. That is not to suggest that *only* the political is important or that the history of this period should be, in effect, politics with the people left out. As an Irish historian of Victorian England has commented: 'people dwell, wash, walk, play, live noisomely or not, live in light or dark, die young or old, as well as struggle for vicarious power or snatch at tokens'.[24] The 'daily banalities' are important, both in themselves and for what they can reveal about a society as a whole. Politics are an *outcome* as well as a *cause* of social change. The society which produced the land war, the Home Rule movement and the nationalist revival was a much more varied one, and more open to a range of often competing and contradictory influences than a picture drawn from an agglomeration of political landmarks would suggest.

2 Land

Aunt Judy: .... *there's harly any landlord left; and ther'll soon be none
at all.*
Larry: *On the contrary, ther'll soon be nothing else; and the Lord
help Ireland then!*

Shaw: John Bull's Other Island

Two issues, more than any others, dominated political debate in Ireland between 1870 and 1922: the first was the self-government question, however defined, and the second was the land question. The periodically disturbed state of the Irish countryside in the nineteenth century guaranteed that agrarian problems were never far from the surface. However, from the late 1870s especially, the Irish land question thrust itself into the centre of the arena with an insistence which demanded immediate and fundamental reform. By 1923 a revolution in the ownership of Irish land had been achieved. In the late 1860s when John Bright, the English radical, suggested the transfer of the ownership of the land from the landlord to the tenant, he was dismissed as an extremist.[1] Within half a century, the policy suggested by him had been successfully implemented by those who at the time had recoiled in horror at his assault on property rights.

The land settlement of the years 1870-1903 effectively replaced landlordism with a peasant proprietorship or more accurately owner occupancy. As such it was a response to one interpretation of what the root of the problem was. Rightly or wrongly the land question insofar as it concerned land tenure and land ownership was seen as being essentially political. In the classic statement of Michael Davitt's *The fall of feudalism in Ireland*, the Saxon landlord was replaced by the Celtic peasant. Landlord-tenant relations, though never generally as bad as sometimes suggested, were certainly a significant source of conflict and tension and contributed to underdevelopment and crisis. However, the continuance of agrarian poverty, inefficiency and unrest long after 1903 suggests that land tenure was only one aspect of a much wider malaise. Congestion and small farm size, inefficient methods, lack of capital investment and indeed landlessness were as important in some parts of the country as the land tenure system itself. These problems were not

14

consistently addressed until the 'land question', in the sense of ownership of the land, had been 'settled'. In other words, the land settlement was in fact the settlement of the land tenure question only.

The land tenure system

In 1870, more than three quarters of the population lived in rural areas. Those engaged directly in agriculture fell into the categories of landless labourers, tenant farmers or landlords. In the early 1870s there were approximately 410,000 agricultural labourers. Badly affected by the famine and later by the decline of tillage, their numbers declined steadily throughout the period.

Tenant farmers and their families accounted for about half the rural population. The size of their holdings varied considerably with many having less than five acres. The average farm size was twenty to thirty acres, although with the consolidation of smaller holdings this increased during the period. Such figures are misleading, however, as they conceal both the large numbers of smaller holdings and important regional variation. In 1871, just under 50 per cent of holdings were fifteen acres or less while 73 per cent of the holdings were thirty acres or less. In Connacht, the great majority of holdings were under fifteen acres in 1871 whereas in Munster farm sizes were larger, although here too there was considerable variation in some areas. Such diversity points to the danger of too rigid a categorisation of classes in rural Ireland. Many tenant farmers lived on uneconomic holdings and their sons worked as labourers. They had more in common with landless men than with prosperous tenant farmers who occupied holdings of a hundred acres or more. While both played important parts in the conflict which developed, their economic interests were not always the same.

In contrast the number of landlords was small, just over 20,000 in 1870. However, here too there was considerable variation — 302 landlords owned estates greater than 10,000 acres; 3,459 between 1,000 and 10,000 acres; and 15,527 owned 1,000 acres or less. Over half the land was owned by less than 1,000 major landlords. At the time of the land war, Lord Lansdowne owned 120,000 acres in six different counties while the duke of Devonshire owned 60,000 in Cork, Waterford and Tipperary. Below these was a larger group with more modest holdings ranging between 1,000 and 5,000 acres. Despite the size of their holdings, the economic position of many in this group was not strong. The Encumbered Estates Court established after the famine had shown just how insolvent many of them were and facilitated a transfer of property from many traditional landlords to new landlords, most of them Irish. Some of these generated as much hostility as absentee landlords because of their more business-like and aggressive approach to their new property.[2]

Landlords and tenants benefited from a period of prosperity in Irish agriculture, which with the exception of the depression in the early 1860s, lasted from the famine until the land war of the late 1870s. Prices and production increased, particularly in relation to livestock. Land reform was called for periodically and some changes were made but the system seemed relatively stable.

Until 1860, relations between landlord and tenant were based on tenure rather than contract. Long leases, which had been common before the famine, were less frequent afterwards. The majority of tenants were tenants at will, holding their land from year to year. While this may seem to have placed them in a more vulnerable position, they considered themselves to have an interest in their property derived from customary rights which had built up over the years and which were in practice superior to the conditional rights conferred by a formal contract. Under tenant right, or Ulster Custom as it was known, the right of the yearly tenants to undisturbed possession was accepted as long as they paid their rent. They could sell their interest in the property or pass it on to their heirs. Tenant right was openly accepted by landlords in Ulster and also in some other parts of the country. It gave existing tenants some security of tenure and a source of income if they chose to move. It also meant of course that an incoming tenant could find himself saddled with the payment of rent to the landlord and the value of the tenant right to the outgoing tenant.

A number of steps were taken during the nineteenth century to simplify the procedure for the eviction of tenants which had hitherto been a cumbersome and costly process. After the Napoleonic wars, the procedure for evicting leaseholders was simplified. Eviction for non-payment of rent was extended to yearly tenants in 1851. Finally in 1860, the Deasy Act defined the relationship between landlord and tenant as being based on contract. The notion of tenant right was ignored. Eviction procedures were further simplified. A tenant could be evicted for non-payment of one year's rent or without cause by service of notice to quit at the termination of the yearly tenancy.[3]

In practice, while capricious evictions were sometimes carried out and, more frequently, evictions to allow consolidation of holdings and perhaps a move over to pasture, the vast majority were for non-payment of rent. While there was some rackrenting, the average increase in rent between the famine and the land war was 20 per cent. Rents did not keep pace with the rise in agricultural prices in the same period. The numbers of evictions were correspondingly small for most of the period, certainly compared to the wholesale clearances during and immediately after the famine. The annual rate was well below 1,000 until the depression of the late 1870s. Then it rose quite sharply, exceeding 5,000 in 1882. It remained high for much of the decade and thereafter declined.[4]

Much the same pattern is evident in the figures for agrarian crime such as breaking down of fences, driving off of animals, attacks on landlords and their agents. The period of the land war saw a major upsurge in this kind of crime. Generally, however, there is a tendency to exaggerate the extent of Irish agrarian crime and to overestimate the activities of the various agrarian secret societies which surfaced from time to time. It is doubtful that the rate of such crime was any greater than in comparable societies elsewhere. Moreover, a considerable proportion of agrarian crime had little to do with landlord-tenant relations but involved squabbles between tenants, or neighbours or even within families.[5] Nonetheless, in a society where substantial sections of the peasantry were only a series of bad harvests away from destitution, agrarian crime does act as an accurate barometer of economic depression.

The Deasy Act and the agricultural depression which followed inevitably produced a demand for reform of the land system. Whatever the frequency and cause of eviction, the famine clearances had scarred the folk-memory to such an extent that they were a continuing and potent source of resentment. For example, at Ballycohey, County Tipperary, in August 1868, a policeman and a bailiff were killed when a tenant successfully resisted a threatened eviction. Local sympathy lay firmly with the tenant and it proved impossible to secure a conviction of those responsible for the shooting.[6]

The Fenian rising drew further attention to Irish problems and convinced Gladstone to address the Irish land question when he came to power in 1868. Despite his declaration that his mission was to pacify Ireland, the Gladstone Land Act of 1870 was a modest affair. It legalised the Ulster Custom or similar customs wherever they existed. Elsewhere, evicted tenants were to be compensated for disturbance and for any improvements made by them to the holding. Incredibly, however, the act did not define the Ulster Custom clearly and the tenant had to prove that it existed in his case. The machinery for operating the act was inadequate. Implementation of its provisions required proceedings before a county court judge. Compensation for improvements and disturbance tended to be low. At least theoretically most tenants still had no security of tenure and their rents could be raised at will. Isaac Butt, the leader of the Irish Party in the house of commons, introduced a bill in 1876 to remedy some of these defects but it was rejected. Defective though it was, it is doubtful whether the Gladstone act would have been amended had it not been for the turn of events in Ireland in the late 1870s.

The new departure and the land war of 1879-1882

The question of why the land war broke out in 1879 has received considerable attention from historians in recent years. Despite its obvious weaknesses, the land system had at least proved durable and the agricultural sector had experienced a modest prosperity in the post-famine period. One partial explanation why the explosion came when it did is the agricultural depression which hit Ireland in the late 1870s. This arose to some extent from a wider depression in British agriculture brought about by increased competition from cheap American grain. More directly it was caused by a series of bad harvests in Ireland which severely damaged the potato crop. However, since the depression of the early 1860s did not produce a land war, depression alone does not provide a complete explanation for the events of 1879-82.

As the agricultural community was not a homogeneous population, the effect of the depression varied. The failure of the potato crop had an immediate and devastating impact on the small holders in the west and that is where the land war began. The impact of the depression on the larger tenant farmers was less intense and immediate, although their prosperity was threatened. Therein lies another cause of the land war. The historian James Donnelly has argued that the prolonged period of prosperity had created 'rising expectations' which, when they were suddenly disappointed, caused the tenants to defend their interests. Although not without its critics, this explanation does help to explain the behaviour of the larger tenant farmers.[7]

The larger tenants had traditionally been active in farmers' organisations and occasionally in reform movements such as the Tenant League of the 1850s. Apart from those who were sporadically involved in agrarian secret societies, the small farmers had no such history of participation. Their involvement in the land war is what gave it its cutting edge. As to the rest of the rural community, the labourers understandably played little part in the war. One unexpected group who did participate and give direction at local level was the business community of the towns, particularly shopkeepers, publicans and journalists, either through commercial self-interest or because they were at a natural point of assembly and discussion for the rural population.[8]

To destitution and rising expectations can be added the general sense of grievance amongst tenants over such issues as insecurity of tenure, lack of compensation for improvements and absenteeism. The one remaining factor, and arguably the most important in achieving the transition from spontaneous unrest to effective revolt, was leadership. What galvanised the various groups and shaped them into a potent force was the temporary coalition of Fenian, radical agrarian and constitutional traditions in the 'New Departure', a phrase coined by the exiled Fenian, John Devoy. Born in Kildare, in 1842, Devoy became a key Fenian organiser. In 1866, he was sentenced to fifteen years penal servitude but was released five years later on condition that he left the United Kingdom. He took up residence in the United States where he saw his role as providing the propaganda, revenue and impetus for a revived national movement in Ireland. The obvious leader of the constitutional side of such a movement was Charles Stewart Parnell, the young MP for Meath and Butt's rival for the leadership of the Home Rule party in parliament. He had attracted Fenian attention by his obstructionist tactics and his claim in the house of commons that the men who had killed a policeman in attempting to rescue two Fenian prisoners at Manchester in 1867 were not guilty of murder. With Fenian help, he had displaced Isaac Butt as leader of the Home Rule Confederation of Great Britain. A series of discussions took place between Parnell and Fenian leaders during 1877 and 1878. As a result, Devoy offered American support for the constitutional movement on certain conditions, the most important of which were:

1   abandonment of the federal demand and substitution of a general declaration in
     favour of self-government;
2   vigorous agitation on the land question on the basis of a peasant proprietary,
     while accepting concessions tending to abolish arbitrary eviction.[9]

Devoy's proposals met with some opposition within the Fenian movement but he pressed ahead. He met Parnell on a number of occasions during 1879. Devoy claimed later that a definite agreement was reached. This seems unlikely although it is clear that Parnell was not averse to informally accepting Fenian support. Indeed Devoy's 'new departure' was not even new: a similar understanding had been attempted by the Fenians with Isaac Butt in 1873. What *was* new in 1879 was the addition of an immediate practical dimension to the understanding by

Michael Davitt and the Land League.[10]

Whatever lingering doubts there may be about the nature of the New Departure, there can be none about the decisive importance of Davitt and Parnell in the conduct of the land war. Like Fintan Lalor, Davitt saw the land and national questions as inseparable. His passion for land reform owed much to his own background. He was born in Mayo in 1846. When the family was evicted, they emigrated to Lancashire where, at the age of eleven, Davitt lost an arm in a factory accident. Recruited into the Fenians, he was sentenced to fifteen years penal servitude in 1870. When he was released in 1877, he rejoined the Fenians and spent some time in the United States. On his return, his attention was quickly attracted to the discontent which was brewing in his native Mayo. He grasped the potential of the situation and placed himself at the head of the growing protest movement.

The inaugural meeting of the campaign, at Irishtown on Sunday 19 April 1879, was organised by James Daly of Castlebar who had been a leading figure in a tenant right agitation in Mayo between 1876 and 1878. Posters headed 'THE WEST AWAKE' announced the meeting and included the following melodramatic call to arms:

> From the China towers of Peking to the round towers of Ireland, from the cabins of Connemara to the kraals of Kaffirland, from the wattled homes of the isles of Polynesia to the wigwams of North America the cry is: 'Down with invaders! Down with tyrants!' Every man to have his own land — every man to have his own home.[11]

Although involved in its organisation, Davitt did not attend the meeting, whether because of prudence or, as was later claimed, because he missed his train. (Daly later remarked cynically that Davitt would have been father of the Land League if he had not missed the train.)[12] A large gathering passed resolutions condemning landlordism and demanding reductions in rent. Another meeting was held at Westport in June. At least partly to guarantee coverage in the national newspapers, Davitt invited Parnell to attend the meeting. Parnell accepted despite a public condemnation of the proposed gathering by Archbishop MacHale of Tuam who was alarmed by the Fenian presence among the organisers and the threat of agrarian violence. Whatever his reservations about attendance, Parnell's speech provided the embryo movement with its programme:

A fair rent is a rent the tenant can reasonably pay according to the times, but in bad times a tenant cannot be expected to pay as much as he did in good times three or four years ago. If such rents are insisted upon, a repetition of the scenes of 1847 and 1848 will be witnessed. Now, what must we do to induce the landlords to see the position? You must show them that you intend to hold a firm grip of your homesteads and lands. You must not allow yourselves to be dispossessed as your fathers were dispossessed in 1847. You must not allow your small holdings to be consolidated. I am supposing that the landlords will remain deaf to the voice of reason, but I hope they may not, and that on those properties where the rents are out of all proportion to the times a reduction may be made, and that immediately. If not, you must help yourselves, and the public opinion of the world will stand by you in your struggle to defend your homesteads.[13]

Further meetings followed and the protest acquired new recruits, among them John Dillon and Bishop Duggan of Clonfert. Parnell, though supportive, baulked at the idea of creating a national movement. In August, the Land League of Mayo was established under the auspices of Davitt. The opening sentence of a long declaration of principles declared that 'the land of Ireland belongs to the people of Ireland'. The Mayo example produced a demand for action not just elsewhere in Connacht but in Munster too. Existing tenant societies in these areas came under pressure to take a more active role. Finally, in October 1879, the National Land League was established with Parnell as president and Davitt, A J Kettle and Thomas Brennan, as joint secretaries. Its main aim was ownership of the soil by the occupiers. This was to be achieved through organisation among tenant farmers and defence of those threatened with eviction.

As the depression deepened and the threat of famine loomed larger, the Land League spread. Branches were established in Britain and the United States and a Ladies' League was established under Anna Parnell, Charles's sister. He and Dillon toured the United States raising funds which were used to relieve distress and to provide much needed seed potatoes. Although there were other relief agencies at work, these activities helped the league gain public acceptance.

The league operated on two levels, public and covert. The Mayo tactic of trying to force rent reductions through large public meetings was repeated elsewhere. When this failed, stronger measures were resorted to. The growth of evictions was accompanied by a growth in agrarian crime. Apart from the traditional after-dark activities of the secret societies, intense pressure was wielded openly. Process servers were cajoled, persuaded or physically prevented from serving eviction notices. Some evictions were disrupted by large crowds. Land League courts were established to fix rents and mete out punishments. Those who dared 'grab' evicted farms were exposed to a solid phalanx of community hostility. Ostracism, or social excommunication as it was known, was a potent weapon when used against grabbers. It proved equally effective when used against a land agent, Captain Boycott, who refused the abatement of rents and who in the process gave the movement a name for its main tactic. Even the drafting in of volunteer labour from Ulster to harvest his crops under military protection failed to break the total ostracisation of Boycott who soon left the country.

The bumper harvest of 1880 did nothing to reduce the intensity of the land war. Landlords demanded their rents but were met with the cry 'Hold the Harvest'. The success of Irish party candidates who supported the Land League in the general election of that year and the election of Parnell to the leadership of the party added to the clamour for reform. The new Liberal government's first response was to pass a Coercion Act in 1881. Following the arrest of Davitt, who spent more than a year in prison, Parnell resisted pressure from some of his Land League colleagues to withdraw from the house of commons and lead a no-rent campaign in Ireland. His caution seemed to bear fruit when Gladstone introduced a new land bill.

Gladstone's Second Land Act (1881) was quite a radical measure, which would not have seen the light of day but for the Land League. It enshrined the principle of 'dual ownership' of the land by landlord and tenant. The three F's – fair rent, fixity of tenure, and freedom of sale – were adopted or confirmed. The Irish Land Commission was established to make loans to tenants for the purchase of their holdings and to fix fair rents. Though the act itself had only limited success, the Land Commission became an important agency for dealing with land problems. Land League opinion was divided on the merits of the act: the moderates felt that it was a reasonable measure of reform while the radicals, including the Fenian element, felt it should be rejected out of hand on the grounds that it did not meet their demands and that its implementation was in untrustworthy hands. As a compromise, it was agreed by a Land League convention in Dublin that the act should be tested by referring selected cases to the rent tribunal. However, this was not sufficient to satisfy the government. With unrest in Ireland continuing, in October 1881, Parnell and the other leaders of the Land League were imprisoned in Kilmainham Jail in Dublin.[14]

This turn of events threatened to provoke an even greater crisis in Ireland. A no-rent manifesto was issued calling for non-payment of rents by tenants until their demands were met. The government responded by suppressing the league. The Ladies' League then stepped into the breach and the campaign continued The government had calculated that firm action would restore order. In fact crime increased. However, with chaos seemingly unavoidable, both sides drew back. Indirect negotiations between Parnell and Gladstone produced the so-called Kilmainham Treaty in April 1881, an informal agreement that Parnell would accept the Land Act and end the campaign in return for the amendment of the act to extend the fair rent clauses to leaseholders, measures to protect tenants with heavy arrears of rent and, of course, the release of the prisoners.

The Kilmainham Treaty marked a watershed in Parnell's career and in the land agitation. Parnell's flirtation with semi-revolutionary agitation was ended, although that did not become clear for some time. Likewise, the league itself rapidly disintegrated. While the land agitation continued in new guises, it never regained the same drive and cohesion which it had between 1879 and 1881. That was probably inevitable once the league spread from its heartland of Connacht. The coalition of interests which the National Land League represented made it likely that once substantial reform was granted, the small holders would be abandoned.

The Plan of Campaign

The significance of the Kilmainham Treaty was obscured by the murder shortly afterwards in the Phoenix Park of the new chief secretary, Lord Frederick Cavendish and the under secretary, Thomas Burke. Cavendish had replaced W E Forster who had resigned in protest against Gladstone's appeasement policy. The Invincibles, who carried out the murders, were mostly Fenians or ex-Fenians. Some of them were members of the Land League, although the league itself was not implicated. Parnell, who had been privately saying that Ireland was on the eve of a great breakthrough both on the land and political questions, was deeply affected by the murders. He considered retiring from politics altogether but was dissuaded by Gladstone among others. Nevertheless, the murders did have an important impact: they made a conciliatory policy on the part of the government much less likely for the time being at least and they defused some of the criticism of the Kilmainham Treaty by Irish radicals. In the longer term, they also confirmed Parnell's reluctance to continue his close involvement with semi-revolutionary politics.[15]

Parnell's reticence and Davitt's reluctance to abandon the alliance with him meant that the land war in the sense of a centrally controlled movement slowly ground to a halt. Nonetheless, evictions and agrarian crime continued. Davitt and John Dillon tried unsuccessfully to persuade Parnell to revive the agitation by reviving the Land League under another name. When, in October 1882, the Irish National League was founded with Parnell as president it was a very different organisation from its predecessor, both in its aims and methods. Although it incorporated most of the aims of the Land League, its platform was much wider, embracing the wider political question. It was focussed more on parliamentary agitation than on land. A disillusioned Davitt later described the change of emphasis as a 'purely parliamentary substitute for a semi-revolutionary movement'.

Meanwhile, Gladstone's act was being implemented. Despite the reservations of the Land League, the establishment of a fair rent tribunal attracted considerable interest from tenants when it became clear that reductions averaging 20 per cent were being granted. This itself caused problems as a backlog of cases soon built up. A further problem was caused by the lack of guidance as to what constituted a fair rent and how it should be assessed. Decisions were often inconsistent and were guaranteed to upset one side or the other. Appeals against the initial finding were common. John Dillon's prediction that the act would prove 'a milch cow for the lawyers' was borne out by the rapid growth of expensive and time-consuming litigation.

Popular though the act was, it became clear that it did not provide the final solution to the land question that Gladstone claimed it would. One effect it had, however, was to so frustrate some landlords that they were ready to accept the transfer of ownership of the land at a fair price. In 1883, a motion in favour of a land purchase policy was supported by Liberals and Tories in the house of commons. When the Tories returned to power in 1885, they passed a land purchase act with the support of the Irish parliamentary party. Land purchase was not a completely new policy. The Irish Church Act of 1869 and the Gladstone acts of 1870 and 1881 all had limited land purchase clauses under which state loans could be provided to enable tenants to buy their holdings. However the so-called Ashbourne Act of 1885 was the first to introduce the principle of making loans for the full amount of the purchase price.

An initial sum of £5 million was placed at the disposal of the Land Commission to provide loans for land purchase where agreement had been reached between landlord and tenant. The commission was also given power, through their Landed Estates Court, to buy estates for resale to tenants. The entire purchase money was to be advanced to the landlord by the commission minus a guarantee deposit of one fifth to protect the state against the eventuality of default by the tenant. The tenant was to repay the purchase price in annual instalments over a period of forty-nine years. The act was amended in 1887, 1888 and 1889 to provide further funds. In all £10 million was provided allowing just over 25,000 tenants to purchase their holdings, while the Landed Estates Court purchased 101 estates for resale.[16]

Whatever the long term merits of the Ashbourne Act it did nothing to tackle the renewed crisis which engulfed rural Ireland during 1885 and 1886 and which marked the second phase of the land war. Indifferent harvests and foreign competition depressed agricultural prices and made it difficult for tenants to pay their rents. Even judicial rents – rents fixed under the 1881 Act – were now considered excessive. The rent commissioners were forced to take the depression into account in dealing with new cases but this was of no use to the majority of tenants. Some landlords granted rent abatements while others could not or would not. Inevitably the cycle of evictions and agrarian crime began again. This, in turn, produced a major upsurge in membership of the Irish National League. The time seemed ripe to revive the agitation of 1879-81. Parnell, now more interested in Home Rule, refused to countenance such a step. During the autumn of 1885, rent strikes developed in various parts of the country. They were encouraged by leading members of the Irish party such as Dillon, William O'Brien and Timothy Healy but the National League, under Parnell's influence, was lukewarm. A year later, with the failure of Gladstone's Home Rule bill and the defeat of the Liberals, Parnell sought to placate the militants in his own party by introducing a tenant relief bill to stay evictions for non-payment of rent while a fair rent was being fixed. The defeat of this bill opened the way for a less moderate approach.[17]

The 'Plan of Campaign', hatched by Timothy Harrington, secretary of the league, Dillon, O'Brien and others, was launched in October 1886 without the *imprimatur* of Parnell. It was really a refinement of the abortive 'No Rent Manifesto' of 1881. Under the plan, tenants on estates where rents were considered excessive, were to seek an abatement. If this was not granted, they were to pay what they considered a fair rent into an estate campaign fund which would be used to pursue their case. Evicted tenants were to be supported from the fund; negotiations with the landlord were to be undertaken by an estate committee and any breaches of what was in effect a strike were to be dealt with by boycotting.

The Plan of Campaign lasted from 1885 until 1891 when the disputes on most of the outstanding estates fizzled out from lack of funds and because of the split which followed the fall of Parnell. It was adopted on 203 estates, a larger number than sometimes supposed, but still less than 1 per cent of all Irish estates. Its main impact was in Tipperary, Kerry and Galway, and to a lesser extent other parts of Munster and Connacht. It had little impact in Leinster or Ulster. As a form of collective bargaining, it was successful in the sense that it extracted reductions in rent on a majority of estates involved. Many of the battles were long and bitter and extremely expensive for tenants and landlord. The conflict on the Smith Barry estate in Tipperary illustrates this point well. Smith Barry's estates were targeted for attention when he led a group of landlords in frustrating a settlement which seemed likely on the Ponsonby estate in Cork because of the bankruptcy of the owner. In Tipperary, two-thirds of Smith Barry's tenants failed to pay their rents in 1889. Within a year, 154 had been evicted. Those evicted included shopkeepers with thriving businesses. They moved their premises from Tipperary town and set up in business nearby. New Tipperary, officially opened in April 1890, was a symbolic gesture reminiscent of some of the efforts of the Chartists in England fifty years earlier. It was, however, a most expensive gesture. By mid 1891, at least £40,000 had been spent by the tenant side on the Tipperary campaign.[18]

The Plan of Campaign was not as successful as the original Land League campaign. Although in practice it was organised by leading members of the Irish party and National League, it never enjoyed the official support of either. Parnell, in particular, tried to restrict its growth. This caution was shared by the catholic bishops, despite the initial support of some of their number, and the active participation of many priests. Their position was made particularly delicate by the 'rescript' issued by Pope Leo XIII in April 1888 condemning the plan and the practice of boycotting. While many of the organisers rejected this interference and responded with condemnations of clerical interference in political matters, responses which were both radical and unusual for the nationalist movement, the rescript and the debate that followed only served to highlight the lack of wholehearted support for the plan.

The Conservative government was intent on breaking the campaign. Arthur Balfour was appointed chief secretary early in 1887 and immediately set about crushing resistance. A harsh coercion act was quickly passed. It gave the authorities wide summary powers to deal with boycotting, intimidation, resistance to eviction, unlawful assembly and incitement. The difficulty of getting convictions from local juries was met by empowering the attorney-general to transfer such cases to other districts. The severity of these measures created resentment but they certainly gradually weakened the resolve of the tenants.

Land purchase

The Conservatives also made some attempt to temper coercion with concession. The fall in agricultural prices and indeed the Plan of Campaign had further damaged the financial position of many landlords and made them more favourably disposed towards selling their estates. The funds provided for land purchase rapidly proved inadequate. The Balfour Act of 1891 introduced a new system under which the landlord was paid for his property in a specially created land stock. Equal in nominal value to the purchase price, this stock bore interest and could not be redeemed for thirty years. As with the Ashbourne Act, the tenant's annuity was 4 per cent of the purchase price over forty-nine years. Unlike the 1885 act, however, deficiencies in the 'Land Purchase Account' caused by defaulting tenants were to be made good ultimately not from the landlord's payment but from a guarantee fund, partly endowed from funds normally payable to Irish local authorities. Thus any deficiency would effectively become a charge on the localities. For that reason, limits were placed on the amount of stock that could be issued in each county. Balfour also fixed an upper limit of £33 million on advances. In fact, despite an amending act in 1896, only £13·5 million was advanced, representing sales to 47,000 tenants. The machinery provided by the act was complicated and off-putting and the innovation of paying in land stock also proved unpopular. The value of the stock fluctuated with the market and the volume of sales varied accordingly.

The defects of the Balfour Act were finally resolved by the Wyndham Act of 1903 which removed the major barriers in the way of the land purchase policy and ultimately produced a revolution in the ownership of Irish land. While the act owed much to the vision of George Wyndham, chief secretary at the time, it was a direct product of an unprecedented agreement between landlord and tenant representatives at a land conference in Dublin in December, 1902. The conference took place against the background of increasing agrarian agitation dating from another series of poor harvests in the late 1890s. The rapid growth of the United Irish League reflected the disturbed state of the countryside and contributed to it. Boycotting and intimidation reappeared. In 1901-1902, thirteen sitting or former Irish MPs were imprisoned under the Crimes

Act and large parts of the country were proclaimed, thus giving the authorities widespread powers to deal with disorder in those areas. Matters came to a head on the de Freyne estate in Roscommon when, with the encouragement of John Dillon, the tenants organised a no-rent campaign. A group of militant landlords responded by launching a trust fund to prosecute the leaders of the league for conspiracy.[19]

It was to avoid the impending confrontation that Captain John Shawe-Taylor, the younger son of a Galway landlord, issued his historic invitation to named leaders of both sides to attend a conference aimed at producing a land settlement acceptable to landlords and tenants which would put an end to '200 years of land war'.[20] The initiative was given added impetus when, within a matter of days, Wyndham gave his approval by declaring publicly that no government could solve the land question. It could only be settled by the parties directly concerned. While the suggested conference met with considerable scepticism from both sides, not least from those who were not themselves invited, it did assemble and produced an agreed report within a fortnight.

The four landlords originally invited refused to serve. They were replaced by Lord Dunraven, Lord Mayo, Colonel Hutcheson-Poe and Colonel Nugent-Everard, all of whom were known to be moderates. The tenants were represented by William O'Brien, John Redmond, Timothy Harrington and T W Russell. Although the conference agreed recommendations about favourable treatment for congested areas and evicted tenants, the core of its report was the proposition that the difference between what would be a fair purchase price for the tenant and a fair selling price for the landlord should be made up by the state. It was also recommended that the landlord should be paid in cash and not in land stock. This was accepted by Wyndham and incorporated into his 1903 act. Landlords were given a bonus of 12 per cent, to encourage them to sell. The act also introduced the principle of sale of whole estates, with tenants agreeing to common terms rather than piecemeal sale of holdings. The purchase terms for the tenant were also easier than before with the annuity being reduced from 4 to 3·25 per cent and the repayment period being extended to 68·5 years. Provision was also made for the purchase of estates by the Land Commissioners and the resale of untenanted lands to uneconomic holders or evicted tenants.[21]

The Land Act met with a mixed reaction from nationalist leaders. Davitt, Dillon and the *Freeman's Journal* were particularly critical of the bonus to landlords and of the zone system adopted in the act which, it was claimed, inflated the price paid by some tenants. Dillon predicted, correctly as it turned out, that the financial clauses would prove troublesome. The root of his unease, however, lay in his suspicion of the policy of conciliation which he feared was aimed at undermining the nationalist movement and perpetuating rather than destroying landlord privilege. O'Brien for his part was convinced that the land conference marked the dawn of a new era and demanded a new approach from nationalist politicians. While he was successful on the particular point at issue – the United Irish League and the Irish party both endorsed the land conference's report – and tenants availed of the provisions of the Land Act in their thousands, in the longer term he failed. Dillon's view predominated within the Irish party.

The financial provisions of the act quickly needed amendment. The collapse of government credit and the general air of uncertainty caused a crisis. The treasury, which had opposed the financial provisions of the act from the start, used its powers to restrict the amount of funds which could be made available each year to £5 million. Such regulations provoked considerable criticism not only from nationalists but from the Land Commissioners who challenged the legality of some of them. By 1909, sales worth £50 million had been agreed but remained to be paid for. The treasury claimed that it was merely following sound financial principles. The land stock which was floated to raise the cash to pay the vendors was soon having to be sold below par. Such losses were to be met initially by a 'guarantee fund' and ultimately by Irish ratepayers. By 1907, the losses were such that Dillon claimed they might 'bankrupt and destroy the whole community'. The issuing of stock was suspended and it was decided to introduce remedial legislation.[22]

Under the Birrell Act of 1909, losses on land stock for pending agreements were to be made good by the treasury – or in other words, the taxpayer of the United Kingdom – and not by the Irish ratepayer. Payment in stock rather than cash was reintroduced for future agreements and the purchasers' annuity was raised to 3·5 per cent. Further provision was also made regarding the landlord's 12 per cent bonus. Wyndham had provided £12 million for that purpose on the assumption that £100 million would be sufficient to complete land purchase. In 1908, the treasury had reduced the bonus to 3 per cent as it was obvious that sales would far exceed £100 million. Clearly this would have acted as a big disincentive to landlords so Birrell provided more money and introduced a graduated bonus ranging from 3 to 18 per cent, depending on the selling price. The lower the selling price, the larger the bonus: thus there was an incentive for the landlord to sell at a reasonable price.

These changes accelerated the pace of land purchase for a time. The outbreak of the first world war interrupted the process again and there was little progress thereafter until the 1923 act passed by the Irish Free State, which introduced compulsory purchase for tenanted estates. By 1920, £83 million had been advanced under the provisions of the Wyndham and Birrell Acts and sales to the value of another £24 million were pending. Nine million acres had changed hands, with a further two million awaiting transfer.

The limits of land purchase

By any standards this represented a dramatic change in land ownership in Ireland. True, a sizeable minority of holders still paid rent and many landlords parted only with their tenanted lands and retained substantial farms. True, some landlords refused to have anything to do with land purchase and neither Liberal nor Conservative politicians were willing to introduce compulsory purchase except in a limited number of cases. And true, land purchase meant more to larger than to smaller tenants. Yet, despite such qualifications, the land purchase policy was of enormous importance. Politically, it confirmed the decline of landlord power and enhanced the position of the nationalist movement, and of the particular groups within that movement. Socially, it enshrined particular values. A tenant spokesman told the Bessborough Commission in 1880 that peasant proprietorship would 'make the peasant more conservative than the Conservatives'. It was that calculation which lay behind the Conservative conversion to land purchase and thus produced the Ashbourne, Balfour and Wyndham Acts. Gladstone too was prompted by similar motives. While land purchase did not prevent Home Rule, it did help contribute to a social conservatism which limited the political revolution later and had important implications for independent Ireland.[23]

Perhaps the greatest drawback of the land purchase policy was that it made so little discrimination between the different classes of tenant in rural Ireland. Politicians, agitators and administrators were slow to realise that fixity of tenure or even ownership of the land could not prevent periodic famine and endemic poverty. Ownership was an irrelevance for the roughly 30 per cent of Irish farmers whose holdings were less than 10 acres. It was partly in an effort to improve the lot of this group that the Congested Districts Board was established by Arthur Balfour in 1891. This and other attempts to deal with such problems are examined below (pp 57-65).

In addition to uneconomic holdings, much controversy was generated by the conacre or eleven months system whereby untenanted land was rented annually to the highest bidder. Ironically, though the land in question was often extremely poor, the rent could be relatively high because of the competitive element which did not exist to the same extent for leasehold or customary tenants. Graziers competed with small holders and labourers for such land, giving rise to considerable jealousy.

Even after land purchase and despite the efforts of the Congested Districts Board, agrarian unrest continued to be a significant fact of life in rural Ireland and violent outbreaks occurred periodically. For example, in 1907-1908, when sales of land under the Wyndham Act were at unprecedented levels, a major ranch war engulfed the midlands and west of Ireland. The aim of the agitation was to force the break-up and distribution of grasslands. Large cattle ranchers came under attack, with their cattle being driven off in the middle of the night. Uneconomic holders, labourers and evicted tenants sought to press their claims to land.[24]

A decade later, Laurence Ginnell, the Irish party MP who played a leading role in the 1907-1908 outbreaks, sought to persuade the reorganised radical nationalist Sinn Féin party to address the issue. There is no doubt that the rise of Sinn Féin after 1916 was helped by a residue of grievance in this area. During 1917 and again in 1920 there were renewed outbreaks of agrarian trouble with the demand for the breakup of ranches being commonly heard. Members of Sinn Féin and the Irish Republican Army were involved in many of these incidents but when the official response came from the republican movement it was cautious and conservative. Land seizures were condemned. Land courts were established but their main function was to preserve order and replace existing state organs rather than to foment social revolution. The response of the new nationalism to the deep rooted problems of Irish agriculture was little more radical than that of the unionist party in 1891.[25]

Arguably the group who suffered most in rural Ireland after the famine were the farm labourers. Yet they benefited least from the changes which took place in these years. They suffered badly from the decline in tillage which contributed to serious problems of unemployment, low wages and poor housing. Attempts were made to organise them but never with the sort of success which tenant organisations or even English labourers' organisations achieved. Labourers never wielded the same political muscle as tenants. Partly due to the demands of the Irish National League and of Parnell, the Labourers' (Ireland) Act was passed in 1883 to provide for the building by local authorities of labourers' cottages equipped with small plots of land. Fifteen thousand such cottages were built by 1901.

Sinn Féin was little different in its attitude from the Irish party. Against its will, the Sinn Féin Dáil was dragged into a number of disputes between farmers and their labourers. However, as with other agrarian and labour problems, its official position was one of neutrality between classes and its main aim was to avoid diverting attention from the political question. By and large, the farm labourer was a vanishing breed. Though wages and housing improved modestly, employment prospects did not. By 1911, average wages were 10s 9d (53p) per week but the ratio of farm labourers per 100 farmers had fallen from 160 in 1871 to 131 in 1911. Farm labourers were to be found in significant numbers only in the areas of Ulster, Leinster and Munster where larger farms predominated. They had well nigh disappeared from Connacht. Apart from the impact of these changes on the class concerned, the political and social implications have yet to be fully teased out.[26]

Land purchase was not a panacea for the economic problems of Irish agriculture. Indeed it may in some cases have perpetuated lack of competitiveness by, for example, allowing inefficient or uneconomic tenants to buy their holdings for an annuity up to 20 per cent below their already reduced rents. However, similar criticisms can be made of dual ownership. The tendency of many recent historians to treat land purchase as a 'tragic irrelevance' underestimates its social and political significance.[27] Furthermore, even if the real economic problems were not primarily caused by landlordism, these problems were never going to be solved while landlordism lasted, such were the passions generated by that institution. Other solutions to the Irish land question were occasionally canvassed. Davitt favoured land nationalisation rather than peasant proprietorship. Constructive unionists offered state paternalism. However, by 1903, most critical observers realised that the abolition of the landlord system was the *sine qua non* of any further progress.

3 Home Rule 1870-1891

'There is no principle, gentlemen, which seems so simple, but which somehow seems to need so much instilling into some of our greatest statesmen, as the fact that the potato one knows and likes is better than the truffle that one neither knows nor likes.'

Lord Rosebery

The Bilton Hotel on Upper Sackville Street, Dublin, is much less evocative in Irish history than Miss Hayes's more modest establishment in Thurles. Their respective positions in the history books may be explained by the fates of the movements whose inception they witnessed. The Home Rule movement launched at The Bilton on the evening of Thursday 19 May, 1870, dominated the political stage in Ireland until 1914. It was then supplanted by the new nationalism which shaped, and was partly shaped by, the Gaelic Athletic Association established at Hayes's Hotel in 1884. The apparent failure of one and success of the other movement has tended to overshadow the extent to which the first created the conditions necessary for the second.

Home Rule dominated political debate in Ireland in the second half of the century in the same way as Repeal dominated the first half. Both movements were similar, not least in the outstanding leaders they threw up, and in general terms their goals were the same. For subsequent generations of nationalists, 'Repeal' and 'Home Rule', whatever their precise literal meanings, became code-words for Irish independence. It is fair to see at the root of both, what contemporary critics discerned and moderate supporters denied, a movement towards Irish separation from Britain. It would be wrong, however, to attribute to advocates of Home Rule, particularly in the early days of the movement, a conscious attachment to the separatist ideal. The original Home Rule movement was an essentially conservative movement concerned as much to prevent as to promote change. Only gradually, as its ranks swelled and its leadership changed, did it take on a more radical complexion.

Isaac Butt and the genesis of Home Rule

The meeting convened by Isaac Butt at the Bilton Hotel in May 1870 unanimously adopted a resolution calling for the establishment of an Irish parliament with control over domestic affairs and appointed a committee to organise an association dedicated to this end. The Home Government Association, formed in July and publicly inaugurated three months later at the Rotunda, was as much a constructive unionist as a nationalist movement. Although there were a few members of the revolutionary secret society, the Irish Republican Brotherhood (see below, pp 96-100) involved, as well as a sprinkling of liberals and constitutional nationalists, the largest single group among the forty-nine people who attended the Bilton meeting and the sixty-one who formed the executive council of the association were protestant conservatives.[1]

Businessmen such as W L Eason and W L Mackey, landlords such as Edward King-Harman from County Longford, and journalists such as Major Knox, owner of the *Irish Times,* were disillusioned with the union and disturbed by government policy. The merchant presence was particularly marked. The union had neither created economic prosperity nor quelled political unrest. Disestablishment and Gladstone's proposed land legislation seemed to herald an attack on the position of the landed gentry. The instinctive response of some was to demand the devolution of political power from Westminster to an Irish parliament. As such Home Rule was intended to be the guarantee of their political future and not, as it ultimately became, an assault on their position. The main contribution of Isaac Butt to the Home Rule movement and to Irish nationalism was to identify this shift in conservative opinion and to link it with some of the more traditional supporters of Irish nationalism in a somewhat uneasy and ultimately unsuccessful coalition.

Butt's sensitivity to the unease stirring in conservative ranks sprang partly from his own experience of political conversion. Born in Donegal in 1813, the son of an Anglican clergyman, he first came to prominence in the 1840s making a name for himself both as a barrister and a tory. In 1843, he led the opposition to Daniel O'Connell in the famous Repeal debates at Dublin corporation. Even then his exposition of the unionist position was based on reason rather than prejudice. He was a keen critic of economic conditions in Ireland and took a close interest in the land question. He made little mark as a 'liberal-conservative' MP for Youghal between 1852 and 1865, when he lost his seat.

Forced to resume his legal practice, Butt was later to claim that the decisive point in his political formation came with his defence of the

Fenian leaders at their trials when he assumed the role of spokesman for the nationalist case. In the process, he became convinced of the need for some measure of home government for Ireland and for a constitutional movement to achieve it. His subsequent involvement in the Amnesty Association further sealed his identification in the public mind with advanced nationalism, an identification which was to prove beneficial. Butt was respected by the Fenians who looked with a 'benevolent neutrality' on the movement he launched in 1870. He told the Bilton Hotel gathering that though 'the men whom misgovernment had driven into revolt' could not help their efforts, they would not hinder them.[2] Armed insurrection having failed, the Fenians, for the time being at least, were willing to wait in the wings while other methods were tried.

Butt sought to convince Irish nationalists that since simple repeal of the union was not a practical political proposition, Home Rule was a worthwhile alternative. Insofar as it fell short of the desired goal of nationalists, it might act as an instalment. He was even more concerned, however, to placate unionists. He repeatedly urged the landed gentry to take their place at the head of his movement. Only by giving the lead could they keep their catholic tenantry from 'the eddies and whirlpools of rebellion'. He reassured them that the Home Government Association had a single political aim and would not be drawn into other social and economic conflicts such as the land question. In *Irish federalism: its meaning, its objects and its hopes* published in Dublin in 1870, in effect as the programme of his new movement, he argued that Home Rule would act as a bulwark against radical change. Once self-government was granted, the inherent conservatism of the Irish character would assert itself. Even if it did not, an Irish house of lords would be dominated by conservatives, thus counteracting any excesses of the lower house.[3]

Even the term Home Rule itself was a concession to moderation. Because of its association with O'Connell's movement in the 1840s, the term 'repeal' was seen as unrespectable and impractical. The newer term was apparently suggested by Rev. Joseph Galbraith, fellow of Trinity College and one of the founders of the movement, although the term had been used as early as 1858 and 1860 in the pages of *The Celt* and *The Nation* respectively.[4] Home Rule was calculated to emphasise the narrower aims of Butt's movement as opposed to O'Connell's. While Ireland would be given control of her own domestic affairs, her legislature would be subject to Westminster and the position of the crown would not be threatened; Ireland would continue to play her part in imperial affairs and the unity of the kingdom would be guaranteed. Many erstwhile repealers resented the abandonment of O'Connell's policy although they overcame their initial hesitation and drifted into the new movement.

It was Butt's chequered political background and his attempts to reconcile contending forces in Irish society – catholic and protestant – which led to his being labelled 'that grand conjunction' by one contemporary Fenian. He never succeeded in reconciling these forces but he was unwilling to abandon the attempt and throw in his lot with one side or the other. The Home Government association grew steadily in membership and status but it never attracted the wholehearted support of either the landed gentry or catholic nationalists, particularly the catholic clergy. Both sides feared that they would be dominated by the other. After its initial launch, the failure to attract protestant conservatives in substantial numbers became increasingly evident and the balance within the movement shifted towards the liberal nationalist element.

Other related problems were the question of organisation and the role the new association should play. These twin problems were never satisfactorily resolved. Butt's programme attracted widespread popular enthusiasm. Dublin corporation and local authorities in various parts of the country expressed their support. Home Rule Associations were established throughout Ireland and in the major towns and cities of Britain. Some sitting MPs endorsed the programme and candidates supporting Home Rule were successful at several by-elections. Butt himself returned to parliament in 1871 as the member for Limerick. However, all of these developments took place as much in spite of, as because of, Butt and his colleagues. Butt insisted that his association was not intended to be a popular organisation. The new associations were not branches of a national political movement and were not centrally controlled. Those candidates who stood on a Home Rule platform at by-elections did so largely on their own initiative and sometimes more than one Home Ruler contested the same seat. It was Home Rule, not the Home Government Association, that seized the popular imagination. What Butt had on his hands was a policy without a party.

The defeat of Gladstone's Irish university bill in February 1873 and later the fall of the Liberal government marked a major landmark in the Home Rule movement. As long as the Irish bishops entertained hopes of concessions on education from Gladstone they were unwilling to risk alienating his government. Their disillusionment with his bill made them less cautious in their attitude to Home Rule. On the other side, the hope of a return of the tories made the task of attracting protestant conservatives much more difficult.

There was now a growing demand that the new movement be placed on a more popular basis. In response, a national conference was summoned in Dublin in November 1873. Attended by 900 delegates, many of them making their first appearance on a national political stage, the conference quickly endorsed the Home Rule programme. What proved more contentious was the central problem of organisation. Butt had already made some attempts to organise those MPs who supported Home Rule into a parliamentary party. A proposal at the November meeting to form Home Rule MPs into a parliamentary party pledged to Home Rule and acting together on all other issues was now strongly opposed by the MPs present, including Butt. They claimed it would unduly restrict their freedom of action. It was clear that while they were willing to support Home Rule they were not yet ready to abandon their other political allegiances or their personal independence. However, in deference to those who accused them and the Home Government Association of being 'a private association of gentlemen', it was agreed to set up a new organisation, the Home Rule League.[5]

The establishment of the Home Rule League was a gesture towards the creation of a popularly based organisation but there was still a long way to go before an effective Home Rule party emerged. The League was an unduly centralised body and did not encourage the development of branch or constituency organisations. Membership was open to those supporting Home Rule who paid the £1 annual subscription. It was run by a hundred-strong council which met monthly in Dublin and an executive of twenty-one elected by the council. The relationship of the League to the Home Rule MPs and its role in selecting or endorsing candidates was unclear. Such matters became of vital importance in January 1874 when Gladstone dissolved parliament and called a general election.

On the face of it, the 1874 general election was a triumph for the new Home Rule movement. In the outgoing parliament twenty-one Irish MPs had pledged themselves to Home Rule. Of the 103 Irish members elected to the new parliament, 59 were Home Rulers, 32 were Conservatives and 12 were Liberals. However, it would be misleading to assume that a cohesive Home Rule party had now emerged. The Home Rule League had been unprepared for the election and was able to do little more than issue advice. In some cases Home Rule candidates were selected at meetings in the constituencies while in others they simply put themselves forward, without undergoing any pre-selection procedure. Many candidates declared themselves Home Rulers, but also tenant righters or in favour of land reform and denominational education. In Waterford County, Pearson Longbottom, an Englishman, stood as a Home Ruler, a Conservative and a tenant righter.[6] In several constituencies, rival Home Rulers stood.

As a result, the fifty-nine Home Rulers who entered parliament in 1874 were not a cohesive group. In their midst were those whose commitment to the Home Rule cause was opportunist or lukewarm and those who felt an equal commitment to other causes. Despite having decided to act together as a Home Rule party in the commons, when they took their places they did not even sit together – the Conservatives amongst them sat on the government side. In Dod's *Parliamentary companion, (1874)* many of the others described themselves as Liberals in favour of Home Rule and took the Liberal whip. Only one, PJ Smyth, an ex-Repealer and Young Irelander, described himself as a nationalist and he soon defected.[7] In view of this, the ineffectiveness of the party over the next few years is more easily understood. Likewise the apparent rout of the Liberals who fell from fifty-seven to twelve seats in Ireland, is misleading. Only gradually, as a disciplined Home Rule party emerged, was it necessary for many Liberals to choose between conflicting loyalties.

It quickly became evident that there was little future in the house of commons for a complaisant, single issue party. Butt believed in the gradual conversion of English politicians to the merits of Home Rule. He was opposed to the pursuit of an energetic, obstructionist policy such as was favoured by his colleague Joseph Biggar, the member for County Cavan who was a Fenian. He was also reluctant to embroil the party in other issues, Irish or imperial, as that would have risked division and alienation of potential support. In 1876, under severe pressure from Irish farmers, he did introduce a land bill to legalise Ulster Tenant Right, but it was opposed by some of his own colleagues. The party's performance generally was lacklustre and directionless. At home, impatience grew with the lack of progress on Home Rule and on other issues. Criticism mounted and with it the demand for a more vigorous policy. Some effort was made by the party to meet this demand during the 1876 session but without any real success.

Part of the problem was Butt's own personality and leadership. Eloquent, hospitable and urbane, his conviviality was both a strength and a weakness. Even had he been disposed to, he lacked the discipline and organisational skills to weld together a smooth running machine, either inside or outside parliament. He was erratic and frequently impecunious.

At a time when public criticism was growing of the non-attendance by Home Rulers at important debates, Butt himself was often absent for financial or health reasons. In serious debt, he was obliged to continue his legal career while leading the party. His fondness for an expensive claret and the other peccadillos which had previously made him such a colourful figure were now cited against his leadership. On more than one occasion, he offered to resign. Significantly, when his colleagues organised a testimonial to alleviate his financial distress, the reaction from the Irish public was less than wholehearted.[8]

When, in July 1876, following the defeat of a moderate proposal by Butt that the house of commons investigate the case for Home Rule, the nationalist journal *The Nation* was openly critical of Butt's tactics and called for a more obstructionist approach, Butt quickly had his leadership endorsed by a meeting of the party.[9] However, the attack on his leadership and his tactics continued, both inside and outside the ranks of the parliamentary party. The following month, the Home Rule Confederation of Great Britain, established in 1873 with Butt as president, endorsed his leadership but criticised his approach.

The confederation was also critical of the Home Rule League for its failure to harness Irish support for Home Rule. After an initial burst of enthusiasm, the league had stagnated. Its activities were severely hampered by financial problems and, with the failure of the parliamentary party to win concessions, popular interest waned or turned elsewhere. The confederation itself was an example of a vibrant organisation. More popular in composition and radical in outlook, it is no accident that among the vice-presidents elected at its 1876 convention were Joseph Biggar and one Charles Stewart Parnell.[10]

The obstruction crisis of 1877-8 determined the future shape and direction of the Home Rule movement. Biggar and Parnell with a small band of supporters within the party adopted the obstructionist approach called for by *The Nation*. With considerable ingenuity they used a range of devices to disrupt and delay the business of the house of commons and bring it to a standstill. Numerous amendments were proposed to government legislation, debate was prolonged for hours on end, motions for adjournment were repeatedly introduced, all with the intention of forcing British politicians to make concessions. In response to the loud condemnation of the tactic in the English press, it was argued that parliament was overburdened anyway and sufficient consideration was not given to pressing matters, not all by any means Irish. The problem, it was argued, could be solved at a stroke by giving Ireland a separate parliament.

Butt strongly disapproved of these tactics and publicly rebuked Parnell on a number of occasions. He accused him of undermining rather than advancing the case for reform. However, Butt was unable to control Parnell, a fact which itself illustrates his lack of authority and the loose nature of the party to which they both belonged. While the obstructionist tactic was not popular within the party, it won considerable support outside. The Home Rule Confederation of Great Britain welcomed the development and feted the obstructionists at meetings throughout Britain. It was claimed that they were striking a blow not just for Ireland but for the ordinary people of Britain whose plight was ignored by parliament. In August 1877, Parnell was elected president of the confederation in place of Butt.[11]

In Ireland, the obstructionists received a similar warm welcome. With the rift between Butt and Parnell growing rapidly, it seemed that a showdown was inevitable. When it finally came at the long awaited national conference of Home Rulers in January 1878, it was something of an anti-climax. Parnell defused the crisis by not contesting Butt's leadership. Like Ireland, he said, he could wait. Butt's was a pyrrhic victory as the conference then proceeded to support the 'energetic' policy advocated by Parnell. So, with Butt's position greatly weakened, the conflict simmered on. In April, he resigned as chairman of the party but was persuaded to reconsider his position.

There was now, in effect, a party within a party, one favouring conciliation and the other an active policy, the main plank of which was obstruction. The passage of the Intermediate Education Act by the government owed something to Butt's influence and seemed to promise a revival in the fortunes of the moderates. However, whatever goodwill was generated by the act was dissipated when it became clear that Butt had promised support for government policy in other areas as a *quid pro quo*. His subsequent defence of Disraeli's imperial policy further undermined Butt's position in Ireland. He was widely condemned and although he survived as leader until his death in May 1879, he was isolated and powerless.

Parnell and the Parnellite Party

In an obituary at the time of his death, T M Healy, one of the rising stars of the new generation of Home Rulers, pointed to the supreme irony of Butt's career: he had generated popular enthusiasm for Home Rule but in so doing guaranteed his own obsolescence.[12] The stagnation which had inspired Butt's efforts in the early 1870s had been replaced in the course of the decade by a new energy which was beginning to manifest itself in social and political affairs in the shape of such developments as the New Departure and the burgeoning land agitation. Paradoxically, the Home Rule parliamentary party seemed relatively unaffected by the changes which it had helped inspire. The obstructionists were only a vocal minority within the party. During the last years of Butt's leadership, it seemed as if the party might become increasingly irrelevant, if it did not go out of existence altogether. Had Butt recovered from his stroke, it might have been at the expense of his party.

Parnell came from precisely the class Butt had hoped to attract into the Home Rule movement. Born in 1848 into a prominent Wicklow Anglo-Irish family, his father, John Henry Parnell, was a liberal protestant and his mother, Delia Stewart, was the daughter of an American admiral who had fought the British in the 1812 war. His English education left him conscious of his Irishness and decidedly Anglo-phobic in outlook. He was nourished and shaped partly by what he reacted against, so that he became the leader of nationalist Ireland while at the same time being in many respects a Victorian gentleman. When Michael Davitt met him for the first time in December 1877, his first impression was of an 'Englishman of the strongest type, moulded for an Irish purpose'. He was an unlikely politician. Shy and retiring, he did not like large gatherings. He was not a good speaker although he could be effective, and he did have a striking appearance, determined character and direct personality which could sway audiences.[13] Unlike Butt, he grasped the value of extra-parliamentary leverage and of a tightly controlled party. This was already evident in 1880. His elevation owed much to his popularity outside the parliamentary party and he did not challenge for the leadership until he had ensured the presence in the party of those who would support him.

Obstruction was popular in Ireland, especially with nationalists. It became increasingly so when the agricultural depression of the late 1870s began to bite and the demand for land reform became more insistent.[14] During 1878-9, when the party was rudderless, Parnell's attentions were focussed not on Westminster but on Ireland and America. It was during this period that he forged the alliance with the Irish agrarian and republican traditions, an alliance which was to transform him from obscure backbench member of parliament to national leader. Unlike Butt, he was willing to harness those two dynamic forces to achieve his ends. Those ends were essentially parliamentary and required the cutting edge of a disciplined parliamentary party such as he now set about creating.

Butt was succeeded as chairman of the party by William Shaw, a liberal protestant banker who had been active in the Home Rule movement from its inception. Parnell's decision not to contest the leadership was a recognition of the fact that the balance within the party was still in favour of the old guard. A general election was imminent and he made it plain that he would be seeking a mandate at that election for his obstructionist policies. In that election, fifty-nine Home Rulers were elected, many of whom were to play a vital role in the decades which followed. Parnell himself was elected for three different constituencies, Cork city, Mayo and Meath. While the balance within the party had now moved perceptibly in favour of the more vigorous policy which he espoused, his victory was not decisive. His subsequent challenge to Shaw for leadership of the party was successful, but only by twenty-three votes to eighteen. While Parnell's support came from the obstructionists, Shaw's came largely from the original Home Rulers, many of whom now sat with the Liberals in parliament and drifted away from the Home Rule parliamentary party as it became increasingly radical.

In the immediate aftermath of the general election, the main emphasis was inevitably on the land agitation; this suited Parnell as little progress was likely on the political issue. The unsuccessful prosecution of the leaders of the Land League, and the dramatic obstruction of Gladstone's coercion bill early in 1881 kept the party in the public eye. In the latter case, the house of commons had its longest ever sitting and the measure was passed only after a departure from established procedures, soon to be changed permanently, to force the closure of the debate. In obstructing the coercion measure, the Protection of Person and Property Act 1881, which gave the authorities the power to suspend the Habeas Corpus Act and imprison without trial persons 'reasonably suspected' of specified offences, more than thirty of the Home Rule MPs were suspended from the house.

Gladstone's 1881 Land Act and the Kilmainham Treaty which followed marked a shift in emphasis on both sides. While publicly critical of the act which established dual ownership, Parnell accepted that it was a major step towards a settlement of that issue. The Kilmainham Treaty which secured Parnell's release from prison was an acknowledgement of that as well as an indication of Parnell's intention to return to more conventional parliamentary politics. Kilmainham also represented an acceptance by Gladstone that Parnell was preventing and not causing social chaos in Ireland and that little could be achieved without his acquiescence. As such, the compact created problems from

Parnell's left wing and Gladstone's right. However, the murder by the Invincibles in the Phoenix Park in May 1882 of the new chief secretary, Lord Frederick Cavendish and the under secretary, Thomas Burke, and the subsequent reintroduction of coercion polarised positions once more and postponed some of the benefits both leaders might have expected from the compact.

The move from agrarian to political agitation was publicly sealed by the establishment of the Irish National League in October 1882. The National League took the place of the Land League which had been declared illegal in 1881 and of the Home Rule League which had become increasingly irrelevant. The Home Rule Confederation of Great Britain was also absorbed. Over the next three years, the new organisation transformed Home Rule from an aspiration professed with varying degrees of conviction by a small number of members of parliament into a national movement with all the trappings of a modern political party. The league added three new important tiers to what was hitherto simply a parliamentary party: local branches, constituency committees and a national executive. The local branches rallied support; the county or constituency committees selected candidates for election and ran campaigns; and the national executive organised, coordinated and directed, under the watchful eye of the parliamentary party.[15]

Parnell was able to control the Irish National League directly unlike the Land League which, despite his presidency, was essentially an independent organisation. While the new organisation had as one of its aims further land reform, its main goal was Home Rule. Despite the outward appearance of democratic structures, Parnell's party was in fact hierarchical and autocratic. A council envisaged in the constitution and similar to that of the Home Rule League was never established so that control was retained by the 'organising committee' of thirty, chaired by Parnell. The committee which was dominated by the parliamentary party exercised wide discretionary powers. The day to day running of the league fell to an even smaller group, most notable of which was Timothy Harrington MP who acted as general secretary.

The constituency committees consisted of delegates from branches and any members of the local clergy who chose to attend. The latter provision caused some consternation especially among protestant Home Rulers but it did help to win the support of the catholic clergy, thus contributing to the popularity of the movement, and paved the way for the agreement of the church in 1885 to support the constitutional movement for Home Rule in return for Parnellite support of catholic educational demands. In practice, most candidates for election were pre-selected by the national leadership who then used a variety of stratagems to ensure that they would be 'chosen' by the constituency committee.[16]

Parnell also set about improving the cohesiveness of the parliamentary party itself. Improved funds, particularly from the Irish emigrant community in America, allowed the payment of needy members, thus removing a major restriction on the type of person who might stand for parliament and, in the process, increasing their dependence on the party. Even more significant was the introduction of a party pledge. Members of Butt's party had been pledged to support Home Rule in parliament but this had little effect. After the 1880 election, a new pledge was agreed which bound members to act together and to abide by the decisions of the majority. In 1884 an even more coercive pledge was introduced which, unlike previous pledges, was taken by party candidates *before* the election. There was no room for the traditional independent member who had been such a feature of Butt's party. The individual member was subservient to the party. If he wished to indulge his own conscience or interests, he was bound to resign. Each candidate pledged that

> in the event of my election to parliament I will sit, act and vote with the Irish parliamentary party and if at a meeting of the party convened upon due notice specially to consider the question, it be decided by a resolution supported by a majority of the entire parliamentary party that I have not fulfilled the above pledge I hereby undertake forthwith to resign my seat.[17]

The years 1883-5 were relatively quiet ones for Parnell and his party, almost indeed an anti-climax after the heady days of the land agitation. Parnell had wearied of mass agitation and his own financial circumstances were perilous. In parliament the party pursued an active and independent line without much success. There was one major development in 1884 which helped transform the situation. The third Reform Act which was designed primarily to reform the parliamentary franchise in Britain had the effect in Ireland of increasing the electorate from 226,000 to 738,000 while leaving the number of Irish seats the same, despite Ireland's declining population. Gladstone shrugged off the protests of those who claimed that the Reform Act would bring social chaos to Ireland, hoping instead that the influx of small farmers and labourers might in fact damage Parnell's position.[18]

This calculation was not unreasonable in that many of the newly enfranchised had gained nothing from the land war, but it proved mistaken. The new voters flocked to Parnell's party and in the longer term the Reform Act can be considered to have radically transformed the political balance in Ireland.

The impact of the Reform Act was immediately seen at the general election of December 1885. Parnell sought and gained a decisive public mandate for Home Rule. His party increased its strength to eighty-six, sweeping the boards outside Ulster (and Trinity College). Even in Ulster, Home Rulers won a majority of seats. The election brought not just an increase in seats but a change in the social composition of the parliamentary party. The dominance of the party by large landowners had been broken at the 1880 election but it still remained a predominantly upper class party. Most of the new members in 1885 came from lower down the social scale, with the result that the party was now almost evenly divided between large landowners, merchants and higher professionals (barristers etc.) on one side, and farmers, shopkeepers, and lower professionals (journalists, etc.) on the other.[19]

The first Home Rule bill

As well as providing Parnell with a decisive mandate, the general election gave the Home Rule party the balance of power in the commons with the Liberals having 333 seats and the Conservatives 251. Parnell had demonstrated his independence by helping to bring down Gladstone's administration in June 1885, by supporting a minority Conservative government and even advising Irish supporters in England to vote against the Liberals. He was now in an unprecedentedly strong position when he demanded the 'restoration' of an independent Irish parliament. Yet even he must have been surprised at the speed with which Gladstone, once again prime minister, moved to introduce a Home Rule bill in March 1886.

Gladstone's conversion to Home Rule was sudden but not completely unexpected. Earlier in his career, as chancellor of the exchequer, he had been a strong advocate of closer integration of Ireland and Britain and sought to promote more financial and administrative uniformity. The land agitation had convinced him of the impossibility of such a course. He had hoped in 1870 that remedial legislation and strong government would pacify Ireland and allow sensible liberals to take the initiative from the agitators. By 1882, he had to admit that this policy too had been a failure and a new one was necessary. Early in 1885, Joseph Chamberlain attempted to go some way towards meeting Irish demands with his 'central board' scheme which would have devolved certain limited powers to an Irish board and at the same time reformed Irish local government, but this was rejected as inadequate by Parnell. The only remaining alternatives seemed to be either coercion or concession of the Irish demand for Home Rule. Gladstone was unhappy with the former and after the failure of Chamberlain's scheme privately conceded that some form of self-government was inevitable sooner or later.[20]

Gladstone's motives have been the subject of considerable debate. He certainly felt a strong moral obligation to settle the Irish question. His sense of mission motivated him to proceed quickly and to carry on even at the risk of splitting his own party. His experience of the Eastern question had also made him more sympathetic and sensitive to Irish nationalism. At the same time, he viewed the Irish question as a disruptive force in British politics and a threat to the Liberal party because of its reliance on the Irish parliamentary party. Granting Home Rule would facilitate better government in Britain as well as in Ireland.

Gladstone had little direct experience of Ireland and was not well informed about conditions there. In the crucial months during which he resolved to proceed with Home Rule, his advisers warned him of imminent social chaos in Ireland unless something was done. More than anything else, it was that somewhat alarmist advice which persuaded him to introduce Home Rule forthwith and to accompany it with another Land Act aimed at solving the land question. The two acts were part of the same package, designed to avert calamity in Ireland.[21]

While Gladstone's sympathy for Irish nationalism was real, it would be misleading to see him as a supporter of a popular nationalist movement. Like Butt and to a lesser extent Parnell, he feared the consequences of such a movement and his energetic pursuit of a settlement of the land question was aimed at removing the cleavage between landlord and tenant, thus allowing Irish landlords to take their rightful place as the leaders of a self-governing Ireland.[22] His intention, in short, was not to unleash the forces of Irish democracy but to enshrine social conservatism.

The decision to introduce a Home Rule bill inevitably focussed attention on a question which had long been clouded in doubt: precisely what did Home Rule mean? Clearly it meant the establishment of a separate legislative institution for Ireland but with what powers and in what relationship with the imperial parliament? Isaac Butt had shied away from any detailed elaboration of what was entailed by Home Rule. Parnell too was reticent in this area. There was little discussion within the party on the matter. Butt envisaged a subordinate Irish parliament which did not necessarily involve repeal of the union. Parnell, on the rare occasions he addressed the issue, offered Grattan's parliament of the late eighteenth century as a model. Forty years earlier Daniel O'Connell had done likewise and later Arthur Griffith, founder of Sinn Féin, was to follow suit. But Grattan's parliament almost certainly meant different things to all three. Grattan's parliament was unreformed and was the preserve of the protestant ascendancy. Furthermore, although Ireland at the time was technically a separate kingdom with a supposedly independent parliament, legislation could be vetoed by the privy council in London and the Irish executive was not responsible to the Dublin parliament. Grattan's parliament was more a symbol than a serious political objective. Whatever its value as a rallying cry, it did nothing to clarify the meaning of Home Rule. Did Home Rule mean repeal of the union? How were the financial relations of Britain and Ireland to be regulated and was Ireland to cease to have a representation in the imperial parliament? What form was the new Irish assembly to take? All of these questions, which had previously been avoided, now became contentious issues.

Perhaps the most common objection to Home Rule was that it would lead to complete separation. In rallying popular support in Ireland, Parnell was inclined to stress how much Ireland was demanding while in reassuring the opposition the emphasis was on how little. In rejecting Chamberlain's scheme, he stirred an audience in Cork with the oft quoted declaration that

> ... no man has the right to fix the boundary to the march of the nation. No man has a right to say to his country: 'Thus far shalt thou go and no further', and we have never attempted to fix the *ne plus ultra* to the progress of Ireland's nationhood, and we never shall.[23]

However he had just qualified that apparent *carte blanche* to separatism by saying that they could not ask for less – or more – than the restoration of Grattan's parliament. He would have agreed with his colleague John Redmond's definition of Home Rule, perhaps significantly given to an Australian not an Irish audience in 1883:

> I mean by Home Rule the restoration to Ireland of representative government, and I define representative government to mean government in accordance with the constitutionally expressed will of a majority of the people, and carried out by a ministry constitutionally responsible to those whom they govern. In other words, I mean that the internal affairs of Ireland shall be regulated by an Irish parliament - that all imperial affairs, and all that relates to the colonies, foreign states and common interests of the empire, shall continue to be regulated by the imperial parliament as at present constituted. The idea at the bottom of this proposal is the desirability of finding some middle course between separation on the one hand, and over-centralisation of government on the other.[24]

Unlike some of his followers, Parnell was not a separatist. He told his own electors in Wicklow, in October 1885, that though it would be impossible to guarantee that Home Rule would not ultimately culminate in separation, the separatist demand came largely from misgovernment under the existing system and that Home Rule would weaken that demand.[25] He privately presented a Home Rule scheme to Gladstone which, he assured him, did not involve repeal of the union. While he could not propose such a scheme publicly, he undertook to work for its acceptance.[26]

Gladstone's Home Rule bill, introduced in April 1886, was an extremely modest measure. It provided for the establishment of a legislative body in Ireland composed of two 'Orders' which would normally sit together and each of which would have a suspensory veto over measures introduced by the other. The first Order was to consist of the twenty-eight Irish peers who already sat in the house of lords and seventy-five other representatives elected on a restrictive property franchise. The lower Order was to consist of existing Irish MPs and 101 new representatives. Further provision was made to protect the interests of the protestant minority by restricting the assembly's powers relating to religion. Matters relating to foreign policy, defence, trade and policing were also specifically reserved to the imperial parliament in which Ireland was to have no representation. Customs and excise duties were reserved to Whitehall, thus effectively precluding any resort to protectionism. Ireland was to make a contribution of one-fifteenth to imperial expenditure. The balance of Irish revenue was to be at the disposal of the Irish executive, which was responsible to the Irish assembly. This, Gladstone contended, represented an improvement on Grattan's parliament.

The bill was hastily drafted and was defective in a number of areas. Its financial clauses were criticised by both nationalists and unionists. They would have imposed a burden on Ireland and left the new assembly with considerable problems. Limited though the bill was, Parnell did accept it as a final settlement. In Ireland, the reaction from nationalists was far from euphoric but generally favourable. Whatever the outcome, its introduction was seen as a victory for Parnell and his party.[27]

Gladstone had hoped to have all party support for his Home Rule measure. There were some modest grounds for optimism in this regard. Prior to the election Parnell had talks with Lord Carnarvon, the lord lieutenant, who was known to be sympathetic to Home Rule while Lord Randolph Churchill was also favourably disposed to some concession.

Many Conservatives shared Gladstone's fear of class upheaval and some of them were attracted by the idea of a preemptive strike to consolidate the position of the ascendancy. In the event, however, any hopes of a bi-partisan approach to the question came to nothing. Perhaps if Gladstone had moved less quickly, as Parnell expected, and allowed time for more discussion and reflection, the outcome might have been different. Instead Home Rule became a party political issue, indeed, as time went on, the most important single issue dividing the two main British parties, with enormous consequences for the future of the Liberals and of Ireland. Home Rule became an encumbrance to the Liberals while it provided the Conservatives, in danger of losing direction in a rapidly changing society, with an ideal rallying point.

The opposition to the Home Rule bill centred on a number of main issues – the unity of the empire, the lawlessness of the Irish and the position of the Ulster unionists (see below, pp 118-22). With the Conservatives opposing the measure and likely to block it in the house of lords, its chances of passing were slight but these vanished completely when the Liberal party split on the issue. Gladstone's deep commitment to settling the Irish question was not shared by all of his colleagues. The bill was opposed from two quarters within the Liberal party, by the right-wing led by Lord Harcourt and, on the radical side, by Joseph Chamberlain, still feeling slighted by the rejection of his earlier scheme and worried that Gladstone's bill went too far.

Faced with the mounting criticism of the bill, Gladstone promised that it would be amended. This gesture failed to placate the opposition and the bill was defeated on its second reading by 341 votes to 311, with 93 Liberals crossing the floor. In the election which followed, Parnell's position in Ireland was consolidated but the Liberal party was hopelessly divided and the Conservatives returned to power with Liberal Unionist support.

The fall of Parnell

The identification of Home Rule with the Liberals and particularly with Gladstone meant that any further progress in that area would have to wait Gladstone's return to power. Although Parnell and, indeed, many members of the Liberal party did not like it, the futures of their two parties were now inextricably linked. With the Conservatives in power between 1886 and 1892, their Irish policy was one of resolute government tempered by occasional concession. It is hardly surprising then that for the immediate future attention shifted away from the political issue of Home Rule and back to the land question.

Parnell disapproved of the Plan of Campaign not only because he had no desire to return to mass agitation but also because he saw it as a distraction from the political issue. As a result he took little part in that campaign which at least had the effect of confirming Gladstone in his view that social chaos in Ireland was not far away. Parnell's obvious coolness towards the land agitation enhanced his position with English Liberals, though this was soon to be called into question from another quarter.

In 1887, *The Times* published a series of articles entitled 'Parnellism and Crime' which sought to link Parnell with the revolutionary nationalist movement. A key part of the case against Parnell was a letter purportedly written by him approving of the Phoenix Park murders. Despite Parnell's disclaimer, *The Times* repeated the allegations. When Parnell demanded a select committee of the house of commons to clear his name, the government refused and instead appointed a judicial commission of three judges. This was widely seen as a move to discredit Parnell and the nationalist movement as it placed the land league and the nationalist movement under a spotlight designed to establish their role in fomenting agrarian crime and vindicating the view that the problems of Ireland were caused largely by revolutionary agitators. The Special Commission which sat during 1888 and 1889, examining hundreds of witnesses, might have seriously damaged the Home Rule movement had it not quickly emerged that the letters on which the accusations largely rested were the crude forgeries of a Dublin journalist, Richard Pigott, who committed suicide shortly after he was exposed.

His vindication seemed to leave Parnell's standing higher than ever but no sooner had one shadow been lifted than another more ominous one appeared. In December 1889, Captain William O'Shea filed a petition for divorce from his wife, Katherine, citing Parnell as co-respondent. The case which was not defended was finally resolved the following November, with O'Shea being granted his divorce and Parnell stigmatised as the guilty party. The lurid picture which emerged from the newspaper accounts, giving the impression of the Irish leader engaging in a sordid, surreptitious affair and painting O'Shea as an innocent victim was extremely misleading but it severely damaged Parnell's reputation and standing.

Captain O'Shea was far from being an innocent victim. He had been living apart from his wife for several years. Parnell had met Katherine for the first time in 1880 and they had begun to live together for brief periods the following year and permanently in 1886. She bore him two children and probably a third who died. Despite his evidence in court, O'Shea was almost certainly aware of the relationship long before 1886 and used it for his own advancement. He adopted the role of intermediary in the Kilmainham Treaty negotiations and in 1886 persuaded Parnell to impose him as an unpledged candidate for a safe nationalist seat in Galway, in the teeth of fierce opposition from Tim Healy, John Dillon and local nationalists. He resigned the seat shortly afterwards. Probably mistakenly, Parnell suspected him of involvement in *The Times* forgeries. His motivation for suing for divorce now was probably financial as much as petty vindictiveness. An inheritance which he had long expected to receive from his wife's aunt went exclusively to Katherine. By commencing divorce proceedings he may have hoped to receive his share (for a lump sum he was willing to allow his wife divorce him) or, if not, build a case for the overturning of the will.[28]

Parnell's initial reaction to the divorce writ was almost casual. He assured his friends that he would be vindicated, presumably in the expectation that O'Shea could be persuaded to withdraw the writ or be exposed for what he was.[29] He then dismissed it as part of a continuing conspiracy to ruin him. However, he was unwilling to defend the case, probably because he wanted the divorce more than O'Shea. At any event, his aloofness only served to increase the anxiety and ultimately the disappointment of his colleagues.

Parnell's sin was not his relationship with Katherine O'Shea. It was not even, as Professor Lyons has suggested, that he was found out. It was that what had been for many years common knowledge among senior Liberals and nationalists had now entered into the public domain.[30] And, at least in the short term, it was the reaction in England which was decisive. For the moment the Irish catholic bishops remained silent. It was Gladstone and the demands of the 'nonconformist conscience' which precipitated his downfall. Following stirrings within his own party, Gladstone intimated to the Irish parliamentary party, that unless Parnell resigned, Home Rule would be indefinitely postponed. When the party initially confirmed Parnell's leadership, Gladstone made his position public. A further meeting of the party was hastily convened in Committee Room Fifteen at the house of commons. Following a long and rancorous debate at the end of which those present were asked to choose between Parnell and Home Rule, the party split with a group of forty-five, led by Justin McCarthy, opposing Parnell and twenty-seven remaining loyal.

The focus now turned to Ireland. The Catholic hierarchy declared against his leadership and the weight of clerical influence was predominantly against him. No doubt this weighed heavily with some people as did Gladstone's virtual ultimatum. Others now took the opportunity to express criticisms rarely heard before: Parnell was aloof and autocratic; he was a landlord with little sympathy for the small farmer etc. The battle was short, intense and extremely bitter. Parnell was triumphantly received by his supporters on his return to Dublin but in the months that followed the popular reaction was predominantly unfavourable. Pro- and anti- Parnell candidates contested a number of by-elections with the Parnellites being decisively defeated in each case. During all of this time, Parnell's health, which had been bad for a number of years, visibly deteriorated. After one particularly wearing series of speeches, he returned exhausted to England and died on the night of 6 October 1891, in the arms of his beloved Katherine, now Mrs Parnell.

The circumstances of his fall from power make an assessment of Parnell more difficult. Faced with the opposition of a majority of his colleagues and of the clergy, he sought to mobilise popular support by a series of speeches in favour of small farmers, working men and a more radical policy. In Belfast, he was critical of clerical influence and sympathetic to the worries of northern protestants. How seriously to take such speeches is a difficult question: they tend to show him in a more radical light than may be justified. It may be, as Paul Bew puts it, that free from the restrictions of his previous position, he could now express himself more freely. On the other hand his critics, most notably Davitt, argued that the Parnell of 1890-91 was an opportunist trying to exploit whatever weapons remained at his disposal. Davitt points to the fact that while he attempted to rally working people's support in this period, he had earlier been dismissive of any involvement with them.[31] Whatever his reservations about clerical interference, he had cooperated with the clergy earlier in his career. And while his speeches took on a republican tone after the divorce crisis, in 1886 he had accepted Gladstone's modest proposal as a final settlement even though Gladstone claimed that it did not involve repeal of the union. Similarly his new-found interest in the smaller farmer rests uncomfortably alongside his earlier lack of interest in their plight.

Parnell was no social radical. He had no desire to see the victory of radical agrarianism under Home Rule. For that reason in 1886, he cooperated with Gladstone's efforts to produce a land bill distinctly favourable to landlords (which was ultimately scuttled by Parnell's followers for that reason) with a view to reconciling them to Home Rule and persuading them to play their part in a Home Rule parliament. Much to the disgust of Davitt, he argued privately that such a parliament should not introduce any revolutionary changes in the land system. He expressed admiration for Bismarck's Germany where the conservative statesman was undercutting social democracy and labour organisations and in the process entrenching conservatism by a programme of social reform.[32] Paternalistic benevolence and social harmony, with the landed elite in control, were at the heart of Parnell's vision of a new Ireland.

Parnell was a constitutional nationalist who grasped the secret of mobilising popular opinion in Ireland. The nationalist movement which he helped to create, though at his death hopelessly divided, outlasted him. The irony is that the Parnell myth which grew and exercised considerable influence on the generation that followed had its greatest impact outside of constitutional nationalism. For the Home Rule movement itself his legacy remained divisive for a long time to come.

The second Home Rule Bill

In pragmatic terms, the result of the 1892 general election seemed to confirm the wisdom of those nationalists who, forced to choose between Parnell and Gladstone, opted for the latter. In Ireland, the anti-Parnellites led by Justin McCarthy won seventy-one seats while the Parnellites under John Redmond won only nine. More significantly, Gladstone's Liberals were victorious in Britain. Despite objections from within his own party and the continuing schism within the Home Rule party, Gladstone had kept Home Rule in the forefront of Liberal policy and a new Home Rule bill was introduced early in 1893.

More carefully drafted than its predecessor, the new measure was no less modest in its provisions. Gladstone's 'Bill to Amend the Provision for the Future Government of Ireland' opened with a specific reassurance that the supremacy of the imperial parliament was in no way diluted by what was proposed. An Irish parliament was to be established, the lower house of which was to be composed of 103 members elected on the existing franchise and from existing constituencies. The upper house was to be composed of forty-eight members elected on a restrictive property franchise, designed to protect landlord interests. Disagreements between the upper and lower house were to be resolved by fresh elections or majority vote of both houses. Foreign affairs, trade, customs and excise and defence were reserved to the imperial parliament. Land legislation and policing were also reserved although it was envisaged that control of both would pass to the Irish parliament eventually. Irish members were to continue to sit at Westminster, but in reduced numbers. It was originally proposed that they would vote only on matters affecting Ireland, but this was considered to be unworkable and this restriction was abandoned.[33]

The financial clauses again proved extremely difficult to frame, it being well nigh impossible to establish an acceptable and reliable basis on which to calculate Ireland's imperial contribution. When it emerged that the Irish revenue figures on which the provisions of the bill were based were in fact miscalculated, that section of the bill had to be recast, much to the embarrassment of the government.

During its progress through parliament, the bill produced unprecedented unionist opposition. Not only was Home Rule opposed in principle: over eighty days, every clause was fought line by line in a campaign reminiscent of Parnell's obstruction tactics a decade earlier. For their part, the nationalist camp was hopelessly divided, a fact which hardly enhanced the Irish claim for self-government. The anti-Parnellites were lukewarm about the bill but felt obliged to support it as an improvement on 1886 while the Parnellites, although more critical, were reluctant to oppose it. In September 1893, the bill finally passed the house of commons by a majority of thirty-four. A week later, following a peremptory debate, it was rejected by the house of lords by 419 votes to 41.

Gladstone was willing to fight the lords' veto by going to the country for another mandate and then, if necessary, swamping the upper house with new peers who would support Home Rule, but his colleagues had no stomach for such a fight.[34] Gladstone retired and Home Rule was relegated to the back burner by the Liberals. The change of heart came too late to prevent their defeat at the next general election. The defeat of Gladstone's second Home Rule bill was seen by many observers as inevitable. Its main significance was that it passed the house of commons. It was the lords' veto which now stood in the way of Irish self-government. Until the veto was removed, Home Rule was unlikely to reach the statute book.

4 The New Conservatism and the Anglo-Irish Twilight

What trash to be bawling in the streets about the 'Green Isle', 'the Isle of the Ocean', the bold anthem of 'Erin-go-Bragh'! A far better anthem would be 'Erin go bread and cheese', 'Erin go cabins that will keep out the rain', 'Erin go pantaloons without holes in them'.

Sydney Smith

The period between the death of Parnell and the 1916 rising is often seen as a 'featureless valley'. In this scheme of things, the torch dropped by the fallen Parnell is taken up by Patrick Pearse and his colleagues. This view of a state of paralysis in Irish affairs was one felt by some contemporaries and owed much to petty divisions within the nationalist movement. However, it is a view which is only partly accurate. The period witnessed developments in the social, economic and political sphere which were important in themselves and in their long term impact. In many respects, it was an age of experiments, the failure of which had important implications. Following a second attempt at a Home Rule settlement by Gladstone, new solutions to Irish problems were explored. These proved no more effective than previous efforts and by 1911 Home Rule was back at the top of the political agenda.

Constructive unionism

At the root of the Home Rule movement was the belief that many of the fundamental social and economic ills of the country sprang directly from the Act of Union. This analysis was vehemently rejected by unionists but their case was weakened by the absence of a credible alternative diagnosis for Irish problems or prescription for their solution. That dilemma was at the root of the so-called constructive unionist movement which emerged in Britain and Ireland from the 1880s onwards.[1] Arthur Balfour, chief secretary from 1887 to 1891 was one of the first exponents of such a policy. Gerald Balfour, chief secretary from 1895 to 1900, followed in his brother's footsteps, as did George Wyndham, chief secretary from 1900 to 1905. All three were British politicians whose main concerns were British. On another level, constructive unionism was a reflection of the concerns of Irish landowners seeking a *rapprochement* with the new Ireland. As such it was part of the same tradition which had inspired the Home Rule movement in the 1870s.

The term constructive unionism is misleading if it suggests a cohesive, organised party. Constructive unionism was a diverse movement, embracing, on the one hand, senior government ministers preoccupied with British, not Irish, politics, and on the other, improving Irish landlords whose main concern was Ireland. Nevertheless, while motivations varied, there was a common outlook based on the conviction of what a constructive policy might achieve.

Constructive unionism was also in many respects the product of the same impulses which had created the 'new conservatism' in Europe, particularly in Germany under Bismarck. Conservatives everywhere were coming to the realisation that the best way to preserve the essentials of the old order was to adjust to the newly emerging society and to seek to control rather than blindly oppose it. Thus conservative statesmen such as Bismarck promoted a state paternalism aimed at resolving social conflicts and undercutting radical politics. Yet, while Ireland shared this wider European experience, there is much that was distinctive in the Irish situation. Elsewhere, the new conservatism developed largely in response to industrialisation while in Ireland the focus was predominantly rural. In Europe, the new conservatism sought to manipulate nationalism; in Ireland constructive unionism sought to kill it.

Gerald Balfour summed up the basis of constructive unionism as follows:

> Apply suitable remedial measures, say the Unionists, to the social and economic conditions of the country, and it is not unreasonable to hope that political discontent – or, in other words, the demand for Home Rule – will gradually die away of itself.[2]

Balfour listed the remedial measures which were tried, including the building of light railways to remote parts of the west, peasant proprietorship, local government reform, state aid, encouraging and supplementing self-help and cooperation. As such the policy was simply a development of that prescribed by his brother, Arthur Balfour, when he came to Ireland as chief secretary in 1887. The disturbed state of the country at that time had convinced Gladstone of the necessity for Home Rule. Balfour, a firm advocate of resolute government, came to a different conclusion:

Cromwell failed because he relied solely on repressive measures. This mistake I shall not imitate. I shall be as ruthless as Cromwell in enforcing obedience to the law, but at the same time I shall be as radical as any reformer in redressing grievances and especially in removing every cause of complaint in regard to the land. It is on the twofold aspect of my policy that I rely for success.[3]

Thus conciliation was added to the traditional tory policy of coercion. The firmness of Arthur Balfour's commitment to coercion enabled him to gain acceptance within his party for conciliation. This policy survived until the devolution crisis of 1904 when all pretence of interest in concession was dropped. Gerald Balfour somewhat unwisely labelled the policy 'killing Home Rule with kindness'. Such an open admission of ulterior motive was guaranteed to make nationalists suspicious of the policy. Furthermore, it is by no means certain that all British unionists wished to kill Home Rule for they could see that as long as it remained an issue, the Liberals would be hamstrung and they themselves would have a ready-made rallying cry.[4]

The clearest manifestation of constructive unionism was the land purchase legislation. While land reform was begun by Gladstone in 1870, the legislation which ultimately transferred the ownership of the land to the tenants was passed by the Conservative party. Such a revolutionary step was taken because it was felt to be the only means to gain social peace and prevent turmoil. Thus the party which was traditionally the voice of landlordism endorsed peasant proprietorship as the price for stability. Nor was the policy one imposed completely from outside. Although some landlords resented land purchase, the initiative for the 1903 act came, as we have seen, from a landlord.

The Congested Districts Board

By 1891, it was clear that land purchase was not the complete panacea for Irish agricultural problems that some of its proponents hoped. As we have seen (p.15), many holdings were too small to provide a living for the occupier, especially in the west of Ireland and there remained a substantial number of landless who were unaffected by the transfer of land ownership. To tackle these problems new structures had to be devised which would be flexible and more responsive to Irish needs. The two major examples of such innovation were the Congested Districts Board, established by Arthur Balfour in 1891, and the department of agriculture, established on the initiative of Horace Plunkett in 1899.

After visiting the west of Ireland in 1891, Arthur Balfour agreed to include in the Land Act of that year provision for the setting up of a

Congested Districts Board which was invested with wide powers of a paternal character to devise schemes for the amelioration of social and economic conditions in that region. The operations of the board were confined to electoral divisions with a rateable valuation of less than 30 shillings per head, situated in counties in which twenty per cent or more of the inhabitants lived in divisions of such a rateable valuation. By these complicated criteria, the congested districts in 1891 comprised one-sixth of the area and one-ninth of the population of the country, mainly along the western seaboard. The criteria were relaxed in the Land Act of 1909 so that the entire counties of Donegal, Sligo, Leitrim, Roscommon, Mayo, Galway and Kerry, and six rural districts in Clare and four in Cork, were classified as congested districts, representing over one-third of the country and a population of over one million.[5] Of the 98,000 families resident in the congested districts in 1891, more than 17,000 were defined by the board as 'approaching the borderline of poverty'; 28,500 families lived on holdings of less than £2 rateable valuation while 26,600 lived on holdings between £2 and £4 valuation. The average poor law valuation was £1-0-2 (£1.01p) as against £2-19-8 (£2.98) for the country as a whole.[6]

Balfour was well aware that for the board to be successful it would have to be popularly acceptable and have considerable discretion in the framing and implementing of its policies. He clearly laid down that the board was semi-independent of the Irish government. This 'charter of freedom' caused considerable friction with Dublin Castle and the treasury in London over the next twenty years and the board's autonomy was rarely accepted by Balfour's successors. The board repeatedly clashed with the treasury over its tendency to over-commit itself financially. Especially after 1905, there was a running battle between the board and the treasury with the board regularly exceeding its budget and the treasury refusing to meet the deficit. Most of these squabbles were solved only after political intervention by nationalist politicians. The board's uneasy relations with the central bureaucracy culminated in the board actually taking the treasury to court in a case which went all the way to the house of lords.[7]

The board was empowered to take such steps as it 'thought proper' to promote agricultural development, forestry, the breeding of livestock and poultry, the sale of seed potatoes and oats, migration and emigration, the enlargement and amalgamation of small holdings, the improvement of estates, and the development of fishing, weaving and spinning and any other suitable industries. The board quickly became involved in all of these areas except emigration, an area which was seen to be too controversial. Initially its funds were limited but by 1909 it had a total income of £231,000 *per annum*. It was also entitled to lend and borrow money for productive purposes. Partly because of its limited income, the board concentrated mainly on the purchase of land for improvement and resale to tenants, although it also made concerted efforts to improve communications by building roads and railways and to develop the fishing industry by building piers. Between 1891 and 1921, well over 1,100 estates (and farms) were purchased at a total cost of almost £11 million.[8]

The board has often been accused of being a manifestation of state paternalism which tended to stifle rather than foster local initiative. There was certainly an element of that in the tory approach, as can be seen from the attitude of the earl of Zetland, the lord lieutenant at the time the board was established, who warned Balfour

> I grieve to say that my experience of the Celt leads me to believe that providence has not endowed him with sufficient energy to do more than eat potatoes that are put into his mouth.[9]

The Balfours argued that *laissez faire* had failed and therefore a 'veritable new departure in statesmanship' was necessary. Michael Davitt preferred to see the board as an example of 'enlightened state socialism'. Be that as it may, the centralism of its approach sometimes led to problems.[10]

Nevertheless, the board did achieve considerable success and had an impact on the lives of those most disadvantaged in the congested districts. The accusations of state paternalism are somewhat misleading in that its most significant features were its independence and its virtually 'amateur' status. It was an unpaid board whose members assembled monthly to decide where and how to spend its funds. Not until 1909 did any of the permanent staff become members of the board. The chief secretary was an *ex officio* member and acted as chairman when he was present. Frederick Wrench, the land commissioner, and West Ridgeway, the under secretary, were also *ex officio* members of the original board. The eight nominated members were a motley crew of clergymen, landlords, business and professional men. The clerical element was always well represented. When the board was reconstituted in 1909, the number of members was increased to fourteen, including two bishops and three parish priests. Of these, two in particular made enormous contributions to the work of the board, Fr Denis O'Hara from Mayo and Dr O'Donnell, bishop of Raphoe.

From the beginning, but especially after the return of the Liberals in 1905, an attempt was made to include members from all parts of the congested districts and to appoint representatives of the nationalist population. Though the board was often criticised by nationalists, it was the only government agency which they actually dominated. As a result, it managed to win popular acceptance. That not only made its work easier, it made it more difficult for politicians and administrators to curb its activities.[11]

The department of agriculture and the IAOS

The board was so successful that it was suggested that its operations should be extended to include the whole country but this was never seriously considered. The extreme poverty of the congested districts was deemed to justify such an experiment, but only in limited areas. The long-term development of agriculture throughout the country was felt to require a more conventional approach.[12] Not that the department of agriculture and technical instruction could be classed as conventional. The board was popular, but it was neither democratic nor integrated into the normal structure of government. Horace Plunkett's department of agriculture promised to reconcile these apparently conflicting demands. That it failed to do so was due as much to personality factors as to any defects in his proposals.

Plunkett, who was also the father of the Irish cooperative movement, was born in 1854, the third son of Baron Dunsany. He spent some time ranching in the United States before returning to Ireland to manage his father's estates. Always a controversialist, and once dubbed the best-hated man in Ireland, he had an individual and passionate vision of Irish society. In his book, *Ireland in the new century,* published in 1904, he presented a comprehensive critique of the Irish situation. His central argument was that Ireland and the Irish were characterised by a lack of initiative, an excessive conformity and a propensity for being led. What was needed instead was self-reliance and individual initiative. His criticisms of nationalist politicians for misleading the people into believing that Home Rule was the panacea for all problems, and of the catholic clergy for their authoritarianism and their concentration on the next life rather than the needs of the present, provoked a storm of protests, mostly from those criticised. Whatever the truth of Plunkett's analysis, such public criticism of nationalist MPs and the clergy was unwise from someone whose practical work required their cooperation. The book entrenched an animosity towards Plunkett which undermined much of his work. What was forgotten at the time was that Plunkett was equally severe on his own class whom he accused of being dedicated only to perpetuating their own position and of making no attempt to reconcile the people to the union.

Plunkett was a firm believer in the virtues of self-help. Though he was a member of the Congested Districts Board from 1891 to 1918, he disapproved of its paternalistic approach. His own ideas found expression in the report of the Recess Committee, a gathering of prominent Irishmen which assembled in 1895, in response to his public invitation, to discuss how the development of the agricultural and industrial resources of Ireland might best be promoted. Remarkably the committee produced an unanimous report recommending that a department of agriculture be established with a minister directly responsible to parliament at its head.[13]

The government accepted the proposal, although the necessary legislation was delayed until 1899 in favour of local government reform. The new department owed something to the peculiar circumstances of Ireland, something to current English administrative practice and something to similar models in other European countries. It took over the functions of six existing boards. Though the chief secretary was president, the real head was the vice-president, who, it was understood, would be a member of parliament. This was a new departure, and placed the department on a similar footing to many English departments.[14]

The list of powers and duties transferred to the department at its foundation or shortly afterwards gives a good impression both of the variety of its duties and of the complicated and confused network which it replaced. By order of the lord lieutenant, the following powers and duties were transferred to the department: those of the Veterinary Department of the Irish privy council, under the Diseases and Animals Acts of 1894 and 1896, the Destructive Insects Act of 1877, and the Fertilisers and Feeding Stuffs Act, 1893; those of the registrar-general for Ireland and the Land Commission in connection with the preparation of agricultural statistics and the Markets and Fairs Acts, 1887 and 1891; those of the Commissioners of National Education in connection with the Albert and Munster Institutions which taught agricultural methods; and those of the Inspectors of Irish Fisheries. The administration of the grants for Science and Art and for Technical Instruction was transferred from the English Board of Education in 1901; in 1904 the powers of the Commissioners of Public Works in connection with various Reproductive Loan Fund Acts and the Sea and Coast Fisheries Fund Act were transferred, as were the powers of the English Board of Education in respect of the Geological Survey of Ireland in 1905. The National Museum and the National Library were also placed under the supervision of the department.[15]

Entrusting all these powers to a single department was an attempt to bring 'order and simplicity' to an area previously characterised by disorder and confusion. In addition, the department was entrusted with new powers in relation to the development of Irish agriculture. The expenses of its departmental establishment and the cost of the transferred services were defrayed out of an annual parliamentary vote. For its new functions, it was given an 'Endowment Fund' derived from Irish and imperial sources which yielded an annual income of £166,000.

A major innovation was the introduction of an element of popular control by the creation of a consultative council and advisory boards to assist the department in its work. A Council of Agriculture, an Agricultural Board and a Board of Technical Instruction were established. The president and vice-president of the department were *ex officio* members of each but they were not normally entitled to vote. The Council of Agriculture consisted of 104 members, 68 appointed by the newly created County Councils and 34 by the department. The Agricultural Board had 14 members – 8 appointed by provincial committees of the Council of Agriculture and 4 by the department; while the Board of Technical Instruction had 23, 15 appointed by local authorities, 4 by the department, 1 by the Commissioners of National Education and 1 by the Commissioners of Intermediate Education. The Council of Agriculture, which was bound to meet at least once a year, discussed matters of public interest in connection with the act and the two boards were required to advise the department on all matters submitted to them by the department. They had no specific administrative powers but had a right of veto over all expenditure from the Endowment Fund. Surprisingly, this complicated structure did not lead to prolonged disputes, perhaps because, as Augustine Birrell put it, in practice the council discussed, the board advised and the department did what it thought best.[16] The department was also empowered to cooperate with County Committees of Agriculture in local projects. It was bound, however, to demand a local contribution for such projects, with the result that it was less popular than the Congested Districts Board. Even so, it achieved notable success in this and in the other areas under its control.

Notwithstanding its achievements, the department did not completely fulfil the expectations of the Recess Committee. This was partly because of the overwhelming difficulties which any such department had to face in Ireland. However, it was also related to the controversy which surrounded Plunkett, its founder and first vice-president. 'Killing Home Rule with Kindness' and the whole philosophy of 'constructive unionism' was identified with him more than with any other politician, with the exception of the Balfours. His 'more business, less politics' prescription for Irish ills was poorly received by those who attributed all the economic ills of Ireland to the Act of Union.

Plunkett argued that the Irish question was economic not political. He told Arthur Balfour that a British government which promoted agricultural development in Ireland would reconcile the Irish to the union and at the same time create a market for British industrial produce. In his open letter to the press suggesting the Recess Committee, he frankly admitted his opposition to Home Rule and repeated the opinion that if Ireland was developed industrially and agriculturally, the demand for Home Rule would cease. On the other hand, he pointed out that if it did not cease, Home Rule was more likely to be granted if Ireland was developed. So, he sought support from both sides. The Home Rule party was still divided. Justin McCarthy, of the majority faction, refused to participate in the committee on the grounds that Plunkett was seeking to substitute administrative reform for Home Rule. John Redmond, from the other faction, took the view that nationalists should not decline to assist in the promotion of reform. This division foreshadowed the division on the land conference and the Wyndham Land Act which we have already examined (see above pp28-9). As we shall see, the nationalist movement remained fundamentally divided on what approach to take regarding constructive unionism.[17]

Plunkett's administration of his new department left few grounds for complaint. Despite the opposition of both Gerald Balfour and the lord lieutenant, Lord Cadogan, he insisted on appointing T P Gill, a nationalist MP, to the secretaryship of the department. He made it clear that political patronage would be eschewed in the making of appointments. Neither of these gestures did anything to mollify the opposition to Plunkett, which became more vocal after 1900 when he retained his position despite the fact that he lost his seat in parliament and could therefore not represent his department there. When the Liberals returned, Plunkett resigned as a matter of course. However, following representations from Antony MacDonnell, the under-secretary, that there was no one of sufficient calibre to replace him, he was asked to remain on, at least temporarily. This provoked a torrent of criticism from nationalist MPs who demanded that he be removed. Despite a recommendation from a Committee of Inquiry into the workings of the department that its head should not have a seat in parliament or have ministerial status, Plunkett was replaced by T W Russell, an Ulster Liberal MP for whom the nationalists had expressed a preference. Russell was succeeded in 1919 by H T Barrie, an Ulster Unionist.[18]

The department of agriculture, the Congested Districts Board and the Estates Commissioners represented three different and to an extent rival approaches to the problems of rural Ireland and there was a considerable overlap between their activities. For example, all three were involved in land purchase. Inevitably some rationalisation was necessary. Significantly, the suggestion of Antony MacDonnell, that the board be abolished and its powers given to the department, was rejected by the Liberals in 1909 in favour of a reorganisation which enhanced the powers of the board within its own area and correspondingly limited some of the activities of the department. There is no doubt that this outcome sprang directly from the popularity of the former and the suspicion of the latter.[19]

Plunkett's answer to the weaknesses of the Irish character was agricultural cooperation. Through the cooperative movement, he felt, the natural advantages of soil and climate could be harnessed. On his return to Ireland in 1889, he had travelled the country in an effort to establish cooperative creameries. His first success was in Doneraile, County Cork. By 1894, the number of societies had grown to such an extent that a coordinating body was necessary. Plunkett was the driving force behind the establishment in that year of the Irish Agricultural Organisation Society. Plunkett was president of the society and RA Anderson, Lord Castletown's land agent, secretary. They were joined in their efforts by a diverse group which included Lord Monteagle, from Limerick, Fr Tom Finlay, a Jesuit, and Christopher Digges la Touche, managing director of Guinness's brewery. In 1895 the *Irish Homestead* was launched as the journal of the society, under the editorship first of Finlay and later of George Russell, better known, under the pen-name 'AE', as a poet, painter and mystic. The cooperative movement grew rapidly so that by 1912 there were close to 1,000 such societies, including creameries, credit societies, poultry societies for the marketing of eggs and agricultural societies for the purchase of fertilisers.[20]

Plunkett saw the work of the IAOS and the department of agriculture as being complementary. However, the connection was a source of criticism and damaged both. In the early years they cooperated successfully but T P Gill was increasingly unsympathetic to the IAOS. There were problems elsewhere too. Despite repeated protestations to the contrary, many people saw the IAOS as a political body. When Anderson sought to establish a creamery in Rathkeale, his efforts were thwarted by a local solicitor who

> having elicited the fact that our movement recognised neither political nor religious differences – that the Unionist-Protestant cow was as dear to us as her Nationalist-Catholic sister – gravely informed me that our programme would not suit Rathkeale. 'Rathkeale', said he pompously, 'is a Nationalist town – Nationalist to the backbone – and every pound of butter made in this creamery must be made on Nationalist principles, or it shan't be made at all.' This sentiment was applauded loudly, and the proceedings terminated.[21]

Apart from suspicion of Plunkett himself, the IAOS was resented by merchants and traders who saw the cooperative movement as a threat to their own businesses and the subsidy as unfair competition. They found a sympathetic audience in sections of the Irish parliamentary party who persuaded T W Russell to withdraw the department's grant to the society. After a long fight by Plunkett, this was restored in 1911.[22]

Local government reform

The main emphasis of constructive unionism was on rural development and administrative reform. Both were seen to be interrelated. The representative element in the department of agriculture was facilitated by the major reform in the organisation of local government which had taken place in 1898. Local government reform had long been a demand of Liberal Unionists. Arthur Balfour had opposed the inclusion of Ireland in the proposed reform of British local government in the late 1880s because he feared that the new councils would be dominated by the National League to the detriment of landlords who were at the time fighting the Plan of Campaign. However, the Liberal Unionists had long since been promised reform of local government and delay, once the land agitation abated, risked alienating them and giving a boost to Home Rule. So, in 1890, influenced by West Ridgeway, his under-secretary, Balfour changed his mind. His change of heart provoked an outcry from Irish landlords who saw that popular control of local government, coupled with land purchase legislation, would spell an end to their power. They insisted on the insertion of safeguards in the draft legislation which destroyed its democratic thrust. The bill provided for the setting up of county and district councils but it also contained severe limitations on their power and safeguards to protect the position of the landlords. The compromise was not acceptable to either side so the bill was allowed to drop.[23]

The Local Government Act of 1898 was a more far-reaching measure which had a profound impact on Irish political and social life. While it was a product of constructive unionism, it would seem that Balfour was also motivated by an expedient desire to end an *impasse* over local rating which was blocking the government's legislative programme.[24] The Grand Juries, which were a relic of a by-gone age, and which were dominated largely by the large landowners were replaced by county, urban and rural district councils elected on a wide franchise, including for the first time women. The new councils were to be financed by the treasury and from local rates.

The impact of the act was dramatic. The extent of the transfer of power involved can be seen from the composition of the local authorities before and after the passing of the act. Unionists held 704 seats on the last existing Grand Juries. Nationalists held only 47. On the new county councils, unionists won 265 seats to 774 for the nationalists. The older local authorities showed a similar turnaround. Unionist representation on Boards of Guardians, which controlled the workhouses, dropped from 3,773 to 1,523, or 50 per cent to 18 per cent while nationalist representation grew from 3,639 to 6,689, or from 49·5 per cent to 78 per cent.[25]

The police reported the return of members of the IRB in some cases, but they were a small minority of those elected. The majority were constitutional nationalists of one shade or another. Motions in favour of Home Rule, a catholic university, restoration of evicted tenants and a host of other nationalist causes were ritually passed by the new authorities throughout the country. The question of erecting the green flag over Navan courthouse came before Meath county council. Fist-fights were reported from Galway urban council. However, by and large, the transfer of power was orderly.[26] The reform of local government provided a new stage for the rehearsing of the nationalist case and introduced a new generation of nationalists to politics. It is arguable that it also doomed the cause of southern unionism. Deprived of property and power, they were a class without a *raison d'être*.

Devolution

The period between the passing of the Local Government Act in 1898 and the fall of the Conservative government in 1905 was one of intense activity. Local government reform was quickly followed by the establishment of the department of agriculture, and the Land Act of 1903, both of which were the result of direct negotiations between the relevant interests in Ireland. Similar negotiations were taking place with a view to an agreed settlement of the Irish university question. Many unionists and at least some nationalists saw such direct negotiations as the key to political progress. By 1904, however, the collapse of government credit and the unstable position of the ministry made Arthur Balfour, now the prime minister, unwilling to embark on further experiments in Ireland. The move for educational reform faltered partly for those reasons. These conflicting impulses provide the context in which the Irish devolution crisis of 1904 must be viewed.

The two main instigators of the scheme to devolve limited powers of government to some form of assembly in Ireland were Lord Dunraven and Sir Antony MacDonnell, under-secretary from 1902 to 1908. Dunraven was a moderate unionist landlord and political reformer who believed that the time was ripe for a 'third party' in Ireland. MacDonnell, on the other hand, although Irish born and nationalist in sympathies, was primarily interested in administrative reform. Following a distinguished career in the Indian civil service where he won a reputation as a first class administrator, in 1902 he had been persuaded to come to Ireland as under-secretary by George Wyndham, the chief secretary. MacDonnell accepted the position only on the specific understanding that he would be consulted on all matters of policy and administration and that he would have freedom of executive action within the limits of policy laid down by and subject to the control of his parliamentary chief.[27] That he felt the need for such assurances is indicative of how little discretion could be exercised by relatively senior officials in Ireland.

Within a year of MacDonnell's appointment, Wyndham's experiment seemed to have paid dividends. MacDonnell played an important part in the negotiations which preceded the 1903 Land Act. His efforts at settling the Irish university question were less successful, despite extensive negotiations, so he turned to administrative reform. His first impression of Irish government was how chaotic and uncoordinated it was. Having unsuccessfully tried some minor changes, he was quickly convinced that a fundamental reorganisation involving financial decentralisation was necessary. This would, he believed, increase efficiency and achieve savings which could be used for economic development.

Drawing from his Indian experience, MacDonnell suggested that, subject to parliament, the Irish government should have control of an Irish budget. These ideas found an approving audience in Wyndham and in Dudley, the lord lieutenant, but the position of the government made them of little more than academic interest. However, in the autumn of 1904 they were incorporated in the manifesto of Lord Dunraven's Irish Reform Association. Later, an expanded programme, also drafted by MacDonnell, was published calling for financial decentralisation and the devolution of some legislative functions.[28]

Somewhat surprisingly in view of the fact that he was known to be sympathetic to some form of devolution and that MacDonnell had told him of his contacts with Dunraven, Wyndham immediately repudiated the scheme, thus giving it a prominence it might not otherwise have had. A major controversy arose particularly about MacDonnell's involvement in drafting the scheme. Ulster unionist distrust of the constructive unionist policy came to a head and crystallised around this issue. Ironically, the weakness of the government which had doomed the scheme from the beginning also made it particularly vulnerable to the resultant fall-out. The government's first reaction was to try to get rid of MacDonnell quietly. He was officially only on secondment from the Indian Council, so an attempt was made to force him to return. MacDonnell resisted this because to leave Ireland would have seemed an admission of wrong-doing. Then without giving him an opportunity to explain himself in person and, it would appear, without Wyndham telling his colleagues that MacDonnell had kept Lord Dudley informed of what he was doing throughout, it was decided to censure MacDonnell for acting contrary to the rules of the permanent civil service.[29]

When the controversy showed no signs of abating, the government was left with two choices. The first was to sack MacDonnell. The problem with this was that he could then publish all of the relevant correspondence and thus further embarrass the government. It was also possible that Lord Dudley would resign in support of MacDonnell.[30] The other option, and the one which became more likely as the strain began to tell on him, was that Wyndham should resign. This he did in March 1905.

The devolution crisis which ruined Wyndham's career and severely embarrassed the government, also spelt the end of constructive unionism as an officially sponsored policy. When Walter Long came to Ireland in succession to Wyndham, consolidation rather than innovation was his aim. He was keen to placate the northern unionists. 'What the country needs now', he wrote soon after his arrival, 'is rest and peace, steady, quiet but firm administration, wholesome food and drink. She has had too much quack medicine lately'.[31] Within a matter of months, the government had fallen.

'Quack medicine' was a harsh verdict on constructive unionism. It was always a dual movement involving on the one hand individual reformers such as Plunkett and Dunraven and on the other Unionist politicians in search of a policy. It never looked like killing Home Rule with kindness, if that was ever its goal, but that coalition had produced measures of enormous benefit to Ireland. However, by 1905, not only was a constructive Irish policy not a priority for the Conservative government, it was a positive embarrassment.

The Anglo-Irish twilight

Constructive unionism represented the last throw of the dice for the ascendancy. It was the last opportunity to settle relationships in Ireland on terms remotely favourable to the protestant gentry in Ireland. Thereafter whatever adjustments might take place would be within the context of a Home Rule settlement. From 1905 onwards, despite the urgings of William O'Brien, the Irish party was not interested in cooperation but looked to the Liberal alliance at Westminster for the achievement of its programme. The Conservative party in Britain, having burned its fingers with reform, returned to a policy of anti-Home Rule fundamentalism. Its natural allies in that struggle were the northern rather than the southern unionists.

That is not to say that southern unionists suddenly became reconciled to their fate, only that their position became increasingly isolated. The Irish Unionist Alliance which succeeded the Irish Loyal and Patriotic Union in 1891 as the main focus for opposition to Home Rule was predominantly a southern unionist organisation. It organised public meetings against Home Rule particularly in the period 1911-14, produced dozens of pamphlets arguing the unionist case and assiduously campaigned behind the scenes in Britain in the hope of recruiting British MPs to its cause. The close family connections between the landed communities in England and Ireland facilitated this work and guaranteed southern unionists a sympathetic hearing. Ironically, while many Tories cited the Ulster question as the basis for their objection to Home Rule, they were personally closer to southern than northern unionists. In that sense, the temporary shelving of Home Rule owed something to the efforts of southern unionists.[32]

By the end of the Great War, that influence was aimed more at having a say in the shape of a settlement than in preventing one. For much of the period 1914-18, southern unionist attentions were focussed largely on the war effort and recruiting. When the political issue was addressed, their main concern was to avoid a partition settlement. The war brought a hard pragmatism to British politics where traditional loyalties counted for less. After the 1916 rising Lloyd George came close to negotiating a settlement with northern unionists and southern nationalists based on partition. Southern unionists were galvanised into action and through Lord Lansdowne helped block the scheme. The same rationale lay behind their very constructive contribution to the Irish Convention established by Lloyd George in 1917. Although boycotted by Sinn Féin, the convention was attended by representatives of the other major interests in Ireland, northern and southern unionists and constitutional nationalists. Significantly, the majority report which proposed a modest Home Rule settlement with elaborate safeguards was a product of cooperation between a section of the nationalists and the southern unionists.[33] Such a development might have succeeded in 1911. By 1918 however, both southern unionists and moderate nationalists had been swept aside by the polarisation of opinion.

The first world war was the great landmark for the Anglo-Irish. The storm clouds which engulfed all of Europe had a particularly ominous aspect for that class. The displacement of the Anglo-Irish had begun with the land legislation and the democratisation of local government. But the transition to a democratic society did not necessarily mean the complete displacement of aristocratic power as the English experience was to show. Constructive unionism was, at root, a quest for a *rapprochement* which would preserve intact something of the position of the Anglo-Irish. Its failure left their future in the new Ireland at best uncertain. That much was clear in 1914. What could then only be guessed at was how alien a landscape the new Ireland could be. All of this is beautifully evoked by Elizabeth Bowen in her memoir *Bowen's court* when she describes a garden party at Mitchelstown Castle just after the outbreak of the war:

Almost everyone said they wondered if they really ought to have come, but they had come – rightly: this was a time to gather. This was an assemblage of Anglo-Irish people from all over north-east Cork, from the counties of Limerick, Waterford, Tipperary. For miles around, each isolated big house had disgorged its talker, this first day of the war. The tension of months, of years – outlying tension of Europe, inner tension of Ireland – broke in a spate of words. Braced against the gale of the mountains, licking dust from their lips, these were the unmartialled loyalists of the South. Not a family had not put out, like Bowen's Court, its generations of military brothers – tablets in Protestant churches recorded deaths in remote battles; swords hung in halls. If the Anglo-Irish live on and for a myth, for that myth they constantly shed their blood. So, on this August 1914 day of grandeur and gravity, the Ascendancy rallied, renewed itself... through the grown-up talkers ran and recurred one question – Will this having happened stop Home Rule?

It was an afternoon when the simplest person begins to anticipate memory – this Mitchelstown garden party, it was agreed, would remain in everyone's memory as historic. It was also a more final scene than we knew. Ten years hence, it was all to seem a dream – and the Castle itself would be a few bleached stumps on a plateau. Today, the terraces are obliterated, and grass grows where the saloons were. Many of those guests, those vehement talkers, would be scattered, houseless, sonless, or themselves dead. That war – or call it now that first phase of war – was to go far before it had done with us. After 1918 came the war in Ireland, with the burning down of many of the big houses – some already futureless, for they had lost their heirs.... In the life of what we call the new Ireland – but is Ireland ever new – the lives of my people became a little thing; from 1914 they began to be merged, already, into a chapter of different history.[34]

5 Constitutional Nationalism: Resurgence and Decline

'The greatest feature of the situation, however, is that they have seen the Irish question as one merely of politics and that politics means for them only agitation and Home Rule. They seem to have scarcely any conception of the complexity of social life. They have neglected the intellectual, moral and economic progress of the countryside and the education of the democracy... Whenever fruitful initiative has arisen near them they have shown themselves jealous of it or have set it aside ... They have made no effort to rally Ulster or the oligarchy to Home Rule. Absorbed in the Parliamentary struggle, they have not understood that effort from within can and should favour and forward, outside politics, a national regeneration which Parliament itself is incapable of assuring the country. In short they have reduced Nationalism, as the 'Colony' for their part have reduced Unionism, to a negative rather than a positive policy... The new era makes it necessary that this negative policy should become positive, should grow to maturity, and become at once more responsible and more realistic. Otherwise the ineffectiveness of Constitutional Nationalism may well one day provoke, if indeed it has not already began to provoke, a recrudescence of the extremist and separatist party.'

L Paul-Dubois, 1908

After the Parnellite split, the Irish parliamentary party and the Home Rule movement generally never fully regained the unrivalled position which it previously occupied. It did eventually recover from the trauma of Parnell's fall and ultimately succeeded in having a Home Rule bill placed on the statute book, only to see victory snatched from its grasp by the outbreak of the first world war. The advent of that conflict reshuffled political priorities in Britain. When Ireland next returned to the top of the pack, the Irish parliamentary party had disappeared.

The history of the constitutional movement between the fall of Parnell and the 1918 general election which finally saw its demise can be divided into four parts: the first, 1893 to 1905, was a period of division, reconciliation and reconstruction; the second, 1905-10, saw the Liberals back in power but the emphasis was on reforms other than Home Rule; the third, 1910-14, was the period of the Home Rule crisis; while the last, 1914-18, saw the party deprived of its leverage in parliament and unwilling or unable to direct its energies elsewhere.

Wilderness years

The death of Parnell and the decisive victory of the anti- over the pro-Parnellites at the general election of 1892 should have meant a quick end to the split in the Home Rule movement. That it did not is evidence both of the depth of the divisions which existed and the extent to which they related to issues other than the leadership of Parnell. The most debilitating split was in fact that which developed within the victorious anti-Parnellite camp, led by Justin McCarthy. At bottom this was a leadership struggle, although it was also fuelled by personality differences and very real differences over policy.

The predominance of the leader which had been the strength of the Parnellite movement meant that when he unexpectedly fell from grace there was no obvious successor. Justin McCarthy was at best a stop-gap. Of Parnell's other lieutenants, Timothy Healy and John Dillon were the most prominent. Dillon who was closely associated in the public mind with the land agitation, especially the Plan of Campaign, eventually emerged as the more powerful and became leader in 1896 but only after a prolonged conflict with Healy. Healy was a journalist and barrister and was widely renowned as an able parliamentarian and orator. His vociferous condemnation of Parnell's 'moral deviance' ingratiated him with the clerical opposition to the fallen leader. This close identification with the 'clerical party' actually hampered him later as many anti-Parnellites, anxious to refute the accusation that they were the tools of the bishops and to stress their independence, sought to distance themselves from 'the Reverend Timothy'.

Dillon and Healy clashed repeatedly over matters of policy and organisation. By and large, Dillon shared Parnell's outlook on organisation whereas Healy favoured a much less centralised, less authoritarian approach with local constituencies playing a more active role. The dispute culminated in 1895 with Healy being expelled from the Irish National Federation, which had succeeded the National League in 1891.[1] He proceeded to establish his own People's Rights Association. Though Healy was defeated, Dillon was less successful in his quest to maintain the structure of the Parnellite party intact. The leadership vacuum allowed the growth of a localism which was never fully reversed. As for Healy, he never again wielded real power but his continued alienation from the movement even after the Parnellites had been reconciled in 1900 served to prolong the memory of earlier disputes and to weaken the reunited party.

The in-fighting in the Home Rule movement continued throughout the 1890s. The 1893 Home Rule bill, constituency organisation, selection of candidates, local and general election campaigns, control of newspapers, membership of committees – in short all aspects of the political process – provided the opportunity for indulging again and again in the same mutual recriminations. Not surprisingly, a new generation of nationalists, disillusioned with parliamentarianism, sought fulfilment elsewhere.

Two developments which did give a boost to the Home Rule movement in the 1890s were the report of the Financial Relations Commission in 1896 and the reform of local government. The conclusion of the former that Ireland was overtaxed in relation to her resources seemed to confirm what nationalists had long argued – that the union lay at the root of Irish problems.[2] The reform of local government provided a new forum for the articulation of the Home Rule demand and the politicisation of the local populace.[3]

Above all it was the establishment of the United Irish League by William O'Brien which reinvigorated the Home Rule movement. Like Dillon, O'Brien was closely associated with the land agitation. Disillusioned by the divisions of the 1890s, he had withdrawn from politics only to reappear at the head of a new radical agrarian movement, the UIL. The league was founded at Westport in January 1898. The title was chosen to commemorate the United Irishmen's revolt a century before. It grew out of some poor harvests during the 1890s particularly 1897 when there was a partial failure of the potato crop and a sense of betrayal among tenants and small farmers who felt that the land legislation had benefited only the cattle ranchers.[4] Its activities were initially confined largely to Mayo, Galway, Sligo, Leitrim and Roscommon. While its original aim was the redistribution of ranches to small holders, it became more political and less agrarian in outlook as it spread throughout the country. Its first demand became 'the largest measure of national self-government which circumstances may put it in our power to obtain'.[5] League candidates were conspicuously successful in the local elections of 1899. The rapidity of its growth can be seen from the following figures:[6]

United Irish League Membership

End of year	1898	1899	1900	1901
Branches	94	396	865	989
Members	8,853	44,425	86,119	98,400

Table 2

Police action against league meetings helped to promote its popularity. It also guaranteed that it could not be ignored by nationalist leaders who, with the notable exception of Michael Davitt, were lukewarm at its inception.[7] Rather than be displaced by the league, the various factions agreed after long negotiations to come together in a reunited party. In 1900 John Dillon stepped down as leader, a gesture which placated supporters of Healy, and, in a further fence-mending exercise, it was agreed that the position should go to John Redmond from the small Parnellite faction.[8]

The UIL became in effect the national organisation of the reunified Irish parliamentary party. In the process of saving the party, the league rendered itself subordinate. Though it still officially possessed considerable autonomy and could on occasion display a will of its own, it became very much the creature of the parliamentary party.

O'Brien quickly had cause to regret his magnanimity in handing over his creation. He quarrelled with his ex-colleagues and parted company from them. As we have seen, he had become convinced that the best hope of progress lay in concentrating their attention on Ireland rather than Westminster. He viewed the land conference which paved the way for the 1903 Land Act as an opportunity for extending the olive branch to landlords and for all interests in Ireland to shape their own destiny rather than rely on British politicians. It was a bold vision but not one which appealed either to those who felt more at home in the house of commons than in Ireland, or to the radical agrarian element whose outlook was based more on class conflict than consensus. Within the parliamentary party there were some who shared that view, including its new leader, John Redmond, who supported the Land Conference and the Wyndham Act. John Dillon, on the other hand, viewed such moderation with extreme suspicion and managed to carry Redmond along with him. O'Brien might have been better advised to use his influence from within.

Instead he left the party in 1904 when his conciliation policy was rejected and the balance shifted the other way. With the collapse of constructive unionism, the return of the Liberals and the failure of devolution, the moment for conciliation had passed.[9]

Home Rule in instalments

The general election of 1900 brought an infusion of new blood into the parliamentary party but, with the Conservatives still in power, the prospects for directly influencing government policy were not good. The return of the Liberals in 1905 and their success at the subsequent general election changed that. The alliance with the Liberals was renewed. Even so, most Liberals were reluctant to become embroiled once again with Home Rule and, with a record majority, they were not dependent on Irish party votes in parliament. Lord Rosebery refused to serve in the government unless Home Rule was removed from the political agenda. Others, such as John Morley and Campbell-Bannerman, more dependent on Irish votes or sympathetic to the nationalist cause, preferred vague expressions of support. Insofar as Home Rule had been an issue in the general election in Britain it was the Tories who raised it. When it became clear that the election was going against them, they introduced the Home Rule bogey to rally their supporters. Arthur Balfour told a meeting in East Manchester that Home Rule was 'the great dividing line between the two parties in the State' and warned that if the Liberals were returned Home Rule could not be excluded.[10]

Campbell-Bannerman, the new prime minister, publicly ruled out any attempt to introduce Home Rule for at least five years. Instead, he did promise 'to govern Ireland in accordance with Irish ideas' and to introduce a measure 'to associate the people of Ireland more closely with the government of Ireland' – a phrase borrowed from a speech of Lord Dudley. He told Redmond that this measure would 'be consistent with and lead up to the larger policy'. This policy, which was effectively that devised by Herbert Asquith and Edward Grey some years previously, was quickly dubbed 'Home Rule by instalments'. It involved the resurrection and development of Antony MacDonnell's devolution proposal.[11]

The great advantage of devolution, a term avoided because of its association with the previous government, was that it could be sold to nationalists as an instalment of Home Rule while at the same time unionists could be reassured that it fell far short of self-government. The disadvantage of this approach was that in attempting to be all things to all men it might please no one. That in effect is what happened.

A draft scheme was quickly prepared by Antony MacDonnell with the help of James Bryce, the new chief secretary. It was similar to the ill-fated scheme of 1904 and quickly ran into trouble behind the scenes because of objections from the nationalist leaders. MacDonnell and Bryce saw the scheme essentially as an effort at administrative reform rather than a political measure and resisted the attempts of Redmond, Dillon and T P O'Connor to reshape it into as large an instalment of Home Rule as possible. The nationalist leaders were closely consulted in the preparation of the draft and contributed two memoranda commenting in detail on the proposals. Augustine Birrell, who replaced James Bryce early in 1907, was more sympathetic to the demands of the nationalist leaders or at least more conscious of the need to placate them. Under his and John Morley's influence and despite strenuous objection from MacDonnell, the draft bill was amended to make it more acceptable to the nationalist leaders.[12]

The Irish Council bill was introduced into the house of commons in May 1907. It provided for the transfer of the powers of existing Irish departments to an Irish Council. The council was to consist of eighty-two members, elected on the local government franchise, and twenty-five nominated members. It was envisaged that the council would establish committees to administer the various Irish boards and departments, including a new department of education which was to take over the work of the several boards then involved in the education area. The council was to have no powers relating to taxation, policing or justice and the lord lieutenant was to have a veto over its decisions.[13]

The original proposal had no provision for direct election but this was changed under pressure from Redmond and Dillon. MacDonnell was not opposed to some elected element but he was anxious to create a non-political body owing as little as possible to existing political divisions: as Dillon cynically described it, 'that favourite abstraction of amateur solvers of the Irish problem, non-political businessmen'. On the other hand, the nationalist leaders were insistent on the creation of as large a council as possible, elected on the parliamentary franchise so that they could sell it to their supporters as a Home Rule assembly in all but name. They went so far as to propose that all existing Irish MPs should be members of the council. The bill presented to parliament was a compromise but, while it was a long way short of Home Rule, especially in the limited powers devolved to the council, it was closer to the model requested by the nationalist leaders than to that originally envisaged by MacDonnell.[14]

In introducing the bill, Birrell played down its provisions presumably in an attempt to woo the opposition and on the assumption that nationalist support was a foregone conclusion. Redmond's speech was critical of some of the provisions but non-committal on the measure as a whole. It was felt that this indicated a cautious support. When, shortly afterwards, a convention of the United Irish League in Dublin voted to reject the measure there was considerable surprise. The Irish parliamentary party had at that stage no choice but to fall into line and oppose the bill which was then withdrawn.

To an extent, the debate on the Irish Council bill was more tactical than real because many Liberals and nationalists did not believe that it had any chance of passing the house of lords.[15] Nevertheless the incident is significant. It represented the last opportunity for a compromise solution which might have been acceptable to nationalists and unionists. MacDonnell insisted that a less ambitious measure might have attracted all-party support but was ridiculed for his delusion that 'the Moderates in Ireland who drink tea in the Phoenix Park are capable of compelling the nationalists in the House to accept Moderate Measures'.[16]

The affair also revealed weaknesses in the leadership of Redmond and in the position of the party. Having been regularly consulted about the bill, Redmond was familiar with its contents. Yet he allowed unrealistic expectations to grow among his supporters. When it was finally published, the anti-climax for those who had expected Home Rule by another name was understandable. Furthermore, the surprise rejection of the bill showed that Redmond was out of touch with developments in Ireland and was not able to control his own supporters. As well as disappointment about the impotence of the Irish Council, there was a good deal of alarm in clerical quarters about the proposal to establish a department of education which would give control of that area to popularly elected representatives. Popular control of education was dear to the hearts of Liberals but it raised for many clerics the spectre of secular education. Clerical opposition undoubtedly played a part in the league's rejection of the bill. Yet the danger signals had been undetected or ignored by the nationalist leadership.[17]

The failure of the Irish Council bill ended all hopes of a political settlement for the duration of the existing parliament. In the meantime, the Liberal alliance continued. Campbell-Bannerman's promise to govern Ireland in accordance with Irish ideas meant governing Ireland in accordance with the ideas of the Irish parliamentary party. The relationship with the Liberals was never closer than during these years with the Irish party being treated with considerable deference and acting almost as a satellite of the Liberal party. For instance, the nationalist leaders were regularly consulted about appointments to sensitive positions in Ireland such as membership of the Congested Districts Board. When James Bryce was being replaced as chief secretary at the end of 1906, Campbell-Bannerman discussed possible replacements with John Redmond who approved the appointment of Augustine Birrell.[18] The views of the nationalist leaders were sought and treated with respect on a range of issues. There is no doubt that they influenced the Liberals' tolerant attitude towards agrarian crime. When there was a resurgence of agrarian crime during 1907 and 1908, the government came under strong pressure to deal with it firmly. A proposal from Antony MacDonnell that those inciting 'cattle driving' be prosecuted was overruled on the advice of Birrell who warned that it would result in half of the Irish party being landed in jail.[19]

The partnership also produced a range of productive measures for Ireland. A new Labourers' Act, introduced in May 1906, sought to remedy the defects in the existing legislation for the provision of labourers' cottages. Although the bill was amended by the house of lords, it still remained an important measure which provided a much-needed impetus to local authorities to provide housing for labourers.[20] Similarly the Town Tenants Act which extended the principle of compensation for improvements to town tenants owed much to the Irish party. Originally a nationalist bill with little hope of passing, it was 'adopted' by the government in an amended form. Most of its progressive elements were removed by the house of lords, but the act as passed did improve the position of town tenants. The measure was given immediate significance by a serious case which had arisen in Loughrea. Lord Clanrickarde, a controversial absentee landlord who refused to sell any of his land or cooperate with the Estates Commissioners, served notice to quit on a local shopkeeper, allegedly because of his activities as secretary of the local branch of the UIL. Under the existing law, the tenant would receive no compensation for having built up a thriving business. The aggrieved tenant barricaded himself in his shop and a potentially explosive situation was averted only after the direct intervention of senior members of the government.[21]

The Evicted Tenants' Act of 1907, the University Act of 1908 and the Land Act of 1909 were further fruits of the Liberal alliance but the first two also show some of the limitations of that alliance. The restoration of tenants evicted during the land agitation was a cause close to the hearts of the nationalist MPs. The land conference had recommended and the 1903 Act provided for the restoration of evicted tenants. However, the number actually restored was small. Over 8,000 such tenants had applied to the Estates Commissioners for reinstatement . Of these roughly 1,000 were reinstated and 3,000 applications were rejected. Undoubtedly many of the claims for reinstatement were spurious but there was a genuine sense of grievance in many cases. As originally introduced, the Evicted Tenants' bill was a radical measure which provided for compulsory reinstatement, even where the holding was now occupied by another tenant. However, the bill was emasculated by the lords and this provision was removed. It was clear that even with a record majority in the house of commons the Liberals were unable to guarantee the passage of any legislation strongly opposed by the landed interest in Ireland. The moral drawn by the usually mild John Redmond was that if reform was to be achieved, they would have to make their movement 'sufficiently strong and menacing' to persuade the opposition.[22]

The shadow of the lords' veto certainly hung over the negotiations of the Irish University Act, which set out to remedy the inadequate provision of university education in Ireland, particularly for catholics. Considerable progress had been made on this subject by Antony MacDonnell while the Conservatives were still in power. In 1906 the matter was raised again and, following an inconclusive commission, James Bryce announced the government's support for a 'federal university' to consist of Trinity College, Dublin, a new college in Dublin with a 'Roman Catholic atmosphere' and the three Queen's colleges of Belfast, Cork and Galway. Although nobody was very enthusiastic about the scheme, it was acceptable to most of the parties involved with the exception of Trinity College which launched a vigorous campaign in opposition to any dilution of its own independence. The hostility of Trinity made it unlikely that the Bryce scheme would pass the house of lords. Largely for that reason, Birrell abandoned it and, despite the objections of MacDonnell, its main architect, substituted the proposal which was ultimately passed as the 1908 act. Trinity College and Queen's University Belfast, which was given its independence, were excluded from the new National University of Ireland which was comprised of the University Colleges of Cork and Galway and the new University College Dublin.[23] Although this was the outcome closest to catholic demands, the result was not due to nationalist pressure. Ironically, it was also the outcome least favoured by liberal non-conformist opinion in England which was instinctively opposed to the creation of what would in practice be denominational universities.[24]

The third Home Rule bill

The budget of 1909 marked the beginning of a new stage in the Liberal alliance. The unprecedented rejection of a money bill by the house of lords brought to a head the question of the relationship between the two houses and ultimately opened the way for Home Rule. It was not only Irish legislation which had suffered at the hands of the house of lords. With the Unionist opposition in the commons severely depleted after the 1906 general election, the Unionist majority in the lords adopted a more aggressive role. The Liberals had been unable to pass any legislation of a controversial nature without substantial amendment by the lords. Their response was a policy of 'filling the cup': allowing the lords to continue on their course until it was manifestly intolerable. They passed a series of resolutions in the commons asserting the supremacy of the lower house. The rejection of Lloyd George's reforming budget of 1909 left them with no option but to seek to establish that supremacy in practice.

In the general election which followed in January 1910, the Liberal majority over the Unionists was reduced to two, with Labour and the Irish parties holding the balance of power. The election also saw the brief emergence of a small group of dissident Irish MPs under William O'Brien and Tim Healy who opposed the Liberal alliance. Initially the Irish party refused to support the budget unless an assurance was given that a measure dealing with the lords' veto would be passed during 1910. When Asquith refused, it seemed for a time as if the Irish party might oppose the budget which was unpopular with some sections in Ireland, particularly the publicans who exercised considerable influence with the party. Following negotiations, some minor changes were agreed in the budget but on the main Irish objection – the increased duty on spirits – there was no concession. Realising that defeat of the government would be disastrous for the Home Rule cause, the Irish party backed down. The incident imposed severe strain on the Liberal alliance but it was never likely that Redmond would assert his independence to the extent of bringing down the government.[25]

There remained the more fundamental question of the lords' veto. A constitutional conference was summoned to resolve the issue but without success. At the conference, the Unionists proposed that questions of constitutional change, such as Home Rule, should be put to a plebiscite but this was rejected by the Liberal delegates. It was clear to all concerned that a removal of the veto would open the way for Home Rule. At the cabinet, Lord Grey unsuccessfully proposed that any legislation to curtail the veto would only be used in the first instance and 'perhaps exclusively' for reconstruction of the house of lords, thus further postponing Home Rule.[26] Eventually, following pressure from Redmond, Asquith agreed that, following the abolition of the veto, a Home Rule bill would be introduced within the life of the new parliament.[27]

When the lords rejected the government's proposals to reform its powers, a new general election was called. This left the state of the parties virtually unchanged. Faced with a government threat to flood the upper house with new peers, thus guaranteeing a majority for its proposals, the lords finally gave way. The Parliament Act of 1911 removed their veto on legislation: they could delay but not defeat government measures. That act, a landmark in English constitutional development, made the introduction of Home Rule inevitable.

With the lords' veto abolished, Redmond's reward for loyalty and patience could not be long delayed. In October 1911 a committee of the cabinet was appointed to deal with Home Rule. In 1886 and 1893, the prime minister and chief secretary had assumed joint control of the Home Rule bill but 'significantly' Asquith assumed the predominant role now, with Birrell being relegated to a secondary position.[28] When the first draft came before the cabinet it was associated with 'Home Rule all round' or devolution for the rest of the United Kingdom. The rationale for this was not to make the bill more acceptable to Ulster but to get over the thorny problem of Irish representation at Westminster after Home Rule was passed. Not surprisingly, the nationalist leaders protested that this would delay Home Rule by generating needless controversy. The idea was quickly dropped and only reappeared temporarily when it was proposed by Lord Loreburn late in 1913.

Various drafts of the bill were submitted to the nationalist leaders for comment. In the main, their objections centred on the need to create the appearance of a powerful Irish parliament – even if, in some cases, it was no more than the appearance. For instance, they were adamant that the Irish parliament should be defined as having full powers with named exceptions rather than simply listing its powers, even though it would amount to the same thing. With the exception of the financial clauses which had caused such difficulty in 1886 and 1893 and which were now drafted by a special committee, a conscious effort was made by the government to keep the bill as close as possible to the 1893 bill which had received the support of the house of commons.[29]

The Government of Ireland bill was introduced by Asquith in April 1912. It provided for the establishment of a parliament in Ireland, consisting of a house of commons with 164 elected members and a senate with 40 members. Originally members of the senate were to be nominated but this was dropped at the committee stage of the bill in favour of the 1893 provision for election on a property franchise. Disagreements between commons and senate were to be settled by majority vote of both houses sitting together. As demanded by Redmond, the role of the new parliament was to provide for the 'peace, order and good government' of Ireland with the exception of certain reserved powers and subject to the supremacy of the imperial parliament. The reserved powers were fewer than in 1893 but they included all matters relating to the crown, war and peace, the army and navy, defence, foreign affairs and foreign trade. Control of the police was temporarily reserved and land purchase permanently. As in 1886 and 1893, the endowment of any religion was forbidden. Ireland was to continue to be represented at Westminster but in considerably reduced numbers.[30] Executive authority was to lie with an 'executive committee of the privy council' composed of ministers who were heads of the various Irish departments. The executive committee was to be responsible to parliament and was, in effect, the Irish government. Its nominal head was to be the lord lieutenant who, although a non-political figure, retained a veto on Irish legislation.

As in 1886 and 1893, the financial clauses were the most difficult to draft and considerably more time was devoted to them than to the Ulster question at the drafting stage. The financial question had become even more complicated since 1893 because of the huge growth in Irish expenditure due chiefly to land purchase and the introduction of old age pensions. By 1911, as we have seen, government expenditure in Ireland exceeded Irish revenue. A committee headed by Sir Henry Primrose which investigated the problem proposed financial autonomy for Ireland which, although it was favoured by nationalists, might in fact have worked to their financial disadvantage. Ireland would have had control over her own revenue and expenditure, with Britain continuing to meet the cost of existing pensions.

Despite the efforts of Birrell who favoured the Primrose proposal, it was rejected in favour of a less radical but more complicated financial scheme drawn up by Herbert Samuel, the postmaster general. The nationalist leaders reluctantly accepted Samuel's scheme on the understanding that it would be reviewed after a period. All Irish revenue was to be paid to the imperial exchequer which would pay the cost of reserved services and transfer to Ireland a fixed amount to cover Irish expenditure. An imperial contribution from Ireland was to be settled when and if Irish revenue balanced expenditure. While customs and excise duties were reserved, the new Irish parliament was given limited powers to vary duties or levy new taxes. Even this limited provision was objected to by some Liberals and was curtailed after a backbench revolt in parliament.[31]

In the event, however, it was the Ulster question which generated most discussion and gave the Home Rule crisis of 1911-14 its passion. The crisis is examined in more detail below (pp125-35). With a comfortable Home Rule majority in the commons and the lords' veto abolished, the Orange Card was seen by tory opponents of the bill as the most effective means of killing Home Rule. Under the terms of the Parliament Act, the Home Rule bill had to pass the commons in three separate sessions if, as was inevitable, it was rejected by the lords. The protracted passage of the bill through parliament contributed to the sense of crisis and heightened tension. For two years, Ireland and the Irish question dominated British politics in a way in which it never did before or has done since. The threat of extra-parliamentary resistance was mobilised to achieve what parliamentary opposition seemed unable to deliver. The irony was that those involved had been among the sternest critics of such tactics when they were used by Parnell and the Irish parliamentary party.

One unexpected effect of Samuel's scheme was that it made it more difficult simply to amend the bill to exclude Ulster. Many of the complicated financial provisions would have required alteration and even then it would have been extremely awkward to operate in practice. Nevertheless, as the date when the bill would finally become law approached, some compromise on the Ulster question became more and more likely. When the outbreak of the first world war put the Irish question into cold storage, it was only the nature of that compromise which remained to be agreed. Home Rule was placed on the statute book but suspended for the duration of the war, with the understanding that some provision would be made for Ulster before Home Rule came into operation.

The decline of the Irish parliamentary party

The outbreak of the first world war was a tragedy for the Irish parliamentary party and the constitutional movement generally. By the time that conflict ended and the time came for the implementation of Home Rule, the Irish party had been swept aside by the Sinn Féin movement and revolutionary nationalism. The radicalisation of Irish nationalist opinion between 1914 and 1918 is often seen as the cause of the decline of the Irish party. This is only partly true. More than anything else, it was the inability or unwillingness of the party to respond to the new circumstances in which it found itself which allowed the initiative to pass to a new generation of militant nationalists.

With Home Rule on the statute book, Redmond promised Irish support for the war effort. He had often declared that a self-governing Ireland would be a loyal ally rather than a threat to Britain. His belief in the empire and support for the war was genuine. Immediately the war broke out, he promised the government in the house of commons that the defence of Ireland could safely be left to the Irish and promised loyalty. He hotly denied Bonar Law's assertion that it was a conditional loyalty and later denounced as libel a claim by *The Times* that Ireland was disowning her own soldiers. He continued:

> In this war, I dare say that, for the first time, certainly for over 100 years, Ireland feels and will feel that the British democracy has kept faith with her... the manhood of Ireland will spring to your aid in this war.

He reiterated this promise in his famous speech at Woodenbridge, Co. Wicklow, when he argued that it would be a disgrace to Irish manhood if it were to shrink from proving itself on the field of battle.[32]

Redmond's outright enthusiasm for the war was not shared completely by all of his colleagues, some of whom were more circumspect in their pronouncements. John Dillon, for example, was advised by a friend that it would not be prudent to encourage young men to go to the front. Dillon was reluctant to be cast in the role of recruiting sergeant and disagreed with what seemed to be Redmond's increasingly 'emotional' involvement in the war. Nonetheless, the Irish party did follow Redmond's lead and commit itself to the war. Several had sons and relatives who joined up. Stephen Gwynn and T P O'Connor argued that by playing a positive role in the war, Ireland could establish herself internationally. Even Dillon, whatever his reservations, endorsed his colleagues' position. He told his constituents that he was England's friend in the war as long as she stood by Home Rule.[33] This was in fact a fair summary of Irish attitudes generally as is borne out by the relatively enthusiastic response to the calls for recruits, especially in the towns and cities. A police report of late 1914 confirms that while a small minority expressed opposition to the war, the predominant response was one of support.[34]

As the war unexpectedly dragged on, it became more and more a liability for the Irish party. Politically, Home Rule seemed increasingly remote. Public confidence in Redmond's conciliatory approach, reflected in the rousing welcome given to Asquith on his visit to Dublin early in the war, began to diminish. The formation of a coalition government in Britain in May 1915 which included both Bonar Law and Carson was a landmark. Redmond's refusal of the invitation to join, while in keeping with his party's tradition of independence, did not foreshadow a return to a more independent position and ran counter to the logic of his views on the war. Redmond's inactivity left others to cash in on Irish disillusion. Bishop Fogarty of Killaloe, for long a supporter of the Irish party, wrote to Redmond expressing a sentiment common among nationalists:

> Home Rule is dead and buried and Ireland is without a National Party or National Press...What the future has in store for us, God knows..[35]

There were setbacks too for Redmond's strategy on the war. He recognised that the most effective way of mobilising Irish opinion was by mobilising the dynamic force of nationalism. His attempt to reconcile nationalism and the call of empire failed, with enormous consequences for both. The formula of friendship for England after England had kept faith with Ireland was appealing but it underestimated the extent to which anti-Englishness was central to Irish nationalism. For Redmond's policy to succeed required considerable tact on the part of the government in its political and military dealings with Ireland. This condition was fulfilled in neither area.

The Volunteer movement had developed in the south of Ireland in November 1913 in opposition to the Ulster Volunteers. (see below, pp 99-100). The following June, Redmond decided that it would be dangerous to leave such a popular para-military group in the hands of those who did not support his party, so he took over control. He successfully demanded that its provisional committee be reconstituted 'on representative lines'. When, three months later, the movement split into National Volunteer and Irish Volunteer factions over Redmond's support for the war, the vast majority sided with the pro-Redmondite National Volunteers.[36] In promising that the Volunteers could be relied on to defend Ireland, Redmond was assigning to them the role of a national army. His attempts to persuade the government to arm the Volunteers, to form new Irish regiments with Irish officers, bands and insignia and ultimately an Irish division – a latter day Irish brigade – were designed to appeal to Irish national pride. In all these areas he met with resistance and sometimes hostility from Lord Kitchener and the War Office. Difficulties over the appointment of catholic chaplains and in prominent nationalists getting commissions were widely attributed to prejudice. Certainly the War Office displayed an animosity towards Irish nationalism which hampered Irish recruitment.

By December 1914, Dillon had become so disillusioned that he resolved to speak on no more recruiting platforms. Redmond also complained repeatedly about the situation. He told Birrell that he felt 'very sore at the way my efforts for recruiting have been thwarted'.[37] In spite of this, his commitment was undimmed. His son and brother joined up and he visited the front in 1915. Early the following year, he was still predicting a resurgence in recruiting which had by now declined to a trickle. In the light of the rebellion which was soon to take place in Dublin, his views are extremely ironic:

> No people can be said to have rightly proved their nationhood and their power to maintain it until they have demonstrated their military prowess, and though Irish blood has reddened the earth of every continent, never until now have we as a people set a national army in the field...those brave sons in the field need not fear for the honour they have won for their country. Their brothers are coming to them. Ireland's armies will be maintained.[38]

The failure to harness the enthusiasm of the Volunteers not only damaged Irish recruitment but also helped to drive the young men into the hands of the militant nationalists. When Redmond foisted himself on the Volunteers, he displayed an awareness of the importance of the extra-parliamentary dimension in the nationalist movement. The political truce in Britain for the duration of the war made that dimension more, not less, important. Yet, once his efforts to use the Volunteers for national defence failed, Redmond consciously allowed the organisation to run down. Dillon on the other hand argued that it should be maintained to pressurise the government and to act as a focus for the enthusiasm of the younger generation.

The National Volunteers themselves slowly became disillusioned with Redmond's policy of inactivity. Discontent centred on the crucial question of organisation. Reorganisation was necessary at all levels because many of the most active Volunteers had enlisted (one estimate put the number at 25,000).[39] The number of affiliated companies was rapidly diminishing but efforts to deal with the problem were blocked by Redmond. After the 1916 rising, senior leaders of the National Volunteers became even more convinced that an active reorganisation policy was necessary if the young men were not to drift into secret societies. County boards were urged to enrol new members and train outdoors. Some Volunteer leaders canvassed for Count Plunkett, the father of the executed 1916 leader, against the party candidate in the by-election in North Roscommon in February 1917. Colonel Maurice Moore, the inspector general of the Volunteers, publicly declared that constitutional and revolutionary nationalists differed on means and not ends, called for both sides to work together and accused Redmond of subordinating the Volunteers to the exigencies of party politics. This finally brought the divisions into the open and caused a second split, arguably as important as the first.[40]

A planned national convention was cancelled three times during 1916-17 at the behest of Redmond. On the third occasion, Moore had threatened to split the Volunteers publicly unless a convention was held on the already symbolic anniversary of the 1916 rising. The national committee of the Volunteers initially agreed but then reversed its decision when Redmond threatened to resign.[41] The fear of conscription which had been introduced in England but not yet in Ireland strengthened the conviction among the Volunteers themselves of the absolute necessity of placing their organisation 'on a sound and permanent footing'. Despite objections from Redmond, meetings of Volunteer companies took place. An officers' meeting on Whit Sunday, 1917 passed motions expressing sympathy with all Irishmen who died for freedom and calling for the release of imprisoned republicans and the reorganisation of the Volunteers.

Acting through the general purposes committee which was more representative of the rank and file than the national committee which was dominated by Redmond, Moore declared the national committee illegal as it had not summoned a convention for over two years, contrary to regulations, and occupied Volunteer headquarters in Dublin, seizing the arms stored there.[42] He then proceeded to summon a convention which decided to rejoin the Irish Volunteers. Redmond belatedly held his own convention to repudiate Moore's breakaway group and to endorse his policy of inaction. Although he claimed to have retained the support of a majority, it is clear that all those interested in an active policy had by now defected from Redmond's Volunteers, in many cases moving over into the Irish Volunteers and bringing their arms with them.[43]

The failure of the Irish party to move to suit the popular mood on the question of the Volunteers was repeated on the general political question. Here again, Redmond and Dillon differed fundamentally, a difference which flowed from their respective attitudes to the war. The latter was more closely in touch with the state of the party in Ireland and as early as 1915 was urging the need for revitalisation. The 1916 rising which he defended in the house of commons, convinced him of the necessity for the party to pursue a more vigorous, independent policy in Ireland. He warned that if the party was to be saved it had to embark on such a policy in Ireland. He considered that the abortive negotiations with Lloyd George in the autumn of 1916 (see below, pp137-8) compromised them on partition without any compensating gain and that Lloyd George's Irish Convention of 1917, which Dillon refused to participate in, could only do likewise.[44] The catholic bishops were alienated by the partition negotiations and the Irish Convention postponed the possibility of any alternative policy for more than a year.

Both Redmond and T P O'Connor, a strong advocate of negotiations with Lloyd George, believed that the radicalisation of Irish opinion could best be dealt with by producing a political settlement and they were willing to sacrifice much to achieve it. In the event, however, Dillon's analysis proved more accurate. When he succeeded Redmond as leader on the latter's death early in 1918, a change of policy was expected. There were some hopeful signs, most notably the success of party candidates in by-elections in Waterford, South Armagh and East Tyrone which interrupted Sinn Féin's series of by-election victories. Dillon hoped for a period of calm during which he could 'reconstitute the party from the bottom up'. He believed that the popularity of Sinn Féin was an emotional response to the executions of the leaders of the 1916 rising and that it depended for its growth on periodic stimulants, such as hunger strikes.[45] In the event, far from a period of calm, Dillon's accession to the leadership coincided with the serious crisis provoked by the decision of the government to extend conscription to Ireland in the wake of the German offensive on the western front in March 1918.

The Irish party bitterly opposed the extension of compulsory military service to Ireland, even though it was linked with a promise to introduce Home Rule, not only because it was fundamentally opposed to conscription but because it knew that it would play into the hands of the revolutionary nationalists. (See below pp108-11) The government's Irish advisers were opposed to conscription for those reasons and because they doubted whether it could be implemented. Against this background, Dillon suspected that Lloyd George's actions were part of a Machiavellian plot to kill the Irish party and Home Rule.[46] Although the Irish party withdrew from the house of commons as soon as conscription was passed and joined with the leaders of Sinn Féin and Labour leaders in a popular movement against conscription, their position in Ireland was undermined. The active policy long since demanded by Dillon came too late. An alternative popular movement now existed. The Irish party's inability to defeat conscription in the house of commons seemed to prove what Sinn Féin had been arguing – that attendance at Westminster was useless. William O'Brien declared that it proved the 'final bankruptcy' of parliamentary methods. Tim Healy, a life-long parliamentarian, expressed the dilemma of the Irish constitutionalist. He told the house of commons:

> I speak almost apologetically, when I get up in this House, about a distant Ireland which you have never seen and about which you do not care a curse...when you are going to coerce the country, when we are discussing matters of life and death, blood and money, we are told...that we are speaking humbug and direct insult is poured on us and our country.[47]

With the passing of the conscription crisis, the Irish party moved quietly back to the house of commons. There was little choice. The radical high ground coveted by Dillon since 1916 was now occupied by Sinn Féin. In the general election of December 1918, Sinn Féin won 73 seats, the Unionists 25 and the once powerful constitutional nationalist party a mere 6 seats.

While it is true that the cohesion and central control of the Parnellite organisation was never regained by the reunified Irish party and that the continued presence of Healy and O'Brien outside the party was a source of weakness, the reasons for the decline of the Irish parliamentary party are to be found largely in the period 1914-18. The absence of opposition before 1916 made it unnecessary to keep in close touch with their constituencies. With Home Rule on the statute book, this aspect was even more neglected. The party was also an ageing party. Like any reforming party, it badly needed renewing and an influx of new blood. In 1910, the average age was over fifty. With few young recruits, this increased steadily thereafter. More than thirty of its outgoing MPs did not seek re-election in 1918 and others stood only after persuasion from Dillon. There was considerable difficulty in getting new candidates and Sinn Féin won 25 seats unopposed. It was also a party socially out of touch with the new Ireland. Though less upper-class in composition than the party of Butt or Parnell, it was more so than Sinn Féin. With the general election taking place on a democratic franchise for the first time, this was probably of some little significance.[48]

The leadership issue was clearly of considerable importance too. The qualities which made Redmond a good choice of leader in 1900 – his acceptability to all sides, his moderation, his inoffensiveness – were less suited to the changed circumstances of 1914-18.This was compounded by Redmond's deep commitment to the war and the empire which increasingly became a liability. Dillon, on the other hand, was never at home in the house of commons and was more closely attuned to developments in Ireland. Had he succeeded to the leadership in 1916 while the advanced nationalist movement was still in disarray, he might have been able to seize the initiative. Instead, Redmond's policy of inactivity condemned the party to irrelevance. The constitutional movement became so much the embodiment of the *status quo* in Ireland that the very process of change seemed to necessitate its destruction.

6   The New Nationalism

Davoren: *I remember the time when you yourself believed in nothing but the gun.*

Seumus: *Ay, when there wasn't a gun in the country; I've a different opinion now when there's nothin' but guns in the country..An' you daren't open your mouth, for Kathleen ní Houlihan is very different now to the woman who used to play the harp an' sing 'Weep on, weep on, your hour is past', for she's a raging devil now, an' if you only look crooked at her you're sure of a punch in th' eye.*

Seán O'Casey: The Shadow of a Gunman

The period 1914-18 which witnessed the decline of the Irish parliamentary party also saw the victory of the new nationalism. The new nationalism differed from the old in its emphasis on the distinctiveness of the Irish cultural identity and the need for economic, social and political self-reliance, and in its distrust of parliamentarianism and party politics generally. It was also more Anglo-phobic than its predecessor which, as the years passed, lost much of its cutting edge and had been absorbed into the political culture of Westminster. The new nationalism was concerned with outlook and identity. The emphasis was on regenerating the fibre of the nation which it was claimed had been weakened by the demoralising impact of the famine, emigration, anglicisation and perennial party squabbling. This crusade – for that is how many of its adherents thought of it – was fuelled by a plethora of diverse organisations, literary, cultural and political, but always there, seeking to direct and manipulate, was the oath-bound, secret society, the Irish Republican Brotherhood, which provided what ultimately became the most important distinguishing feature of the new nationalism, the advocacy of physical force.

Cultural nationalism and Irish Ireland

The first of the new organisations to emerge and the one which probably had the greatest popular impact was the Gaelic Athletic Association established by Michael Cusack in 1884. The clearest statement of the values which inspired not just the GAA but the cultural nationalist movement generally was contained in a letter to Cusack from Archbishop Croke of Cashel, the patron of the new association. He deprecated the 'ugly and irritating fact' that the Irish were daily importing not only English produce but English fashions, accents, 'her vicious literature, her music, her dances, and her manifold mannerisms, her games also and her pastimes'. Ireland's 'grand national sports' were being displaced by 'such foreign and fantastic field sports as lawn tennis, polo, cricket and the like' which, though 'excellent health giving exercise' in their own way, were not 'racy of the soil'. In Croke's view, such games were 'alien', like those who introduced and patronised them. He warned that this process had wider implications:

> Indeed, if we continue travelling in the next score years in the direction that we have been going in for some time past, condemning the sports that were practised by our forefathers, effacing our national features as though we were ashamed of them, and putting on, with England's stuffs and broadcloths her masher habits, and such other effeminate follies as she may recommend, we had better at once, and publicly, abjure our nationality, clap hands for joy at the sight of the Union Jack, and place 'England's bloody red' exultantly above the 'Green'. [1]

Croke's letter with its assault on anglicisation and all things British provides a virtual manifesto of what the cultural nationalist movement stood for. An immediate application of his thinking was the GAA ban on its members playing foreign games, which was relaxed in the 1890s but later reaffirmed.

Croke's assault on anglicisation was taken up by the Gaelic League, established by Douglas Hyde, Fr Eugene O'Growney and Eoin MacNeill in 1893 to preserve and extend the use of the Irish language and to promote the study and publication of literature in Irish. Elsewhere in Europe one of the dominant characteristics of the nationalist movement was the emphasis on language and linguistic nationality. The Gaelic League ensured that Ireland would be no exception. Previous societies of this sort in Ireland had been aloof, scholarly bodies whereas the league sought to reach a wider audience. Unlike the GAA, it was never a mass organisation, but it did spread fairly rapidly after 1898. While primarily a cultural organisation, it provided their first contact with the nationalist movement for a new generation who graduated into more political organisations. Virtually every senior leader in the nationalist movement between 1916 and 1921 had earlier been a member of the Gaelic League. Hyde was insistent that it was not a political organisation and managed to preserve this position formally until 1915 when the IRB secured control of its executive and changed its constitution to favour the demand for political independence. Hyde resigned but he must have known all along that the line between cultural and political movements was very fine. In 1892, he delivered an address to the National Literary Society in Dublin entitled 'The necessity for de-Anglicizing Ireland' in which he pointed to the irony that, while the demand for self-government was growing, Ireland was all the while losing many of the distinguishing features of nationality. The first step in the process of de-anglicising the country was the arrest in the decline of the Irish language. He went on to echo Croke:

> In a word, we must strive to cultivate everything that is most racy, most smacking of the soil, most Gaelic, most Irish, because in spite of the little admixture of Saxon blood in the north-east corner, this island is and will ever remain Celtic at the core...We must create a strong feeling against West-Britonism, for it – if we give it the least chance, or show it the smallest quarter – will overwhelm us like a flood, and we shall find ourselves toiling painfully behind the English at each step, following the same fashions, only six months behind them; taking up the same fads, after they have become stale there; following them in our dress, literature, music, games, and ideas, only a long time after them and a long way behind.[2]

The Gaelic League was only one of a plethora of separatist literary and cultural societies which mushroomed in the 1890s. The Celtic Literary Society, established by William Rooney in 1893 to promote the study of Irish language, literature, history and song, was another. Out of the cultural nationalist movement came a 'veritable renaissance' in both Irish and English literature in Ireland. Much of it now commands attention more for its historical interest than for its literary merit but among the works which proved of lasting merit were those of Pádraig O Conaire in Irish and William Butler Yeats and John Millington Synge in English. In the present context, the sheer volume of the literary outpourings and the leading role played by the Anglo-Irish is what is significant. The establishment of the Abbey Theatre by Lady Gregory, W B Yeats and Edward Martyn in 1904 as part of the effort to create a distinctive Irish literature in English was the pinnacle of the literary renaissance. It also brought to a head some of the tensions within the cultural nationalist movement. The vigorous attacks on Synge's *In the shadow of the glen* in 1903 and *The playboy of the western world* in 1907 by leading exponents of Irish-Ireland exposed the narrow parochialism which in equal measure with lofty idealism was part and parcel of the cultural nationalist movement and ultimately disillusioned some of those who had been mesmerised by the Celtic twilight.

The most colourful expressions of the Irish-Ireland philosophy came from the pen of D P Moran who founded a weekly newspaper,

The Leader, in 1900. In an article entitled 'Is the Irish nation dying', Moran developed the themes first outlined by Croke and Hyde. The over-emphasis on Home Rule, he argued, was diverting attention from the slow death of the nation. To halt this process, Moran prescribed a revival of the Irish language and a development of Irish industries.[3] *The Leader* did much to popularise the central tenets of the new cultural nationalist movement but it also helped expose some of its contradictions. While essentially a movement of the middle class of the towns, it championed a rural counter-culture as a reaction against the bourgeois values of Victorian society. Furthermore while many of the greatest protagonists of cultural nationalism were Anglo-Irish intellectuals, such as Hyde and Yeats, Irish-Ireland as espoused by Moran and others was an exclusively catholic and Gaelic movement. Thus, ironically, those Anglo-Irish who created the literary revival were helping to forge a weapon which would one day be turned on themselves.

Of more enduring importance than Moran was Arthur Griffith and the Sinn Féin or self-reliance movement which he organised. A Dublin printer, born in 1871, Griffith was deeply influenced by the Young Irelander, Thomas Davis. He emigrated to South Africa in 1896 but returned two years later to edit the *United Irishman* established by Denis Devereux and his friend William Rooney. Although its circulation was small, the *United Irishman* quickly became an influential vehicle for the new nationalism. It acted as a forum for the various nationalist organisations and promoted greater contact between them. Griffith recognised the growing nationalist spirit and in 1900 called for the establishment of a national federation to coordinate their efforts. Cumann na nGaedheal, established in September 1900, sought to fill this role but without much success.[4] The National Council, formed in 1903 to oppose the visit of Edward VII to Ireland but which continued in existence afterwards, and the Dungannon Clubs established in 1905 by Bulmer Hobson, added to the proliferation of groups with overlapping membership. The widespread fragmentation was finally halted with the formation of the Sinn Féin League from a merger of the Dungannon Clubs and Cumann na nGaedheal in 1907. The following year, the League merged with the National Council to form Sinn Féin.

Although the new organisation was an amalgamation of different bodies, separatist and otherwise, its programme came largely from Griffith. Griffith had used the pages of the *United Irishman* to develop his ideas on economic self-reliance and abstention from Westminster. He also explored the parallels between the Hungarian and Irish situations which had previously been commented on by none other than Lord Salisbury.[5] Griffith found in the 1867 constitutional settlement in Austria-Hungary a model for Ireland. The creation of two separate independent kingdoms with a shared monarchy would, he argued, restore the constitutional position which had existed in 1782. Dual monarchy was added to abstention and economic self-reliance as the keynotes of the Sinn Féin policy.

Sinn Féin as established in 1908 was a new national organisation and not a coordinating body as originally envisaged by Griffith. This may have been a mistake as the organisation never enjoyed the popularity achieved by the outlook encapsulated in the term itself. In its early years, Sinn Féin enjoyed some popularity, partly because of a disillusionment with the parliamentary party. A few members of the Irish party were attracted by the Sinn Féin policy, and one, C J Dolan, resigned his North Leitrim seat and unsuccessfully contested it for Sinn Féin in 1908. However, Griffith's advocacy of the non-violent methods of O'Connell, which attracted dissident parliamentarians, was less attractive to more militant nationalists and the new organisation fell between two stools. In 1909, it had 128 branches. Thereafter, it declined and played only a peripheral role in events until 1917.[6]

The Irish Republican Brotherhood

In some respects, the new nationalism was not new at all. The Irish Republican Brotherhood which contributed to and benefited from the cultural nationalist movement was making a reappearance not a debut. What converted the new nationalism from a potentially to a genuinely revolutionary movement was the IRB and for that organisation the Irish question was little different in 1916 than in 1867.

The abortive Fenian rising in 1867 was followed by a period of feuding between and within Irish and American Fenian organisations. This was officially resolved in 1876 with the establishment of a joint Revolutionary Directory but it quickly reappeared and was a permanent feature of revolutionary politics.[7] In 1873, the IRB adopted a revised constitution which declared the supreme council of the IRB *de facto* and *de jure* the sole government of the Irish republic. However, it also allowed its members to support other genuinely nationalist movements. The latter was of fundamental importance as it allowed the revolutionary nationalists to capitalise on virtually every popular nationalist movement for the next fifty years.

With the failure of the rising of 1867, many Fenians began to explore ways of advancing the nationalist cause while allowing the physical force movement time to recuperate. As we have seen, attempts were made to forge an alliance both with Butt and Parnell and the leadership of the Land League was dominated by Fenians. However, such efforts were hampered by the constant division and splits within the revolutionary movement. The IRB's supreme council was divided on the subject of support for Butt's Home Rule party. Later Devoy's 'new departure' provoked similar division when the supreme council refused to endorse it. However, individual Fenians were allowed to participate in the agrarian agitation, and they did so in large numbers. The half-heartedness of the supreme council disillusioned Davitt and led to his expulsion from the Fenians. Paradoxically, while the Fenian tradition was of great significance in the land war, the official leadership of the IRB played little part.[8]

The IRB was relatively inactive during these years. There were sporadic bombings and assassinations such as the Phoenix Park murders carried out in 1882 by the Invincibles, a breakaway Fenian group. Otherwise the IRB was content to work through front organisations such as the GAA and the Young Ireland Society, of which W B Yeats was a member. The relationship between the IRB and the GAA serves as a good illustration of the way in which the revolutionary movement operated in these years. An overlap in membership between both groups was to be expected but the involvement of the IRB went beyond that. The GAA helped to spread the separatist ideal and acted as a recruiting ground for the secret organisation. Three of the eight founder members of the GAA were members of the IRB. With the exception of a short period in 1888, the IRB remained the dominant element through its control of the officer board. In 1887, the annual convention was packed by the IRB, leading to a split and the establishment of breakaway clubs. A new convention was held, at which the IRB influence was less strong. Nevertheless, it succeeded in slowly regaining control. This was recognised by the catholic church which feared that control of a popular sporting organisation would give the secret society enormous influence. Some bishops condemned the GAA for that reason and in 1890 there were in effect two GAAs, one controlled by the church and the other by the IRB. Also in the 1890s, a split in the Fenian movement was fought out within the GAA in a manner which severely hampered the growth of the GAA. The take-off of the GAA as a popular, nationalist sporting organisation from roughly the turn of the century coincided with a decrease in the influence of the IRB within it, although the organisation remained an important part of the nationalist movement generally.[9]

On the political issue, the IRB declared that the Home Rule bill of 1886 was inadequate but members were urged not to hinder its passage. The Parnellite split brought Parnell and the Fenians closer with Parnell seeking to balance his loss of power within the parliamentary party by appealing to the 'men of the hillside'. He succeeded in attracting Fenian sympathy because he was seen as a victim of perfidious Albion. Parnell's funeral in Dublin was used as the occasion of a major demonstration orchestrated by the IRB and thereafter Parnell was adopted into the Fenian pantheon of fallen heroes.

The division in the constitutional nationalist movement during the 1890s was matched by a division in revolutionary nationalism. The latter originated in America during the 1880s when Clan na Gael, the IRB's sister organisation established in 1867, split into two main groups, one led by John Devoy and the other which eventually established the Irish National Brotherhood. This conflict which owed more to American than Irish politics spilled over on to the Irish scene with the establishment of the INB in Ireland and Britain during 1894-5. Among the new recruits were Maud Gonne and W B Yeats. A concerted effort was made by advanced nationalists to use the centenary of the 1798 rebellion to generate support but the centenary committee and the '98 clubs were dogged by the IRB/INB rivalry. The split was eventually resolved in 1899 when Devoy managed to reconcile the various factions in America and the INB in Ireland faded from the scene. The IRB continued as before, acting through a variety of fringe groups, supporting the Boers in their war with Britain and helping to organise an Irish brigade, infiltrating Griffith's Cumann na nGaedheal, agitating against recruitment to the British army, and demonstrating against the visit of Queen Victoria in 1900.

The centenary of 1798 and the Boer War produced a surge in Fenian activity but thereafter the movement atrophied. Far from being the guiding hand behind the nationalist revival as some would have it, the IRB by the first decade of the twentieth century looked like becoming an irrelevance. Two events reversed that trend: the first was the entry into the movement of a number of young, energetic nationalists who replaced most of the ageing leaders. Of the new generation, two of the most important were Bulmer Hobson and Denis McCullough. Both were Ulstermen, though from different religious backgrounds, and both had been closely involved with Cumann na nGaedheal, the Dungannon Clubs and Sinn Féin. However, they were impatient with Griffith's ideas on dual monarchy and looked instead to a reinvigoration of the IRB. They were responsible for replacing many of the old Fenians with younger, energetic recruits. One of these, recruited in Belfast, was Seán MacDermott, who was to play a vital role in the reorganisation of the IRB and in the 1916 rising. Their efforts were given a boost by the return to Ireland of Tom Clarke, who though one of the older generation supported the move to purge the organisation of dead weight. The establishment of *Irish Freedom* in 1910, with Hobson as editor, marked the new revival in IRB activity. Until its suppression in December 1914, it made strong claims to be the authentic voice of militant nationalism.

The second event which helped the revival of the IRB was the Home Rule crisis of 1911-14 which produced the conspiratorial climate in which the Fenians thrived. Attitudes to the Home Rule bill among advanced nationalists varied. Griffith and Sinn Féin were critical of the bill's provisions but did not reject Home Rule completely. *Irish Freedom* took the more opportunistic line that if a limited measure of Home Rule was passed it could be exploited by the IRB, and if it was not passed, they could capitalise on the disappointment.[10] In the event, however, it was mobilisation of Ulster unionist opinion against Home Rule which proved most beneficial. The commencement of drilling in Ulster and the establishment of the Ulster Volunteers provided an example which the nationalist movement was not slow to follow. When Eoin MacNeill publicly proposed the establishment of an Irish Volunteer force in 1913, the suggestion was enthusiastically received by the IRB. Eight of the thirteen members of the committee which launched the Irish Volunteers in November 1913 were IRB members.

The Volunteers were not simply an IRB front. Their aim was to 'secure and maintain the rights and liberties common to all the people of Ireland' and their motto was 'Defence, not Defiance'. A conscious effort was made to attract support from Home Rulers. This contributed to their rapid growth throughout the country. By the outbreak of the war they had achieved a membership approaching 200,000. Following the example of the Larne gun-running by the Ulster Volunteers, arms were landed at Howth and Kilcoole in July 1914. Attempts by the authorities to intercept the Howth consignment before it was dispersed were unsuccessful but on their way back to barracks troops fired on a hostile crowd, killing three. This incident, which led to the dismissal of the assistant commissioner of the Dublin Metropolitan Police who was responsible for calling out the military, was a major embarrassment to the government as it allowed militant nationalists to claim that the intervention of the military was in stark contrast to their reluctance to confront the Ulster Volunteers. It seemed to confirm the suspicions raised in March by the failure to deal decisively with the Curragh Mutiny, when army officers indicated their unwillingness to act against Ulster. While most Volunteers knew and cared little about the IRB, the very existence of their organisation contributed to a growing militarism in Ireland. On the eve of the Great War, with no compromise in sight on the Home Rule issue and two large para-military groups drilling openly, the situation was tailor made for the IRB.

As we have seen, the Irish party felt that it was too dangerous to allow a popular, energetic movement such as the Volunteers to remain outside its aegis and in June 1914 Redmond successfully demanded control of the Volunteer executive. His demand produced a division in the IRB with Hobson and others arguing that to maintain the Volunteers as a truly national movement, they had no choice but to accede while MacDermott and Clarke saw it as a sell-out. This split, which resulted in the isolation of Hobson, was an early indication of the new aggressive thinking which now dominated the IRB.[11]

Redmond's success in taking control of the Volunteers shows that in 1914 leadership of nationalist Ireland still lay firmly in his hands. The split in the Volunteers which followed his Woodenbridge speech pledging Irish support for the war illustrates the relative disposition of forces within the nationalist camp. Approximately 169,000 Volunteers sided with Redmond, while 11,000 opposed the war and became Irish Volunteers. Not all or even a majority of these could be considered revolutionary nationalists – the number of members of the IRB at the time is reckoned to have been about 1,600 – but they did form the main basis on which the IRB now sought to build an armed insurrection.[12]

The 1916 rising

In the autumn of 1914, on the initiative of Seán MacDermott and Tom Clarke, the supreme council of the IRB decided to organise a rebellion before the end of the war. A committee was established to plan the rebellion, with MacDermott and Clarke its leading members. It was this committee which engineered the 1916 rising. Although it was officially subject to and occasionally reported back to the supreme council in general terms, the committee proceeded largely on its own initiative. The supreme council was poorly informed and played little part in developments.[13] Instead the committee turned to new recruits to the IRB, the most notable of whom were Patrick Pearse, Joseph Plunkett and Thomas MacDonagh.

All three were more typical of the new generation of nationalists than hard-bitten revolutionaries such as Clarke, and that may explain why they were pushed forward now. If MacDermott and Clarke can be compared in their conspiratorial methods to Lenin and the Bolsheviks who at the same time were resolving to use the opportunity presented by the war to engineer a revolution in Russia, Pearse, Plunkett and MacDonagh are more reminiscent of the poets and journalists of the romantic nationalist movement who led the European-wide revolutions of 1848. They were graduates of the cultural nationalist movement. All three were poets, writers and members of the Gaelic League. Pearse was later to become the figurehead of the nationalist movement generally. He was born in Dublin in 1879. From 1903 to 1909, he edited the Gaelic League's journal *An Claidheamh Soluis* and in 1908 he founded St Enda's, a bilingual school to promote the Irish language and implement his educational ideas. This and his ability as a speaker had attracted the attention of the IRB. His powerful oration at the Wolfe Tone commemoration at Bodenstown in 1913 helped overcome the lingering suspicions among sections of the IRB who had blocked his membership of that organisation because he was accused of being over-ambitious and a Home Ruler. He was recruited to the IRB late in 1913. By the time of his graveside oration at the funeral of the old Fenian O'Donovan Rossa in July 1915, when he uttered the famous words that Ireland unfree would never be at peace, he was firmly at the centre of the movement to organise an armed insurrection.[14]

The strategy adopted by the committee was for the IRB to form the elite corps which would guide the rising but to make use of the much wider group of nationalists who were members of other organisations. Insofar as those nationalists may have considered the future at all, many of them were in favour only of a defensive rather than offensive action. The IRB set itself the task of working on this revolutionary potential, identifying and radicalising those who were amenable and who might play a part later. In May 1915 a military council was established which initially included Pearse, Plunkett and Éamonn Ceannt. Later MacDermott, Clarke and MacDonagh joined. This council did much of the military planning for the rising.[15]

The Irish Volunteers were the obvious vehicle for the rising, organised as they were along military lines with a command structure and rudimentary training. Their policy, as adopted at a convention in October

1914, included the right of Ireland to provide for her own defence, opposition to conscription and the replacement of the Dublin Castle system with a national government.[16] Many of the senior officers were already IRB men: attempts were made to recruit those who were not and to manoeuvre reliable men into key positions. One of these was Éamon de Valera who was promoted to battalion commander only after being vetted by Pearse. De Valera, although an active member of the Gaelic League, was reluctant to join the oath-bound IRB and only did so in 1916 because he found his position in the Volunteers being circumvented by his junior officers who were members.[17] Pearse was director of organisation in the Volunteers and used that position to circumvent the authority of the chief-of-staff, Eoin MacNeill, who was considered unreliable.

The fear that the Volunteers would be proscribed and that conscription would be introduced suited those planning the rebellion as it made it easier to maintain interest in the Irish Volunteers. The Irish Neutrality League and the Irish Anti-Conscription committee, which represented a range of labour and nationalist organisations, helped keep these issues in the public eye. The exclusion of Ireland from the compulsory military service provision introduced elsewhere in the United Kingdom did little to defuse the issue. While all nationalists were opposed to compulsory service, the advanced nationalist position was that the war was not Ireland's concern and opposed voluntary recruitment. Some went even further and sought German assistance for their cause. An approach was made through Clan na Gael in America to Count Bernstorff, the German ambassador, seeking both arms and men. Roger Casement who went to Germany secured a promise of German recognition of an Irish republic. His attempt to establish an Irish brigade from Irish prisoners of war made little progress and only diverted attention from Ireland. A consignment of arms was sent on board the Aud on the eve of the rising but they were intercepted. Casement was arrested shortly after landing in Ireland from a submarine, found guilty of treason and executed. This debacle was a blow but the German connection was peripheral to the main preparations for the rising.

The IRB was not the only group interested in seizing the opportunity presented by the war to create a revolution. James Connolly, the radical labour leader (see above pp 11-12), used the pages of his paper *Workers' Republic* to call for a workers' revolt. In the absence of James Larkin who was in the United States, Connolly was the dominant left-wing figure in Dublin. Like Larkin, Connolly was born in Britain, of Irish emigrant parents. In 1896, he established the Irish Socialist Republican Party. Disillusioned with its failure, he emigrated to the United States in 1903 but returned in 1910 to become an organiser of the Socialist Party of Ireland. Connolly was a socialist but he argued that social liberation for the working class could not be achieved without political liberation and that social and political struggles should march hand in hand. He denounced the war as a 'capitalist war' and strongly opposed recruitment which was high in working class areas. He repeatedly advocated revolution by Irish workers against what he termed 'the bloody Empire on which the sun is ashamed to set'.[18]

Connolly went beyond more than just rhetoric. He was a leader of the Irish Citizen Army established in the aftermath of the 1913 lockout for the defence of Dublin workers. Though extremely small, the Citizen Army was drilled and armed. Connolly published weekly 'Irish Citizen Army' notes in *Workers' Republic*, urging the need for organisation and training in preparation for the coming struggle. Such belligerence alarmed the IRB who feared that Connolly might preempt their own plans. As a precaution, Connolly was coopted on to the Army Council in January 1916. Thus was sealed an alliance which was to have major implications for the incipient labour movement.

The rebellion which took place at Easter 1916 demonstrated how out of touch the Dublin Castle authorities had become. They were not completely unaware of the mood in militant circles but they proved unwilling or unable to act decisively to deal with the situation. Augustine Birrell, the chief secretary, felt that strong action against the Irish Volunteers was not necessary and, in any case, might precipitate the outbreak which it was designed to prevent. He was absent from Dublin during much of the time because of the illness of his wife. His under-secretary, Matthew Nathan, was more alive to the dangers and was responsible for the adoption of a firmer policy against seditious newspapers. However, he too was inclined to take a sanguine attitude. Soon after his arrival in Dublin, he warned against the tendency to see the Irish Volunteers as an insignificant minority but shortly afterwards he himself dismissed them in exactly those terms. During the latter part of 1915 and early in 1916, he was reluctant to agree to the firm action being demanded by some advisers. At the end of March 1916, the government did agree to the deportation of a number of the leaders of the Volunteers and to consider the cases of others. But as late as 10 April, Nathan was insisting that a rebellion was unlikely.[19]

Even at the last minute, decisive action by the government might have prevented the rising. On Wednesday and Thursday, 19 and 20 April, Nathan was informed of rumours that there was to be a rebellion. On the Saturday, he learned about the attempt to land arms in Kerry. He was aware that a mobilisation of the Volunteers was planned for Easter Sunday but when the mobilisation was cancelled he judged that an outbreak was unlikely. The lord lieutenant, the police and the military all urged immediate action but Nathan was not inclined to rush things now that the danger seemed to have receded. He insisted that widespread arrests would have to await the sanction of Birrell. Before that could be obtained, the rising had begun.[20]

The order cancelling the mobilisation of the Volunteers on Easter Sunday, which misled Nathan and effectively destroyed his career, was issued by Eoin MacNeill who had learned of the plans for a rising under cover of the Volunteer mobilisation. In February, Hobson and MacNeill, who opposed anything but a defensive rebellion, confronted their colleagues who denied rumours that they were secretly organising a rebellion. Thereafter MacNeill was systematically deceived. So too were many others who were known not to favour a rebellion. Indeed, some of them were placed under house arrest on Easter Sunday to prevent their attempting to cancel it. Denis McCullough, president of the supreme council of the IRB, was officially informed about the rising only shortly before it took place. A forged document was used to convince MacNeill that a move against the Volunteers was imminent and to persuade him that a preemptive strike was necessary. When he discovered that he was being deceived, he ordered the cancellation of the mobilisation order. The military council appeared to acquiesce but went ahead with its plans the following day.[21]

At noon on Easter Monday, 24 April, the insurgents seized the General Post Office and several other strategic buildings in Dublin, but, inexplicably not Dublin Castle. Pearse then read the Proclamation of the Republic signed by the members of the military council. It summoned all Irishmen and Irishwomen to the flag of the Irish republic. Until the establishment of a permanent government, a provisional government with Pearse as president was to administer civil and military affairs.

The military strategy for the rising, devised originally by Plunkett and apparently revised by Connolly, was inept if there was any intention to engage in a prolonged struggle. Strategic buildings were ignored and the strategy led inevitably to a short, desperate siege. In the main, the planned simultaneous risings in other parts of the country failed to materialise, with the exception of a few minor affrays in Counties Dublin, Meath, Wexford and Galway. With Britain engaged in a major international conflict in Europe, she could not afford a prolonged diversion in Ireland. The size of the insurgent force at the outset has been estimated at much less than 1,000, although the number increased when news of the rebellion broke. They were faced initially by 2,500 soldiers, mostly Irish. By the end of the week, this number had grown to 12,000. More importantly, artillery was brought in to shell the GPO forcing the evacuation of the garrison there and precipitating an unconditional surrender on 29 April. By then, the casualties were approximately 500 dead and 2,500 wounded. Most of these were civilians – army and police fatalities were officially put at 132 while about 60 insurgents died.[22] By 12 May, there were fifteen more dead after the court martial and execution of Pearse, MacDonagh, Clarke, Plunkett, Ceannt, Connolly, MacDermott, William Pearse, Edward Daly, Michael O'Hanrahan, John MacBride, Cornelius Colbert, Michael Mallin, Thomas Kent and Seán Heuston. Many others were sentenced to death but had their sentences commuted.

The failure of the rising had not been unexpected by the insurgents themselves. The view that even an unsuccessful rising could act as an impetus to national regeneration was widely shared by the leaders although not all of them went as far as Pearse in his quasi-religious espousal of the redemptive value of a blood sacrifice. However, while Pearse in his writings expressed unusual views particularly about the sacredness of the struggle in which they were engaged, his rhetoric about the cleansing power of bloodshed has many echoes in pro-recruitment speeches throughout Europe in 1914 and 1915. By 1916, Europe had grown used to sacrifice. Given that the casualties in the rising were only a tiny fraction of the Irish casualties on the Western Front and that most of the blood sacrificed in the former was that of innocent civilians, Pearse might have been proved wrong about the symbolic value of their enterprise had it not been for the prolonged series of executions which softened the initial public hostility to the insurgents. The executions replenished the nationalist pantheon of martyrs in a way in which death in combat would not have done. Then began the process of retrospective legitimisation which had occurred after previous rebellions but which on this occasion took place with remarkable speed.

The victory of Sinn Féin

Within three years of the Rising, Sinn Féin achieved a decisive endorsement at the polls and the IRA, as the Irish Volunteers were now known, had embarked on a guerilla war which was to culminate in the treaty of 1921. It would be wrong however to assume that this transformation was inevitable or that it followed a well-ordered blueprint. While the new nationalism made steady progress after 1916, there was considerable confusion as to what direction it would take and under whose leadership. As we have seen, John Dillon still harboured a belief that the Irish party could reassert its control by adopting a more radical policy. A rival claim to leadership came from Count Plunkett, the father of the executed 1916 leader, Joseph Plunkett. Following his easy defeat of an Irish party candidate at a by-election in February 1917, he established Liberty Clubs to rally nationalist support. However, these were later subsumed into Sinn Féin which, helped in no small measure by the mistake of the Dublin Castle authorities in describing the rising as a Sinn Féin rising, gradually emerged as the most likely victor in an internal nationalist power struggle.

The increased popularity of Sinn Féin was graphically illustrated by a series of victories over the Irish party at by-elections in South Longford, Kilkenny and East Clare, with Éamon de Valera being successful on the latter occasion. By the end of 1917, Sinn Féin was claiming to have 1,200 branches and 250,000 members nationwide. The latter figure is certainly an exaggeration for propaganda purposes. Police reports which suggested that the number of clubs was 1,039 with a membership of 66,270 are probably closer to the mark.[23] This Sinn Féin revival was matched by parallel reorganisation of the Volunteers which received a major impetus from the release of those imprisoned after the rising from December 1916 onwards. The continuance of martial law, the recurrent threat of conscription and the death of Thomas Ashe in September 1917 after a hunger strike all contributed to the revival of the Volunteers. Secret drilling recommenced and the incidence of arms raids grew steadily.[24]

Griffith's Sinn Féin party was an unlikely vehicle for the promotion of the national resurgence as it was committed to dual monarchy and played little part directly in the rising. This was not lost on the militants who had participated in the rising and who now sought to transform Sinn Féin. What emerged was essentially a compromise. The post-1916 Sinn Féin party owed little to Griffith's original but neither did it become merely the creature of a militant elite. It was in effect a national front which united a number of diverse streams and individuals. The implicit tensions were at least temporarily resolved at the Sinn Féin convention of October 1917. A divisive election for leadership was avoided when both Griffith and Plunkett stood down in favour of Éamon de Valera, the senior surviving leader of the rising. Born in New York in 1882, the son of an Irish mother and a Spanish father, he was raised in Bruree, County Limerick. A professor of mathematics, he joined the Irish Volunteers at their foundation and was sworn into the IRB by Thomas Mac Donagh. Although he was sentenced to death for his part in the Rising, the sentence was commuted to penal servitude for life. After imprisonment in Dartmoor, Maidstone and Lewes, he was released in June 1917. His election to the presidency of Sinn Féin dramatically illustrated the change in emphasis within that organisation. It was he who was responsible for the subtle compromise formula enshrined in the constitution to reconcile the old and new Sinn Féin. Its aims were defined as the securing of international recognition of Ireland as a republic but it was added that having achieved that status, the Irish people could by referendum freely choose their own form of government. De Valera's position as the senior public figure in the nationalist movement was confirmed by his election as president of the Irish Volunteers.

Despite this reorganisation, there was some danger that the advanced nationalist movement might run out of steam. Sinn Féin was now a well organised political party with a well defined (though perhaps naive) programme. However, beyond abstention from Westminster and appeal to any peace conference which would follow the war for the international recognition of the republic, it was unclear how its aims were to be achieved. The policy of contesting elections had been embarked upon without much consideration and with serious misgivings on the part of many, including de Valera, who suspected anything that whiffed of involvement in party politics. Three successive by-election defeats early in 1918 resurrected those doubts and had their effect on morale.

It was unclear where the movement was heading. Although there was a good deal of militant rhetoric, another rising seemed to be out of the question. The policy which seemed to be emerging almost by default was, as Constance Markievicz put it, a combination of the policy of Tone and Parnell: a constitutional movement backed by a physical force movement. That was certainly the model favoured by de Valera who may have been indicating his own preference for the future when he told a meeting: 'We fight England for freedom with votes, and then if we fail, with rifles if necessary'.[25] He certainly had a preference for an open rather than a secret movement. He had chosen not to rejoin the IRB after the rising arguing that they were now entering a new phase in the movement.

Others were less sure that the IRB had outlived its usefulness, most notably Michael Collins, who emerged as one of its most powerful leaders when it was reorganised shortly after the rising. Born in Cork in 1890, Collins went to London to work as a clerk in the Post Office when he was sixteen. He joined the IRB in London and returned to Ireland for the rising in which he acted as aide de camp to Plunkett. Imprisoned at Frongoch he was released in December 1916. He became a member of the supreme council when the IRB was reorganised. His 'oration' at the funeral of Thomas Ashe, left no doubt as to his own position. Ashe had been IRB president and a volley of shots was fired over his grave. That, said Collins, was the only speech it was proper to make at the grave of an old Fenian.[26] The IRB sought to ensure that their members were elected to key positions at the conventions of Sinn Féin and the Volunteers in 1917, although with less success in the case of the former than the latter. They dominated the elections to the executive of the Volunteers, with the exception of the position of chief-of-staff which was filled by Cathal Brugha, another survivor of the rising, who was strongly critical of the IRB. Collins himself became director of organisation and used that position to great effect in the following years.[27]

Clearly the exact balance between the open constitutional movement and the physical force wing was still uncertain. Two events in 1918 had an enormous impact on both and helped clarify the balance between them: the first was the conscription crisis and the second was the December general election. The English historian, A J P Taylor has argued that the German offensive on the western front in March 1918 caused Britain to lose Ireland. Although this is a considerable exaggeration, it does point to the important implications of the government's decision to meet the crisis on the western front by extending conscription to Ireland. If the conscription crisis was a disaster for the Irish party, it was an enormous stroke of luck for Sinn Féin and the Irish Volunteers. One Volunteer organiser later recalled that it was a great problem keeping existing companies alive as the memory of the rising faded. He described the effect of the conscription threat as 'electric'. Existing companies doubled in size and numerous new companies were formed.[28] This was confirmed by the police who reported:

The threatened application of conscription resulted in a great volume of support for Sinn Féin. It was the only political organisation directly opposed to recruiting for the Army, and the only political organisation showing any signs of existence at the time the conscription bill was passed. The people, therefore, flocked to its standard and the campaign that followed. Sinn Féin took the lead.... Sinn Féin was the driving force at the back of the movement and all the anti-conscription platforms were in reality Sinn Féin. After the danger of conscription had passed, the great bulk of those who identified themselves with anti-conscription continued to give their support to Sinn Féin, and this accounts in a great degree for its strong position now.[29]

While this report probably underestimates the importance of other factors in the growth of Sinn Féin, the general point is borne out by the police figures for Sinn Féin membership which increased by 24,000 between March and May 1918. By the end of 1918, the police were aware of 1,354 Sinn Féin clubs with 112,000 members.

Sinn Féin Membership 1917-18[30]

	31 December 1917		*31 December 1918*	
Province	*Clubs*	*Members*	*Clubs*	*Members*
Ulster	230	12,534	308	24,103
Leinster	243	15,125	320	23,234
Connacht	239	4,917	310	26,317
Munster	327	23,694	416	38,346
Total:	1,039	66,270	1,354	112,000

Table 3

Sinn Féin's participation in the Mansion House Conference which assembled in Dublin on 18 April to coordinate the campaign against conscription gave that organisation a respectability which it did not previously possess. The cooperation of de Valera and Griffith with the representatives of the Irish party and of Irish labour in the joint campaign allowed de Valera in particular to enhance his reputation. It was he who drafted the anti-conscription pledge taken at church gates throughout the country. It was a skilfully ambiguous formulation, designed to be acceptable to constitutionalists and believers in physical force: 'Denying the right of the British government to enforce compulsory service in this country, we pledge ourselves solemnly 'to resist conscription by the most effective means at our disposal'.[31] He won the support of the catholic bishops for this pledge by arguing that the Volunteers would forcibly resist conscription if the government proceeded, no matter what pledge was adopted. A united nationalist front might persuade the government to back down and thus avert violence.[32]

De Valera's calculation proved correct; faced by the united opposition of nationalist Ireland the government decided not to proceed, although the threat of conscription continued to hang over the country until the end of the war. In the meantime preparations for resistance continued. Anti-conscription committees were established throughout the country. Their plans were confined largely to passive measures but behind the scenes, independent of the committees, the Volunteers were making their own contingency plans which to a considerable extent formed the basis of the later guerilla war. This work was organised by Michael Collins, Cathal Brugha and Austin Stack. Members of Sinn Féin who were also Volunteers were withdrawn from Sinn Féin activities. Arms were smuggled in from abroad and numerous arms raids took place throughout the countryside, during one of which two Volunteers were killed. Police were attacked in Tralee. Training was intensified. Safe houses were identified. The practice of arrested Volunteers refusing to recognise the court or accept bail was reversed. Among the first to benefit from this was Michael Collins who had been arrested for incitement early in April and had refused to accept bail. As soon as the conscription crisis developed, he accepted bail and was released.[33]

Despite the potential gains, Sinn Féin cooperation with the Irish party in the anti-conscription campaign was opposed by many militant nationalists and not surprisingly the united front broke up quickly once the immediate threat of conscription passed.[34] The failure to avert a divisive by-election contest in East Cavan in May, despite intensive behind-the-scenes negotiations, was an open acknowledgement of the breakdown of the nationalist consensus. The victory of Arthur Griffith, who had been selected as a Sinn Féin candidate against his wishes, was assisted in no small measure by the so-called German plot arrests when seventy-three Sinn Féiners, including Griffith and de Valera, were arrested and interned by the government which claimed to have discovered evidence of a Sinn Féin plot for another rising. The failure of the government to publish any convincing evidence to support their claims merely confirmed the widespread public suspicion that no such evidence existed.[35]

The German plot arrests were a major miscalculation on the part of the government. At a critical moment, they tilted the balance within the nationalist movement away from the political and towards the militant, physical force wing. The intervention of the general election at the end of the year obscured this decisive shift but only temporarily. Those arrested were largely political rather than military figures. The Sinn Féin leaders had been forewarned about their arrest and decided for propaganda reasons not to seek to evade capture. A substitute Sinn Féin executive was nominated but it was largely composed of relatively unknown figures. The initiative within the nationalist movement passed to the underground movement and the Volunteers, whose executive, including Collins and Brugha, had escaped arrest. Sinn Féin became little more than a public front. The only significant member of the old Sinn Féin executive to evade arrest was Harry Boland, an active IRB man. This allowed the IRB to exercise a crucial influence in Sinn Féin, including the selection of candidates for the December general election.

Nothing better typifies the changing face of post-1916 Ireland than the 1918 general election. The decision of the Labour party not to contest the election facilitated the declared Sinn Féin intention of using the election as a referendum on independence. Its election manifesto declared the aims of Sinn Féin to be the establishment of an Irish republic. This was to be achieved by withdrawal from Westminster, the establishment of a constituent assembly in Ireland and an appeal to the peace conference. A sentence advocating 'any and every means available to render impotent the power of England to hold Ireland in subjection by military force or otherwise' was censored by the Dublin Castle authorities.[36] The decisive Sinn Féin victory altered the course of Anglo-Irish relations although it was some time before this was officially accepted. The victory of Sinn Féin generated remarkably little immediate reaction in England. The liberal press lamented the demise of the Irish party. On the other hand, the *Spectator* condemned Sinn Féin as 'soul-less selfishness' backed by 'Maynooth machiavellianism' and 'Bolshevik subversion' but recommended a policy of economic development to deal with it. It was left to the *Globe* to clamour for 'blood and iron'.[37] The government was content to wait and see how matters developed. Faced with other pressing problems, the absence of troublesome Irish MPs from Westminster had its advantages.

Sinn Féin's appeal to the peace conference proved to be a largely futile exercise. Abstention from Westminster and the establishment of Dáil Éireann, which met for the first time on 21 January 1919, were of greater importance. At the inaugural session, a declaration of independence was read and a democratic programme introduced. A temporary ministry was established, with Brugha as president in the absence of de Valera who was still in prison. When de Valera took over as president, in April, Brugha became minister for defence. Collins became minister for finance. In terms of social composition, the members of Ireland's first parliament since 1800 were predominantly middle class but from further down the social scale than their predecessors in the Irish party. Forty-three per cent were engaged in professional, 22 per cent in commercial, and 10 per cent in agricultural occupations.[38]

The potential of the Dáil as a forum for political debate was limited by the military conflict which developed from January 1919 onwards. However the Dáil debates and the actions of its various departments provide some clues to the nature of the new nationalism, particularly in its social dimension. As originally drafted, the Democratic Programme was a radical statement of social principles but it was toned down considerably. Even so, it remains quite a radical document. It declared that the nation's sovereignty extended

> not only to all the men and women of the nation but to all its material possessions; the nation's soil and all its resources, all the wealth and wealth-producing processes within the nation... and we affirm that all rights to private property must be subordinated to the public right and welfare.[39]

How seriously can this be taken? There is no doubt that the new nationalism attracted support from many agrarian and labour radicals. In practice, however, the national issue predominated. Everything else took second place. Those who hoped that the victory of Sinn Féin might bring radical social change were quickly disillusioned. Agrarian radicals such as Laurence Ginnell and Fr Michael O'Flanagan unsuccessfully pressed for action by the Dáil. A motion in the name of Alec McCabe and Countess Markievicz pledging the Dáil to 'a full and fair distribution of the vacant lands and ranches among the uneconomic holders and landless men' was withdrawn. At local level, many Sinn Féiners and Volunteers became involved in the resurgence of land agitation between 1917 and 1920 but when the central organisation intervened it was to check rather than encourage the agitation. The Land Commission, established in 1920, sought to control and regulate the activities of the Sinn Féin courts and to mediate between contending interests. This may partly be explained by the necessity not to divert attention from the political issue. However, it also derived from the philosophy of Griffith which dominated the practical work of Dáil Éireann. He argued that they could not have a policy for capital or a policy for labour but a policy for the nation. The role of the state was to mediate between rival sections. He told the 1919 Sinn Féin Convention: 'Sinn Féin is not a party. It is a national composition. If it is a party at all, it is a composite party. No parts of that composition may claim its own individual programme until the national ideal has first been attained'.[40]

Of course Griffith was correct: the new nationalist movement was a composite party which sheltered within its rank conservatives such as himself and radicals such as Constance Markievicz. Insofar as any social policy was officially articulated it tended to be Griffith's. However, by and large social issues were avoided as far as possible. Equally the movement sheltered those who like himself were fundamentally constitutionalists and those whose first loyalty was to the physical force tradition. That division was quickly to become of enormous significance.

The effectiveness of the Dáil in establishing itself as a *de facto* government has been grossly exaggerated. Ministers were appointed, courts established, edicts issued but, with the outbreak of the Anglo-Irish war, much of this was of necessity public posturing. The Dáil met infrequently and neither it nor the cabinet could exercise real control over the fighting men who increasingly seized the initiative.

The Soloheadbeg ambush in which two policemen were killed and which is generally seen as the opening shot of the Anglo-Irish war coincided with the opening of the First Dáil. It was a conscious attempt by those concerned to reassert the predominance of the military wing of the nationalist movement.[41] The drift into guerilla war was gradual, haphazard and largely unplanned. Throughout 1919, there were sporadic arms raids, attacks on police barracks and ambushes. Most of the incidents took place in Munster and were the result of the initiative of local Volunteer leaders. Soloheadbeg which involved nine Volunteers was more typical of the scale and type of engagement than the Kilmichael ambush in Cork in November 1920 when Tom Barry's flying column comprising about forty Volunteers wiped out an Auxiliary patrol.

During 1920, the conflict intensified and the military took the place of the police as the main targets. Only gradually did Volunteer headquarters succeed in coordinating local efforts but its control was never more than partial. While individual Volunteer commanders such as Tom Barry and Seán Treacy acted largely on their own initiative, the dominant figure at national level was Collins who was director of organisation and of intelligence. Ruthlessly efficient, Collins cultivated senior police officers who provided valuable information. His elite 'Squad', established in September 1919, was responsible for the assassination of a team of secret service officers in Dublin, on 'Bloody Sunday', 21 November 1920, which led to the reprisal attack on players and spectators attending a Gaelic football match at Croke Park.

Ironically, the victory of Sinn Féin in December 1918 and the establishment of Dáil Éireann a month later coincided with a shift in real power away from the political wing of the nationalist movement, a shift which was facilitated by the absence of de Valera in America from May 1919 until December 1920. The Sinn Féin party played little direct part in events until after the Treaty split in 1922. Even the Dáil was relegated to a secondary position. Its importance was largely symbolic until the quest for a settlement brought the initiative back to the political leadership.

7 'What answer from the North?': The Ulster Question 1870-1920

The increasingly vociferous nationalist demand for Home Rule and later independence from Britain generated an equally virulent response from those for whom the Act of Union had become a touchstone of their identity. As the nationalist demand grew in intensity, so too did resistance among unionists, particularly in Ulster. The unionist community in the rest of Ireland was more dispersed and consequently more vulnerable to the winds of change. The transfer of the ownership of land, the democratisation of local government and the persistence of the nationalist movement convinced many southern unionists that some change was inevitable. These same factors convinced their northern cousins of their own isolation in an increasingly alien country. The southern unionist resignation to the inevitability of change was completed by the cataclysm of the first world war which hastened the advent of the Anglo-Irish twilight in the south of Ireland. For northern unionists that cataclysm marked not so much the dying rites as a baptism.

The emergence of a renewed awareness of and emphasis on the Irish nationalist identity in the late nineteenth century was paralleled by a similar development among northern unionists. Neither identity was new, of course. Ulster particularism goes back at least to the plantation of Ulster in the early seventeenth century. In the decades and centuries which followed the plantation, the English and Scottish settlers developed a hybrid identity which drew in similar measure from their background, their religion and their new environment. The precise importance of these ingredients could vary sufficiently from time to time to allow both an upsurge of presbyterian radicalism in the late eighteenth century and conservative unionism in the late nineteenth.

The two key features of Ulster particularism were religious and economic. Ulster was the only one of the four provinces to have a protestant majority. While there were some isolated regions of the other three provinces – such as County Dublin and County Cork – where the numbers of the protestant population were relatively large, in no county did they exceed 30 per cent of the total. In 1871, the combined church of Ireland, presbyterian and methodist population was 13·8 per cent of the total in Leinster, 6·2 per cent in Munster and 4·9 per cent in Connacht. In

Ulster the picture was dramatically different as can be seen from the accompanying table. The protestant population was both larger and more broadly based in terms of class. In the immediate post-famine period there was still a small catholic majority in the province as a whole. In the decades that followed, the numbers of both catholics and protestants declined because of emigration but the number of catholics declined faster with the result that by 1871 there was a slight preponderance of protestants. This preponderance grew as the period progressed. There was of course considerable regional variation with counties Cavan, Donegal, Fermanagh, Tyrone and Monaghan containing catholic majorities, counties Antrim, Armagh, Derry and Down containing protestant majorities.

Religious denomination as percentage of Ulster population 1871 and 1911[1]

	Roman catholic	Church of Ireland	Presbyterian	Methodist	Others
1871	48·9	21·5	26·1	1·6	1·9
1911	43·67	23·19	26·64	3·09	3·41

Table 4

Ulster – or at least parts of it – had also experienced considerable industrial development. The linen industry, which was not originally confined to Ulster, took deepest root there. To this was added in the nineteenth century the shipbuilding and the engineering industries. Improvements in the port of Belfast and the growth of the Harland and Wolff shipyard from the 1850s facilitated Belfast's development as a major industrial centre linked closely with Clydeside and Merseyside. Central and eastern Ulster had both a relatively large urban population and a high density of rural population. Skilled industrial employment, especially in Belfast, was dominated by protestants. Agrarian disturbances, although not unknown, were less frequent than elsewhere in Ireland.

The Ulster protestant community was not monolithic. There were major social and religious differences between presbyterians and members of the church of Ireland for instance. In politics there was a strong liberal unionist tradition in Ulster which was only superseded after the nationalist electoral triumph of 1885. There were also important class divisions. The Orange Order had long been a predominantly working-class organisation looked on with disdain by many unionists for reasons both of religion and class. It had fallen into decline until it was revived by disestablishment, the land war and above all Home Rule. As the Home Rule movement gathered steam so did the popular appeal of the Orange Order. The land agitation of the late 1870s revealed fundamental differences between landlords and tenants – protestant as well as catholic – as evidenced by the establishment of the Ulster Tenants' Defence Association by T W Russell, the Liberal Unionist MP for South Tyrone. Ulster tenants, no less than those in Connacht or Munster, demanded land reform and ultimately land purchase. In 1885 a normally safe unionist seat in North Fermanagh was lost to a Parnellite because of a split between unionist landlords and tenants. The next two holders of the seat, both unionists, strongly supported the tenant cause. Indeed as late as 1903 Edward Mitchell, an Independent Unionist who strongly advocated compulsory land purchase, defeated the official Unionist candidate, James Craig, later prime minister of Northern Ireland.[2]

Divisions were also evident in urban areas, particularly in Belfast. Landlord-tenant divisions were mirrored by employer-employee divisions. Ulster may have been relatively more prosperous than the rest of Ireland, but it was not immune from the grim social conditions common in new industrial areas. The harsh conditions in working-class areas of Belfast were often commented on by contemporaries. Linen workers complained bitterly about the ill-effects of constant exposure to flax dust. Wage levels, which were actually reduced in 1875, were a constant source of dispute. The industry was subject to periodic depressions and consequent unemployment such as in 1893. The growth of labour representation at municipal level from the 1890s reflects these tensions. So too does the emergence of the Independent Orange Order in 1903 under the guidance of Tom Sloan, ex-shipyard worker and an Independent Unionist MP.[3] Unionism then, like nationalism, embraced a very broad church. It contained within it significant religious and class tensions. However, these differences were masked by the perceived threat to the common protestant identity posed by a vigorous catholic nationalist movement.

Ulster opposition to the first Home Rule bill

Disestablishment of the Church of Ireland, the land agitation and the various land acts, the 1884 Reform Act which extended the franchise and the related Redistribution Act of 1885 – all caused unease in Ulster. Many unionists feared such reforms might prove the thin end of the wedge. Lord Salisbury, the Conservative leader, identified a widespread fear when he complained that their effect would be to shatter the power of the landed gentry without providing any viable alternative basis of government. Salisbury feared disorder and chaos: even more threatening from a northern unionist point of view was the prospect of domination by a majority catholic movement. The emergence and spectacular growth of the Home Rule movement turned this unease into outright opposition.

Neither Butt's Home Government Association nor the Home Rule League generated a concerted response from unionists beyond abuse of Butt by speakers at Orange gatherings and the dismissal of Home Rule in the house of commons by Conservative MPs from Ulster. With the growth of the land agitation and under the more vigorous leadership of Parnell, the Home Rule movement assumed more threatening proportions. Parnell and Davitt had sought to broaden the basis for Land League support by agitating among tenant farmers in Fermanagh and Tyrone. They also attempted to promote the Home Rule movement in Ulster. Tyrone was contested unsuccessfully by a Parnellite candidate in the autumn of 1881. In June 1883, Tim Healy dramatically won a bye-election in Monaghan. The latter success prompted an all-out attempt to win support in Ulster.

The so called 'invasion of Ulster' was to have mixed results. A series of public meetings were organised which provoked a backlash from the Orange Order. Rival meetings were staged and tensions raised. At a meeting in Roslea, Co. Fermanagh, serious confrontation between huge nationalist and Orange crowds was only narrowly averted. Lord Rossmore who had organised the Orange demonstration was later removed from the commission of the peace and political demonstrations were prohibited. However, the scene had been set for future confrontation. By the beginning of 1886, the Irish National League was claiming 287 branches in Ulster, while on the other side the revival of the Orange Order represented an ominous development.[4]

The 1885 general election served to increase unionist fears. This first test of the new reform act and the revision of constituency boundaries proved a triumph for Parnell. After a lively and sometimes violent campaign, Home Rulers won 17 of 33 seats in Ulster, a gain of 14. The result seemed to confirm the Parnellite argument that even in Ulster unionists were only a vocal minority. However, the nationalist victory was aided considerably by the disunity of the opposition. A common front to oppose Home Rule, such as emerged in the shape of the Irish Loyal and Patriotic Union in the south of Ireland, was more difficult to achieve in Ulster because of the divisions which existed between Orangemen, conservatives and liberals. The main casualties of the 1885 election were the liberals who failed to gain a seat in Ulster. The middle ground in Ulster politics became and remained a precarious position to occupy. The process of polarisation which culminated in partition had begun.

The disorganisation within the unionist camp may have helped convert Gladstone to Home Rule for Ireland. When he decided to introduce a Home Rule bill he had no reason to anticipate significant resistance from Ulster. His closest advisers and cabinet colleagues shared the nationalist equation of unionism with orangeism and bigotry. Ulster presbyterians could be and were being won over. Only James Bryce, a Belfast presbyterian who was later to become chief secretary for Ireland, sounded a warning note. The Home Rule scheme would, he advised, unite Ulster protestants and might lead to civil war.[5] The predominant view was more sanguine and it was not felt necessary to make any special provision for Ulster.

Even the vocal opponents of Home Rule in Britain were not primarily concerned with the problems of protestant Ulster. Indeed some of them, most notably Randolph Churchill who provided Ulster unionists with their rallying cry: 'Ulster will fight and Ulster will be right', felt as little sympathy for Ulster as did Gladstone. Before he emerged as the champion of protestant Ulster, Churchill was widely believed to have nationalist sympathies. His primary objection to Home Rule was that it represented a threat to the unity of the kingdom and the empire. That theme predominated in the house of commons debate on the bill although it was linked, for tactical reasons, with the Ulster question. That the link was tactical rather than ideological was openly admitted by Churchill who confirmed to a friend that he had decided that if Gladstone tried to introduce Home Rule, 'the Orange card would be the one to play.' 'Please God', he wrote, 'it may turn out the ace of trumps and not the two.'[6]

Ulster was to be used as a weapon in a wider imperial game to defeat Home Rule. For this finesse to work, Ulster opposition had to be nurtured. That is what Churchill set about doing, addressing meetings in Britain and Ulster. At Paddington, on 13 February, he warned that an

Irish parliament would have Parnell as its chief speaker and Archbishop Walsh, the catholic archbishop of Dublin, as its chief priest. He promised that England would not leave Irish protestants in the lurch. A week later at the Ulster Hall he took that theme further when he not only justified Ulster resistance but predicted that Ulster would not stand alone – she would be joined by many in positions of influence in England. 'I am not of the opinion', he added,'that this struggle is likely to remain within the lines of what we are accustomed to look upon as constitutional action.'[7]

The extravagance of his language may have owed more to the excitement of the occasion than to any cool-headed assessment of the likely outcome of the crisis. However, within a fortnight he reiterated much of the content of the Ulster Hall speech in a widely publicised letter:

> If political parties and political leaders should be so utterly lost to every feeling and dictate of honour and courage as to hand over coldly the lives and liberties of the Loyalists of Ireland to their hereditary and most bitter foes, make no mistake on this point – Ulster will not be a consenting party. Ulster at the proper moment will resort to the supreme arbitrament of force; *Ulster will fight, Ulster will be right*; Ulster will emerge from the struggle victorious, because all that Ulster represents to us Britons will command the sympathy and support of an enormous section of our British community, and also, I feel certain, will attract the admiration and approval of free and civilised nations.[8]

Churchill consciously raised the religious as well as the political issue in his speeches to mobilise support. Home Rule, he stated repeatedly, would mean oppression of his co-religionists. This theme was taken up by others. Lord Salisbury claimed that protestants were threatened with 'absolute slavery' under Parnell. However, once the bill was defeated, the newly found concern for Ulster protestants diminished. By September Churchill was referring dismissively to 'Belfast beggars'[9] but Pandora's box which he had helped to open was less easy to close.

In Ulster opposition to Home Rule was far from being simply tactical. In the short time between the announcement of Gladstone's intentions and the introduction of his bill into the house of commons, a considerable protest was raised in Ulster. As in the south of Ireland and England, the implicit threat to imperial integrity was a frequent theme in the protests, although the emphasis in Ulster was on the threatened dilution of the British heritage. Even more commonly raised was the accusation that Home Rule would mean Rome Rule. Whatever the validity of that fear, it was raised frequently enough to leave little doubt that it was a widespread apprehension. The third major plank of unionist opposition was the negative social and economic impact which it was claimed would inevitably flow from a weakening of Ulster's links with Britain and her domination by her predominantly rural neighbours in the south of Ireland. Fenianism, the land war and now Parnellism made such a prospect unpalatable.[10] With some refinements, these three objections remained the basis of the Ulster unionist case against Home Rule during the campaigns against the bills of 1893 and 1912.

Much of the early organisation of meetings against Home Rule was undertaken by the Orange Order which received a huge impetus as a result and an influx of members from all classes. The Ulster Loyalist Anti-Repeal Union was also established to lead the protest. The religious fervour of the movement has often been commented on. In many ways it resembled O'Connell's emancipation movement of the 1820s with its religious overtones and emphasis on clerical involvement.

There was some talk about armed resistance and tentative steps were taken to acquire arms and to start drilling. But the immediate crisis had passed before much of substance had been done. What preparations were made tended to be defensive rather than offensive in that they were designed to protect Ulster protestants from attack if Home Rule were passed, rather than being part of a rebellion to defeat Home Rule.[11] There was serious rioting in Belfast from June to September. Beginning in the shipyards, it involved attacks on the police, shops and pubs, and fighting between rival mobs. By mid-September almost fifty people had been killed, making these the worst disturbances in Ireland in the nineteenth century not excluding the various risings or the land war.[12] However the riots, which took place largely after the threat of Home Rule had passed, primarily reflected increased sectarian tension rather than any emerging resistance movement.

Despite the belligerence so powerfully encapsulated in Churchill's slogan, it is doubtful whether Ulster would indeed have fought in 1886, had the Home Rule bill been passed. Whatever violent resistance there would have been, would most likely have been isolated. A strong unionist movement was only beginning to emerge in 1886. Not until the beginning of 1886 were steps taken to establish a unionist parliamentary party at Westminster. In June, Ulster liberals finally turned their back on Gladstone and established the Ulster Liberal Unionist Committee. However, they were not yet ready to throw in their lot irrevocably with the conservatives.

The real importance of the 1886 crisis lies in the fact that it set the scene for later conflicts. Once established, the pattern varied little. What did vary was the intensity. Polarisation increased and the middle ground continued to narrow until it ultimately disappeared. In the process, the Ulster identity began to take shape. Loyalty to the crown was a byeword but it was seen to be a conditional or 'contractual' loyalty which depended on the maintenance of the integrity of the kingdom and the empire.

The events of 1886 also sealed the commitment of the Tory party to the unionist cause. The cause of Ulster and imperial integrity became inextricably linked. The term 'unionist' was formally added to the title of the Conservative party. Home Rule had split the Liberal party and led to its downfall. The Orange card had proved to be an ace. It would be hard to resist playing it again.

The 1893 Act

The resignation of Lord Salisbury's government in 1892 and the ensuing general election brought renewed fears in Ulster, since the return of Gladstone would inevitably put Home Rule back on the political agenda. Once again, unionists were galvanised into action. On this occasion, they were better prepared, while the nationalists by contrast were divided as a result of the Parnellite split. The Unionist MPs at Westminster had also become a better organised group, under the guidance of Colonel E J Saunderson, a Cavan landlord. Again they gained considerable support from British Conservatives in their campaign. Randolph Churchill, although suffering from ill-health, came out of retirement to join the campaign. Arthur Balfour attended a march-past by 100,000 unionists in Belfast. A massive demonstration – the Ulster Unionist Convention – was held in the Botanic Gardens, Belfast, on 17 June 1892. It attracted a crowd of over 20,000 people, with many thousands more unable to gain admission to the specially built hall. The duke of Abercorn brought the crowd to its feet with the declaration that 'we will not have Home Rule'.[13]

The convention marked the beginning of a period of intense organisation among unionists. The Ulster Convention League arose from the enthusiasm generated by the convention. At the beginning of 1893, a Unionist Clubs movement began and spread rapidly throughout the province under the aegis of a Unionist Clubs Council. More influential was the Ulster Defence Union which was established in March to coordinate opposition to the Home Rule bill and which brought most strands of unionist opinion, liberal and conservative, political and Orange together in one organisation.[14]

How far would the resistance have gone? At the Ulster Unionist Convention, Thomas Sinclair, one of the most prominent Liberal Unionists, expressed the view that unionists would resist a Home Rule parliament by passive means. As in 1886, others talked of armed resistance. In 1892, Frederick Crawford, later to play a prominent part in arming the Ulster Volunteer Force, established the secret Young Ulster movement to fight Home Rule. A condition of membership was said to be possession of a revolver or a rifle and 100 rounds of ammunition. Some arms were imported and a little isolated drilling took place. By and large, however, there seemed to be an emphasis on maintaining respectability. The Belfast riots of 1886 had damaged the unionist cause and efforts were made to ensure that these would not recur. It was widely believed that if unionists stood firm and retained Conservative support Home Rule would not reach the Statute Book. Thomas Sinclair's message met with a positive response. It was unlikely that Ulster would fight, unless attacked.[15]

The firmness of the unionist resolve helped persuade the house of lords to reject the bill. Had Gladstone immediately fought and won an election on the issue, as he had intended, the crisis would have continued. However, his resignation in 1894, and replacement by Lord Rosebery, who was not a Home Ruler, promised an end to the crisis for the moment. This was confirmed by the victory of the Conservatives at the subsequent general election.

From the second to the third Home Rule bill

The period between the second and third Home Rule bills was a period of relative calm compared to the high drama of the previous decade. The fact that the Conservatives were in power from 1895 to 1905, the decline of the nationalist movement and the disillusionment of the Liberals with Home Rule meant that there was no immediate threat to the union. However, there were important developments in these years.

The unionist identity which began to emerge in 1886 grew and matured. *The Northern Whig* newspaper, commenting on the Unionist Convention of 1893, noted that 'there sat men of opposed political creeds: still Liberal, still Conservative, on this occasion and in this cause they know but one name - that of Unionist[16].' While there continued to be social, political and religious divisions, this overriding common loyalty survived and grew. The continued growth and prosperity of Belfast contributed to and reflected the maturing northern unionist identity. Between 1871 and 1911 its population grew from 174,000 to 387,000 which matched that of Dublin. Many visitors commented on how it resembled English or Scottish industrial towns more than other Irish towns. Its public architecture of which the most notable example was the City Hall, completed in 1906, self-consciously sought to assert Ulster's independent identity.[17] The *Ne Temere* decree of Pius X in 1907, which required all children of a mixed marriage to be brought up as catholics seemed to confirm many of the worst fears of northern protestants. In the following year, the establishment by a Liberal government of Queen's College Belfast as an independent university rather than its inclusion in the federal National University symbolised the growing separate- ness of Ulster.

While this process was going on, the continuance of the land purchase policy by the Conservatives sealed the decline of the southern unionists. Their willingness to cooperate with nationalists in constructive policies marked them off from their northern counterparts. The major political controversy in this period was the devolution crisis of 1904-5. The involvement of prominent southern unionists in the formulation of MacDonnell's scheme did little to soothe northern unionist fears that this was an attempt to introduce Home Rule by another name. They were vociferous in their condemnation of George Wyndham and ultimately forced his resignation as chief secretary. His successor, Walter Long, was chosen partly because he would be acceptable to Ulster unionists and he took great pains to placate them as much as possible. They continued to pursue Antony MacDonnell and resolved not to support the government on any votes on the administration of Ireland until he was transferred.

Their campaign intensified when the Liberals returned and the Irish Council bill was introduced. Home Rule by instalments was as objectionable to unionists as the Gladstonian version.[18] Devolution did not provoke the popular outcry that Home Rule had, but it did encourage a renewed spate of organisation. The Ulster Defence Union was revived in the shape of the Ulster Unionist Council in 1905. Unlike its progenitor, the council proved both durable and influential. It was in effect an umbrella organisation representing the whole spectrum of unionist organisations. When in 1911 the storm clouds began to gather once more, the task of organising Ulster resistance fell to the Ulster Unionist Council.[19]

Ulster and the third Home Rule bill

The turmoil generated by the first and second Home Rule bills, though intense, was extremely short lived. More than anything, what distinguishes the crisis which developed over the third Home Rule bill is its protracted nature. While it is true that it did not reach a climax until 1913-14 and was only then taken really seriously by the government, the organisation of resistance had been going on for at least four years. The veto of the house of lords had been the ace up the sleeve in the previous campaigns. The abolition of the veto guaranteed an intensity to Ulster unionist resistance on this occasion. The provision that a bill rejected by the lords would have to pass the commons three times before becoming law ensured that resistance would have time to gather pace.

Added to this were two other important factors – organiation and leadership. The earlier unionist campaigns had been haphazard and poorly organised, especially in 1886. By 1911, unionist organisation had improved immeasurably, under the auspices of the Ulster Unionist Council. Moreover, whereas in 1886 and 1893 there was no dominant leader, the latest crisis threw up two – Edward Carson and James Craig. Of the two, Carson was the most unlikely leader. Born in Dublin in 1854, he had a distinguished legal career both in Ireland and Britain. He was MP for Trinity College, Dublin from 1892 until 1918 when significantly he switched and was elected for the Duncairn constituency in Belfast. A brilliant advocate, he succeeded Walter Long as leader of the Irish Unionist members in the house of commons in 1910. He was an unlikely leader, not least because he suffered from ill-health. He was not primarily interested in Ulster at first but sought to use it to defeat Home Rule for all of Ireland. Increasingly he was seen as the major public spokesman for the Ulster unionists. He adapted to that role, developing a most effective style of rhetoric which belied his cautious legal background. If Carson was something of a figurehead, Craig was the driving force, providing both the links with the heartland of Ulster unionism and a grasp of detail and organisation lacking in his leader. MP for East Down since 1906, Craig was the son of a presbyterian whiskey millionaire and possessed considerable financial resources which were to prove useful. Together with Bonar Law, the new leader of the Conservatives in Britain, Carson and Craig represented a formidable triumvirate. Perhaps because of his Ulster connections and presbyterian background, Bonar Law was more sympathetic to Ulster than Arthur Balfour, his predecessor.

Just how prepared the unionists were to resist the third Home Rule bill can be seen from a manifesto issued by the Grand Orange Lodge of Ireland in December 1910:

> Brother Orangemen,
> We address you at a grave crisis in the history of Ireland. Mr. Redmond and the party servants of the American fenians procured for their schemes the help of the Socialists and Radicals of England. Under cover of an attack upon the House of Lords they are striking a deadly blow at the Union. If they obtain a majority at this election, Home Rule may be carried over the veto of the Second Chamber in two years. In these circumstances you have two duties to perform: You must use every effort to defeat them at the polls, neglecting no opportunity of influencing votes in Great Britain. But you are equally bound to prepare for a struggle in this country if we should fail to carry the elections.
> Already steps are being taken to enrol men to meet any emergency. Orangemen must set the example to other Unionists by volunteering their service....[20]

The manifesto was sent to every Orange lodge in Ireland with a form seeking particulars of members of the lodge who, in the event of Home Rule becoming law, were willing to take 'active steps' to resist its enforcement. In the event, the UUC not the Orange Order spearheaded the campaign. The duke of Abercorn was president of the council and Carson, as leader of the Irish unionist MPs, vice president. It was on the initiative of the UUC that the Unionist Clubs were reorganised throughout Ulster from early in 1911. A Women's Association was also established. The first great public launch of the campaign was a rally in the grounds of James Craig's house, Craigavon, ostensibly to introduce the people of Ulster to Carson, their new leader. Upwards of 100,000 people were present to hear Carson denounce Home Rule as 'the most nefarious conspiracy that has ever been hatched against a free people'. 'We must be prepared', he told them, 'the morning Home Rule passes, ourselves to become responsible for the government of the protestant province of Ulster.'[21] Somewhat incongruously, this was, it seems, only the second time Carson had addressed a meeting in the province.

Carson sought the approval of the meeting for proposals to move towards the creation of an alternative government. Two days later, the UUC decided to resist Home Rule and nominated a committee under Carson to draft a constitution for a provisional government. The public nature of these actions show that they were to an extent propaganda exercises but the decision to establish a provisional government was more than that. A detailed scheme providing for a government under Carson's leadership was drawn up and approved in September 1913.[22]

Following the Craigavon meeting, the public and private organisation of Ulster resistance proceeded quickly. The public aspect of the campaign was dominated by a series of monster meetings and public demonstrations designed to mobilise opinion both in Britain and in

Ireland. On Easter Tuesday 1912, shortly before the introduction of the Home Rule bill, a massive demonstration was held at Balmoral in the Belfast suburbs. The opening of the meeting by the Church of Ireland primate, Archbishop Crozier, and the moderator of the presbyterian church, and the presence of seventy British Conservative MPs, including Bonar Law, demonstrate the extent of the support Ulster resistance was receiving.

Bonar Law told the gathering that Ireland was not a nation but 'two peoples, separated by a deeper gulf than that dividing Ireland from Great Britain'. He pledged his party's support for Ulster resistance, whatever form it might take. Nor was this a message tailored specially for an Ulster audience. Three months later, at a rally at Blenheim Palace, he labelled the govern- ment as a 'revolutionary committee' which had 'seized upon despotic power by fraud' and added that he could 'imagine no length of resistance to which Ulster can go in which I should not be prepared to support them, and in which, in my belief, they would not be supported by the overwhelming majority of the British people'.[23]

The *carte blanche* given by Bonar Law encouraged unionist resistance, if such encouragement was needed. The next great public gesture came with the organisation of the Solemn League and Covenant in the autumn of 1912. Great care was taken in drafting the covenant to make it as broadly acceptable as possible and it was shown to the leaders of the main protestant churches for approval. Based loosely on the Scottish Presbyterian Covenant of 1580, it stressed both civil and religious liberty and the unity of the empire and pledged those who signed to resist Home Rule: Being convinced in our consciences that Home Rule would

> be disastrous to the material well being of Ulster as the whole of Ireland, subversive of our civil and religious freedom, destructive of our citizenship, and perilous to the unity of the Empire, we whose names are underwritten, men of Ulster, loyal subjects of His Gracious Majesty King George V, humbly relying on the God whom our fathers in days of stress and trial confidently trusted, do hereby pledge ourselves in solemn Covenant throughout this our time of threatened calamity to stand by one another in defending for ourselves and our children our cherished position of equal citizenship in the United Kingdom, and in using all means which may be found necessary to defeat the present conspiracy to set up a Home Rule Parliament in Ireland. And in the event of such a Parliament being forced upon us we further solemnly and mutually pledge ourselves to refuse to recognize its authority. In sure confidence that God will defend the right we hereto subscribe our names. And further, we individually declare that we have not already signed this Covenant. God save the King.[24]

Meetings were held throughout Ulster to explain and promote the covenant and on 28 September, 'Ulster Day', the covenant was signed. That the covenant was more a declaration of intent than simply an expression of opinion was evidenced by the fact that it was to be signed by men only. Women signed a 'Declaration' endorsing the stand of the men. Interestingly the covenant was opened for signature in Dublin and various British cities but only by those of Ulster birth. Over 470,000 Ulstermen and women signed either the covenant or the declaration.

This massive demonstration of resolve could not but, and was partly intended to, impress public opinion in Britain. It was clear that parliamentary opposition alone could not now defeat Home Rule. It had to be linked with a mass movement particularly in Ulster which might sway public opinion and force the government to think again. It was widely believed that once the government was convinced of the impossibility of coercing Ulster it would back down. The threat of force might therefore ensure that force need not be resorted to. This is not to say that those nationalists who argued that the unionists were bluffing were correct. What evidence there is suggests that they were in deadly earnest.

Sporadic drilling had been taking place since at least 1911. Many of the anti-Home Rule meetings held in 1911-12 were accompanied by military style parades. In January 1913, the UUC decided to formalise a development which had already become widespread by establishing the Ulster Volunteer Force. Volunteer was a name with echoes in Irish history which suited the unionist insistence that they were engaged in a defence of the constitution rather than in rebellion. Open only to those who had signed the covenant, the UVF was organised in each county of Ulster along military lines. Its rapid growth reflected the need felt by many to be doing something while the Home Rule bill moved slowly through its parliamentary stages. Unity and control was assisted by the fact that so many country gentlemen came forward to act as commanders.

Initially the UVF had to make do with whatever arms were available from private individuals, from gun-clubs (of which there were large numbers) and from some small-scale arms importation. Until December 1913, when the government moved belatedly to close a loophole, the importation of arms was legal. In 1914, as the passage of Home Rule loomed closer, it was decided by the UVF to import arms on a huge scale. At the end of April, 35,000 rifles and 5 millions rounds of ammunition, purchased in Germany, were landed at Larne. This operation was both a spectacular propaganda success and a practical boost to the UVF. It also marked a new and ominous turn in the Irish crisis.

The government could no longer postpone addressing the Ulster question. Asquith's initial inclination had been to postpone discussion until the bill was before the house of commons for the third time and the cabinet's early advice about the situation in Ulster seemed to justify that approach. In February 1912, Sir David Harrel, a former under-secretary for Ireland, told Birrell, the chief secretary, in a letter circulated to cabinet, that he felt that Ulster resistance would be kept 'within the bounds of political warfare'. Harrel had spent time as an RIC man in Belfast and his opinion carried weight.

The growing incidence of drilling, rifle practice and purchase of arms was regularly reported by the police but with no great alarm to begin with. As one RIC inspector in Fermanagh commented regarding drilling near Lisnaskea in 1911, it was 'got up for bluster and bravado, in order that it would get into the press of the United Kingdom to show what determined fellows the Orangemen are.' By February 1912, the RIC reported, there had been 119 cases of drilling.[25] Birrell, who had been instructed to make 'careful and confidential' inquiry into the nature and extent of Ulster opposition, passed on the police reports to his colleagues. Though he pointed to the showmanship of much of the opposition and urged that it be seen in perspective, he was seriously worried. His concerns were shared by Lloyd George and Churchill. Asquith accepted that there was a possibility of violence in Ulster but argued that a dilution of Home Rule might cause worse trouble elsewhere in Ireland. The prevailing view in cabinet was that the dangers of civil war were exaggerated. This remained the position down until the autumn of 1913 when opinion turned towards the necessity for a political compromise over Ulster.[26]

Asquith's 'wait and see' policy applied to steps to deal with sedition in Ulster as well. As Ulster opposition grew during 1913 and 1914, so did the likelihood that the government would have to intervene. In October 1913, Birrell asked the cabinet whether Carson would be allowed 'preach and practice sedition and mutiny' right up to the passage of the bill. The answer was yes because to arrest Carson would have been, in Asquith's words, to 'throw a lighted match into a powder barrel'.[27]

There was some doubt as to whether in fact drilling was illegal. Certainly the government felt hampered by the absence of suitable legislation for dealing with the situation, much of the earlier Tory coercion legislation having been repealed or allowed lapse by the Liberals, at the behest of the Irish nationalists. Even after the banning of the importation of arms at the end of 1913, the government was reluctant to clamp down on para-military activity in Ulster for fear of provoking even greater trouble. After the Larne gun-running the cabinet was advised that the ringleaders could be prosecuted for seditious conspiracy. It was decided that 'immediate and effective action' was essential but this was postponed for diplomatic reasons when Bonar Law and Carson began to make more conciliatory public statements, and no action was taken.[28]

The 'Curragh Mutiny' represented an even greater challenge to the authority of the government. In his speech at the Balmoral demonstration Carson had predicted that many army officers would resign rather than participate in the coercion of Ulster. These were prophetic words. Late in 1913 the government began to consider the possibility that intervention by the army might be necessary if the unionists would not accept a reasonable compromise. Major General Nevil Macready, whose previous responsibilities had included the use of troops in aid of the civil power in England, was sent to Ireland as a precautionary measure in November. No other military precautions were taken, however, despite urgings from Birrell and David Harrel, among others.

In early March, coinciding with the rejection by the unionists of the latest compromise proposal, came alarming police reports from Ulster indicating that the UVF had plans for seizure of arms at police barracks and military depots. A cabinet sub-committee, established to handle the matter, agreed that Sir Arthur Paget, commander-in-chief of the troops in Ireland, be advised to have such places secured and that some other precautionary measures be taken. Paget initially declined to send extra troops to Ulster as he feared it would precipitate, not prevent, violence. Following a number of discussions with the cabinet subcommittee, Paget's orders were confirmed: troops were to be moved to Ulster as reinforcements.[29]

In attempting to head off one crisis, the government helped to create another one. Paget gave his commanders to understand that operations of 'an offensive and aggressive character' were intended against Ulster and that any officers who could not obey such orders would be dismissed. Though he had not intended to, Paget had in effect offered his commanders the alternatives of obeying orders or being dismissed and some of them, in turn, did likewise with their officers. Asked to make a direct choice between obeying orders and loyalty to Ulster, fifty eight officers in the Third Cavalry Brigade, led by Brigadier General Hubert Gough, indicated that they would opt for dismissal. Many more opted to follow orders, only with great reluctance. The crisis which was thus precipitated was unnecessary as no offensive action had been envisaged and offering alternatives to the soldiers made disaffection more, not less, likely.

Worse was to follow. The government feared that the 'mutiny' might spread so it was extremely keen to reassure Gough and his men that there had been a misunderstanding. Gough was summoned to London for a reprimand, but he was quick to exploit the government's embarrassment. Encouraged by unionist sympathisers in the army like Major General Henry Wilson, he demanded and received written assurances from Seely, the secretary of state for war, and from the war council, that seemed to rule out the use of the army to force Home Rule on Ulster: the army would not be used to coerce Ulster. It had not been the government's intention to give any such assurance and Seely's action was quickly repudiated by Asquith. However, the damage had been done. Gough and Wilson were quickly claiming that the army had succeeded in doing what the politicians had been unable to do – defeat Home Rule.[30]

It was claimed that the affair had exposed and thwarted a Liberal plot to move against Ulster. Although this theory achieved a fairly wide currency in some quarters, there is little evidence to sustain it. It is true that Lloyd George and Churchill in particular were growing increasingly impatient with unionist disinclination to compromise and that Liberal opinion generally was more inclined to impose Home Rule. Moreover, the cabinet had finally come round to the view that sedition could not be allowed to proceed indefinitely without something being done. Nonetheless, the suggestion of a plot against Ulster is unfounded and owes more to a conservative desire to exploit the government's embarrassment than to what actually happened.

The 'Curragh Mutiny' was not of course a mutiny. No orders were given, therefore no orders were disobeyed. Nonetheless its implications were serious. It did seem to show that there were limits to the uses to which the army might be put. The doubts about the government's ability to impose Home Rule were heightened. The incident occurred partly because of the government's belated commitment to take a firmer line in Ulster. Its outcome was to stimulate a renewed search for political compromise.

The search for compromise

While it is true that the cabinet only really began to take the Ulster question seriously late in 1913, it had from the beginning been aware of its divisive potential. A 'prolonged discussion' had taken place as to whether the bill as presented, or by amendment later, should give some Ulster counties an option to exclude themselves. It had been decided that the bill as introduced should apply to the whole of Ireland but that it should be made clear to the leaders of the Irish parliamentary party that

> the government held themselves free to make such changes in the Bill as fresh evidence or facts, or the pressure of British opinion may render expedient...(and) that if in the light of such evidence or indications of public opinion, it became clear as the Bill proceeds that some special treatment must be provided for the Ulster counties, the government will be ready to recognise the necessity, either by amendment of the Bill or by not pressing it under the provisions of the Parliament Act.[31]

Thus the cabinet's commitment was conditional and liable to weaken in the face of opposition. The 'wait and see' policy of Asquith has often been criticised but it did seem logical to postpone amendments until their necessity had been proved and until the bill was on its last stage. Before then it is unlikely that any compromise would have been seriously considered by either side.

The first major initiative on the Ulster question came from outside the cabinet. In September 1913, Lord Loreburn suggested a conference to discuss a federal solution. Some consideration had already been given to the idea of 'Home Rule all round' in 1911, not primarily to make the bill more acceptable in Ulster, but rather to solve the thorny problem of Irish representation in the imperial parliament. Under this arrangement, subordinate assemblies would have been established in England, Scotland and Wales, as well as in Ireland but the idea was opposed then by the Irish party on the grounds that it would cause unnecessary delay and would cloud the issue. Asquith doubted whether it would be any more acceptable now, either to Redmond or Carson.

Loreburn's initiative did at least stimulate more discussion of possible compromises. The cabinet considered and rejected two possible schemes, the first of which would have given Ulster members in an Irish parliament a veto over legislation and the second of which would have allowed them to establish an Ulster parliament with only negative power, i.e. power to reject legislation but not to pass any. It was Lloyd George who suggested the approach which was to dominate discussions until the outbreak of the war. His scheme envisaged the temporary exclusion of part of Ulster for a definite period of five or six years. This, he argued, would reduce support for Ulster resistance for the moment, In the meantime, two general elections would have been held and, if necessary, Ulster exclusion could be prolonged.[32]

Even though Liberal opinion in the country was reported to be hostile to compromise, temporary exclusion of Ulster won strong support in the cabinet. Informal discussions had already taken place with Bonar Law. It was decided that in the event of their being resumed, the government should indicate its willingness to consider not just temporary but permanent exclusion. Redmond urged that any compromise should be postponed until after the bill had passed although he did not rule out temporary exclusion at that stage. In December, Asquith on his own initiative suggested that the unionists be given the right to refer any legislation which they objected to in an Irish parliament to the imperial parliament but Carson refused to negotiate except on the basis of complete Ulster exclusion.[33]

Lloyd George and Birrell, who had expressed his opposition to exclusion, met the nationalist leaders who reluctantly agreed to a plan which would have allowed Ulster counties to opt out by plebiscite for a fixed period as 'the price of a peaceful settlement'. Redmond, in a letter to the cabinet confirming his acceptance, pointed out the risks he and his colleagues were taking.[34] Having achieved Redmond's 'general concurrence', it was decided to introduce an amending bill. This intention was announced in the house of commons on 9 March 1914 but the formulation of the amending bill was delayed by the Buckingham Palace conference.

The Buckingham Palace conference in July 1914 represented the last major attempt to resolve the Ulster and the Irish questions by negotiation before the resort to physical force. Indeed it was the last tripartite conference on the Irish question until the Sunningdale negotiations of 1973. As such it deserves rather more consideration than it is sometimes given. The origins of the conference lay in the desire of the king, George V, to avoid civil war. As the crisis developed in 1913, he had become convinced that a conference might settle the dispute and tried unsuccessfully to get either the Liberals or Tories to call for one. The preferred Tory position was that a general election be held, while Asquith, who consistently refused to contemplate an election, could see little hope of a conference succeeding where intensive behind-the-scenes negotiation had failed. Nevertheless the belief that even the most intractable of problems could be solved by round-table negotiations finally won the day. While the king's invitation was accepted by all sides, the conference was not approached with any great optimism. Bonar Law felt progress was impossible unless the nationalists would make further concessions and he was unwilling to pressurise the unionists. Asquith was equally pessimistic but thought that at least it would postpone and might avert open conflict.[35]

The conference was attended by Asquith, Lloyd George, Bonar Law, Lord Lansdowne, Edward Carson, James Craig, John Redmond and John Dillon. In an opening address the king declared that it was unthinkable that they should be 'brought to the brink of fraternal strife upon issues apparently so capable of adjustment' and urged all the parties to approach matters in a 'spirit of generous compromise'. The chair was then taken by the speaker of the house of commons. Almost as a matter of form, Redmond asked whether any settlement not based on exclusion of Ulster might be considered and said that if it was he would be willing to consider very large concessions. This was rejected out of hand by Carson. From the outset, exclusion of Ulster was taken for granted by all of the participants: the points of contention were the area to be excluded and for how long. These two points – not the principle of exclusion – were to be at the heart of all subsequent negotiations, even those in 1921.

At Redmond's insistence, the area to be excluded was discussed first. In the event, the time limit was not seriously addressed as agreement was not reached on the first issue. Redmond ruled out exclusion of all of Ulster and suggested that the area to be excluded be decided by 'county option' i.e. each county to be allowed to opt in or out by plebiscite. Assuming counties with catholic majorities would opt in and those with protestant majorities would opt out, this would have meant four counties – Antrim, Armagh, Down and Derry – and Belfast borough opting out of the Home Rule settlement, while five counties – Cavan, Donegal, Fermanagh, Monaghan and Tyrone – and Derry borough would have opted in. The excluded area would have had a population of 1,005,250 (711,767 protestants and 293,483 catholics) while the included area would have had 576,446 (179,113 protestants and 397,333 catholics).

Carson recognised that exclusion of all of Ulster was unlikely but, with the backing of Lansdowne and Bonar Law, took the view that no agreement based on county option was possible. Instead he proposed a block vote of six counties, a procedure designed to ensure the exclusion of Tyrone and Fermanagh. This was unacceptable to the nationalists. In an effort to break the deadlock, other options such as vote by poor law

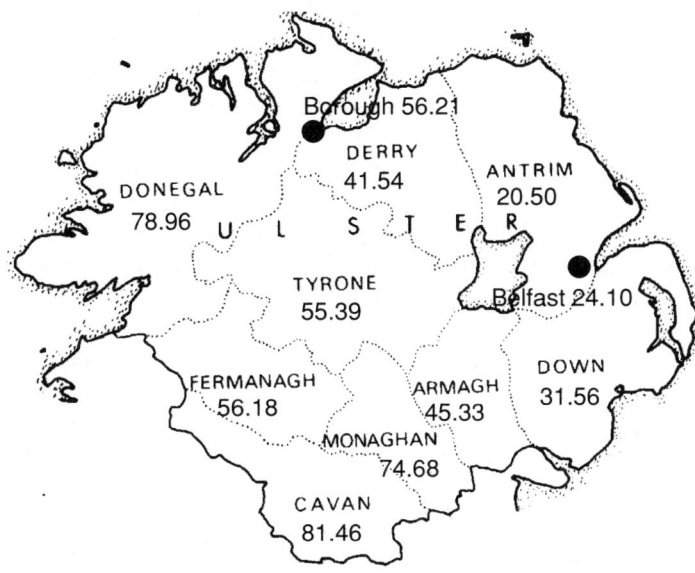

Distribution of Roman Catholic Population in Ulster, 1911
(population percentages)

unions or parliamentary constituencies were explored but all foundered on the unwillingness of either unionists or nationalists to consider losing part or all of Tyrone and Fermanagh. There the conference broke down.

The usual judgement on the Buckingham Palace Conference by contemporaries and historians has been that it was a futile exercise which achieved nothing and that no resolution of the problem was possible short of civil war.[36] However, after the years of barricade rhetoric it was surely progress that the leaders of Irish nationalism and unionism had come to the negotiating table, even if only to identify their fundamental differences. By the end of the conference it was clear that these were not quite as insurmountable as might publicly have appeared. In fact, at the conference both Carson and Redmond made concessions, albeit ones which had been signalled before in private negotiations.

The key to the deadlock was held by Bonar Law. At the conference, Bonar Law asked Redmond to agree to the postponement of the Home Rule bill until after an election. If the Tories lost, or won narrowly, he would concede Home Rule. It is doubtful whether Bonar Law expected Redmond to accept this offer and anyway he was confident that the

Tories would win any election. But if the offer betokened a willingness to compromise, his energies might have been better directed elsewhere. As long as the northern unionists had a *carte blanche* from the Tories no settlement was likely. Asquith was willing to pressurise Redmond who had already conceded a good deal. Similar pressure from Bonar Law on the unionists and towards exclusion of, as far as practicable, only those areas with protestant majorities might have produced results.

When the Buckingham Palace Conference broke down, the cabinet decided to proceed with its Amending Bill, but, on the basis of a suggestion made by Carson at the conference, with the replacement of automatic inclusion after a fixed term with a fresh power of option.[37] Whether this policy would have won the acceptance of either side was uncertain. The deadlock was broken only by the outbreak of the war; the Amending Bill was replaced by the Suspensory Act which postponed the operation of Home Rule for the duration of the war and it was promised that an Amending Bill providing for Ulster exclusion would be introduced before Home Rule came into operation.

Partition

It has been argued that there was nothing predestined about the partition settlement of 1920-21; that the way in which partition came about and the form it took were determined by the events of the decade which spanned the great war.[38] This is undoubtedly true. Ulster opposition was to Home Rule *per se* and the original intention was to defeat Home Rule for all of Ireland, not to win Ulster exclusion. When in June 1912, the exclusion of part of Ulster was first seriously proposed by a Liberal back-bencher, Agar-Robartes, the principle of dividing Ireland was opposed by both nationalists and unionists. However, as we have seen, once serious negotiations began with a view to reconciling the irresistible force of Irish nationalism with the immoveable object of northern unionism, attentions turned quickly to Ulster exclusion. What began as a device for killing Home Rule became an end in itself. On the eve of the war, the questions remaining to be answered were those on which the Buckingham Palace Conference foundered: what special provision should be made for Ulster, for what area and for how long?

The events of the following six years, in Ireland and elsewhere, only served to entrench Ulster unionism. After 1914, the Ulster unionists never again wielded such influence with the Conservative party but Liberals and Tories alike accepted the need for special provision. The decline of Ulster unionist influence at Westminster was less dramatic than that of the Irish party. The rise of Sinn Féin with its abstentionist policy and the corresponding decline of the Irish party in Ireland further reduced the influence of Redmond. It may be that Redmond might have been better advised to accept the offer of a position in the coalition government when it was offered in 1915, as Carson did. Instead he found himself in a no-man's land – wielding influence neither in Ireland nor Westminster. The replacement late in 1916 of Asquith by Lloyd George exacerbated the problem. Though not originally a Home Ruler in the Gladstonian tradition, Asquith felt a residual loyalty to the Irish nationalist cause, while Lloyd George's approach was much more pragmatic and determined more by present needs than by old loyalties.

The presence in senior government positions of politicians who so recently had been fomenting civil war is eloquent testimony to how dramatically the great war transformed the political agenda. The new respectability of Ulster unionist leaders can only have been increased by the enthusiastic response in Ulster to the call for recruits. No doubt the more sympathetic attitude to Ulster of elements in the army and in the war office helped matters. The problems which arose in the south of Ireland concerning mass recruiting of Irish Volunteers, catholic chaplains and commissions for nationalists did not seem to arise with the same frequency in Ulster.

The call of the empire which between 1885 and 1914 had played such a major part in anti-Home Rule rhetoric now became a literal call and was responded to enthusiastically. The 36th (Ulster) Division formed in October 1914 was composed largely of members of the UVF. It was the last of the three Irish divisions to go into action. Ironically the baptism by blood foreshadowed on so many platforms from 1911 to 1914 took place not in Ulster but on the western front. At the Somme in July 1916 the division suffered over 5,500 casualties in one day before being taken out of the battle. By the end of the war, the 36th had suffered 32,186 casualties.[39] The events of the Somme, in particular, had a searing impact on the unionist consciousness, the battle of the Somme taking its place alongside the battle of the Boyne in the folk memory.

The other Irish divisions also suffered major casualties but this was less important in shaping northern unionist attitudes than events such as the 1916 rising and the nationalist anti-conscription campaign in 1918. From a northern unionist perspective, both seemed to confirm southern Irish disloyalty. In truth, conscription was not all that popular in rural Ulster, among protestants or catholics, but the campaign against it, once it had been passed, was seen as seditious. Moreover, the active role of the catholic clergy in that campaign was cited as proof of the argument that

Home Rule would mean Rome Rule. Conscription showed yet again the difference between the two communities in Ireland.

The agreement to shelve domestic problems for the duration of the war had been based on the expectation of a short conflict. As the war dragged on and especially after the 1916 rising, renewed efforts were made to reach a political settlement. The abortive Lloyd George partition negotiations of the summer of 1916 were partly a response to the insistence of the Irish party that the policy of 'marking time' was fatal.[40] In the event the initiative only served to further weaken the constitutional nationalist position. Lloyd George negotiated separately with Carson and Redmond and produced the outlines of a proposed settlement. Home Rule was to come into operation immediately with six Ulster counties excluded for the duration of the war. Under pressure from Carson the UUC unanimously authorised further negotiations on this basis, while Redmond also had the terms endorsed at a conference of Ulster nationalists in Belfast.

Just when it seemed as if an important breakthrough was imminent the proposals foundered on two different rocks. The first, and least expected, came from within the Conservative party, particularly from the spokesmen of southern unionism. Lord Lansdowne and Walter Long claimed that Lloyd George had exceeded his mandate and they threatened to resign. A settlement would be seen as a surrender to extreme nationalism and might also weaken the war effort by precipitating trouble in Ireland. Furthermore, they asserted, southern unionists were being abandoned to the extremists. Significantly Bonar Law and Balfour both supported Lloyd George's proposals, pointing out that they gave Ulster unionists exactly what they had been demanding at the Buckingham Palace Conference.[41]

The apparent Irish consensus was quickly shattered too. Redmond had been led to expect that Ulster exclusion would be temporary, with an imperial conference deciding her fate at the expiry of the provisional period. Carson, on the other hand, had been assured in writing by Lloyd George that at the end of the provisional period, Ulster would not 'whether she wills it or not, merge with the rest of Ireland'[42]. The basis for settlement vanished almost as quickly as it appeared.

The affair represented a major setback for Redmond. At the Belfast conference, there had been considerable hostility to his proposal, particularly from the clergy present. It was openly claimed that he carried the day through the personal influence of Joseph Devlin, the leading Belfast nationalist politician and through 'gerrymandering by a rigged

Convention'. His public acceptance of partition was widely criticised, especially when it emerged that it would be permanent. The northern bishops denounced partition. Bishop McKenna, for instance, characterised it as 'the grossest insult', while his colleague Bishop McHugh, an erstwhile supporter of the war, now turned completely against the Irish party and gave his blessing to the anti-partitionist Irish Nation League, an organisation which proved a stepping stone on the way to Sinn Féin for many dissident nationalists. As Balfour conceded, Redmond had given considerable ground beyond what he was willing to concede two years earlier by his acceptance of the exclusion of Tyrone and Fermanagh.

On the other side, although no settlement had been reached, Carson had more reason to be happy. Asquith and Lloyd George had accepted the unionist case for six counties and the nationalists were in disarray. Even John Dillon admitted that ' the average man, including a vast number of our loyal supporters, believes that, since the formation of the Coalition, the party acted in a timorous manner and that Carson proved himself more than a match for Redmond'.[43]

The replacement of Asquith by Lloyd George, the split in the Liberal party which followed, and the enhanced position of the Conservatives in the coalition all helped to reassure northern unionists. The new balance of power was evident in the decision taken by the cabinet early in 1917 to prepare a new Home Rule bill for implementation after the war. Derry, Antrim, Down, Armagh, Tyrone and Fermanagh were to be allowed to opt out unless a majority of 55 per cent in any of these counties voted for inclusion. Even the cabinet committee charged with the task of framing the measure accepted the illogicality of calling for a 55 per cent vote rather than a simple majority.[44] This particular scheme was shelved with the establishment of the Irish Convention.

While the convention was primarily a means for placating American opinion and the Irish party, it did pose some threat to the northern unionists. As Lloyd George had offered immediate Home Rule with six county exclusion or a convention, it was likely that the efforts of the convention would be aimed at producing alternatives other than one based on partition. The UUC accepted the invitation to participate on the understanding that no alternative was excluded and that the findings were not binding. It took the additional precaution of establishing a committee to advise the delegates, a sensible step which helped keep them in line for the protracted duration of the convention which lasted from July 1917 to April 1918.

At the convention considerable common ground was found between some of the constitutional nationalists and the southern unionists. This was reflected in the majority report which proposed a modest measure of Home Rule for all Ireland. The Ulster unionists consistently blocked all proposals not providing for Ulster exclusion and issued their own minority report.[45] Lloyd George promised to act if 'substantial agreement' was reached but this was clearly not forthcoming. Even so, northern unionists were concerned. There had been considerable impatience on all sides in Britain at the way in which they were blocking progress at the convention. They came under considerable pressure, particularly from Lloyd George, to consider some form of all-Ireland solution with safeguards for Ulster for the sake of the war effort and the empire.

The government did not relish the prospect of being seen to afford the Ulster unionists a veto over a compromise acceptable to southern unionists and moderate nationalists. In the event, the conscription crisis in April 1918 overshadowed the convention's report but it only served to accentuate the problem. Faced with what it saw as the necessity of extending conscription to Ireland despite strong nationalist opposition, the government opted for the so-called dual policy: Home Rule in return for conscription.[46] Nationalist resistance to conscription at any price and a dramatically deteriorating situation in Ireland rapidly made it clear that neither Home Rule nor conscription was viable.

Despite misgivings, the Conservative members of the government did accept the decision to introduce Home Rule. In an attempt to break the deadlock at the Convention, Lloyd George had suggested an all-Ireland parliament with safeguards for Ulster. He now told his colleagues that he would not introduce conscription unless this line was followed. His colleagues agreed in principle and a cabinet committee was established to draw up the bill. Under the chairmanship of Walter Long, a former chief secretary who had close contacts with southern unionists, it consisted of four Conservatives, three Liberals, one Labour represent-ative and General Smuts.[47] The committee quickly set to work but got bogged down on the issue of federalism which had been revived by F S Oliver, a well-known unionist journalist and long-time proponent of federalism or Home Rule all round. He had succeeded in converting Austen Chamberlain, later a member of the cabinet committee, and, at least conditionally, Edward Carson who could not suggest such a solution himself but would accept it if it was pushed by someone else.[48] Lloyd George too was attracted by this possibility of a way around the Ulster difficulty and had suggested it to the Ulster delegation at the convention.[49] So the new committee was established against a background of growing interest in federalism. Long proposed and Chamberlain agreed that any bill which they prepared should be consistent with a federal arrangement for the United Kingdom as a whole.[50] Six of the members of the committee were in favour of drawing up a bill consistent with federalism, with another agreeable if it did not cause delay.[51]

The possibility of 'Home Rule all round' was discussed at the cabinet and soundings were taken among members of the house of commons and in the country. Surprisingly broad support was reported but it was generally accepted that no move could be made in that direction until the end of the war and that the most that could be done now was to make the Home Rule bill compatible with Home Rule all round later.[52] Lloyd George was unwilling to push the issue unless there was unanimity. The committee decided to draft a bill embodying the majority proposals of the convention. There was general support for 'loading' representation in the Irish parliament to protect minority interests rather than the alternative which was to create an Ulster committee within an Irish parliament. Later this decision was reversed with a majority favouring an Ulster committee. To facilitate any later move towards federalism, customs and excise were to be reserved to the imperial parliament.[53]

Given the state of near rebellion in Ireland, there was an air of unreality about these discussions. Although they proceeded for a number of weeks, it was abundantly clear by late May that the dual policy was no longer tenable. Its importance should not be underrated however. The solution envisaged was an all-Ireland one, with safeguards for Ulster. Federalism was something of a side issue but it did help reconcile Conservatives to the decision to establish an all-Ireland parliament. Against the backdrop of the successful German offensive on the western front, the atmosphere was one of crisis. Sacrifices were being called for on all sides. Since the convention, there was a growing impatience with Ulster intransigence. However, the moment passed quickly. A solution based on an all-Ireland parliament was not again considered. The coalition manifesto for the 1918 general election once more reverted to the policy of giving Ulster a *carte blanche* in advance by promising that a solution unacceptable to Ulster would not be imposed.

When, after the end of the war, the Conservative-dominated coalition again came to address the Irish question it took up not where Long's committee had left off but where Lloyd George had left off in 1916. The major difference now was, of course, that Redmond was dead and the

Irish party had been obliterated by Sinn Féin who were engaged on their abstentionist policy. The establishment of Dáil Éireann with Sinn Féin MPs attending that assembly and Ulster unionists continuing to attend Westminster seemed to amount in practice to Ulster exclusion anyway. With the commencement of the Anglo-Irish war, it was unlikely that the British government would try to persuade the unionists to change their minds.

The government might have let the matter slide indefinitely but for the fact that Home Rule was actually on the statute book and was due to come into effect once the war was over and when special provision was made for Ulster. A cabinet committee was established in October 1919 to draft a new bill, again under the chairmanship of Walter Long. The committee quickly rejected all options except Ulster exclusion. The question of the area to be excluded proved as thorny an issue as ever. The committee rejected the obvious solution of county option, as it was unacceptable to unionists. Any alternative would, however, include counties with nationalist majorities in the excluded area. In the year of the Versailles Treaty, this would have been something of an embarrassment. Partly to get over this difficulty, and perhaps also because of a weariness with the whole Irish imbroglio, the committee produced a radically new proposal, two new parliaments – one in Dublin and one in Belfast.[54]

Home Rule for Ulster lessened any appearance of Britain seeming to override the wishes of the local inhabitants, it eased the problem of the area to be excluded and it was in accord with Long's federalist principles. It had not, of course, been asked for by the Ulster unionists who for so long had based their case on the unity of the empire, but they were closely consulted in the formulation of the bill. After some discussion, the idea was reluctantly accepted by them on the grounds that it gave them greater control over their own destinies than was possible if they remained directly subject to Westminster.

The government's official position was that it favoured ultimate unification of the two parliaments, if both were agreeable. To this end, a Council of Ireland was to be created to administer some minor matters concerning north and south and which might eventually, with the agreement of both parliaments, lead to unification. In addition, the cabinet committee had originally proposed that nine counties rather than six come under the Ulster parliament again with a view to easing the way towards later unification. However, this proposal was strongly and successfully fought by Ulster unionists. While four counties was considered too small, nine was considered too large as it would have given only a very narrow unionist majority which might with time be overturned. This was the predominant view of the unionist leaders but it created a great deal of hostility, particularly among unionists in what were to become the border counties. James Craig, now the most influential spokesman of Ulster unionists, strongly urged the government that only six counties should come under the control of the Belfast parliament.[55]

The Government of Ireland bill was introduced on 26 February 1920. After bitter debate, it was accepted by the UUC in March. Its passage was punctuated by serious rioting in Belfast from June to September. It received the royal assent before Christmas and came into effect on 3 May 1921. Foreign affairs, external trade, posts and telegraphs, income tax and customs and excise were all reserved to the imperial parliament. The Northern Irish parliament consisted of a senate of twenty-six members, and a house of commons of fifty-two, elected by proportional representation.[56]

The new parliament was opened by the king in May 1921. As he performed the ceremony he must have been struck by the irony that those who had since 1886 been loudest in their condemnation of Home Rule had now become the proud beneficiaries of a new Home Rule parliament. He may also have reflected that serious rioting which had greeted the opening of the Home Rule era also marked its closing. Any hopes that the 'settlement' marked the dawning of a new era of peace and reconciliation seemed already to have been dashed.

8 Settlements and Divisions

Shortly after the opening of the new Northern Ireland parliament in Belfast a cartoon appeared in *Punch*, the satirical English magazine, under the title 'Ireland's King'.[1] It showed two Irish women, conversing over a ditch which was intended to represent the border. One was bare-footed, wore a shawl and struck a belligerent pose. The other wore shoes, was generally better dressed and knitted while she talked. Somewhat unnecessarily for those familiar with *Punch* stereotypes, an even more direct clue to the women's origins was given: the first, named Dublin, had a coat of arms on her petticoat to indicate her southern origins while the second, named Belfast, had a Red Hand of Ulster on the pocket of her dress. The cartoon and its accompanying caption are revealing. It suggests in effect that all that was necessary now for a settlement in the south of Ireland was for the southern Irish to put their own house in order. However, the cartoon may reveal more about opinion in England than in Dublin or Belfast. It is the missing character, 'London', who is most significant. With the thorny question of Ulster 'out of the way', at least temporarily, attention turned towards a settlement in the rest of Ireland. That shift in opinion is clearly reflected in *Punch*.

Coming to terms with Sinn Féin

It was not until June 1920 that the British government seriously accepted that the Irish question had moved on since 1914 and that some accommodation would have to be reached with Sinn Féin, the new voice of nationalist Ireland. The end of the first world war might have been expected to bring Ireland back to the centre of the political stage in Britain where it had been in 1914. As we have seen, for various reasons this did not happen: demobilisation and post-war reconstruction were more pressing than Ireland; after the 1918 general election the Conservatives dominated the coalition government; and ironically the replacement of the Irish parliamentary party by Sinn Féin, which in the longer term presaged a serious turn of events in Ireland, in the shorter term eased the pressure on the government to reach a political settlement.

Insofar as any consistent Irish policy was followed between 1918 and 1920, it was one of preserving 'orderly government'.[2] There was considerable uncertainty as to what that policy might entail. Both

IRELAND'S KING.

DUBLIN. "THEY TELL ME 'TWAS A GRAND TIME YE HAD WID A VISIT FROM YOUR KING!.

BELFAST. "IS IT JEALOUS YE ARE? BY THE SAME TOKEN HE'S YOUR KING TOO; AN' HE'LL PAY YE A VISIT FAST ENOUGH IF YE'LL BE AFTER PUTTIN' YOUR HOUSE IN ORDER AN' ASKIN' HIM."

coercion and concession were tried to no great effect. The government stopped short of the 'all out war' being urged by the likes of Henry Wilson. Instead, as Wilson put it, 'the government, without the faintest idea of where they are going...sometimes threaten, they sometimes run away, with the result that in Ireland...chaos reigns supreme'. Ironically, Wilson's diagnosis may indeed have been correct although he had the soldier's disregard for what was politically rather than militarily viable. He argued that the government would have to either 'reconquer the country or lose it'. [3]

'All out war' was not a realistic political option, yet the cabinet was slow to accept the need for negotiations with Sinn Féin. Instead it vacillated. Dáil Éireann was proclaimed in September 1919 but the introduction of martial law was baulked at until the end of 1920. In the interval, the government had placed its hopes in the Government of Ireland bill. Long before it reached the statute book, the rapidly deteriorating security situation had shown that the measure which purported to be a 'generous solution' had little relevance in the south of Ireland.

Throughout 1920, Lloyd George persisted in the belief that the problem lay not in the inadequacy of the Government of Ireland bill but in the disturbed state of Ireland. He continued to see the Irish question in pre-first world war terms and assumed that if order was restored, Home Rule would settle the issue. His Irish advisers were less certain. Lord French, the lord lieutenant, recommended either all-out war or a truce to allow a more radical settlement to be negotiated. Nevil Macready, who was sent to Ireland as commander-in-chief, agreed that the imposition of martial law might ease the problem in the short term but it would not solve it. He shrewdly judged that there might be political problems in maintaining a 'military' policy for any length of time and advised that only a political solution, based on dominion style Home Rule had any hope of success.[4] Lloyd George rejected this advice in favour of a policy of restoring order.

It was decided by the cabinet that the Irish government would be given whatever assistance was deemed necessary in the implementation of this policy. Considerable doubts arose as to whether the Irish government was indeed up to its task. Hamar Greenwood took over as chief secretary early in 1920. In May, following an investigation, Warren Fisher, permanent secretary of the treasury issued a scathing indictment of Dublin Castle which he concluded was not up to the job of formulating and implementing policy.[5] As a result the Irish government was strengthened by the addition of a number of handpicked civil servants from England. Foremost amongst these were John Anderson who became joint under-secretary and Alfred Cope who, though only assistant under-secretary, played a very important role over the next two years. This group brought an unprecedented effciency to the Irish administration at the top level but the change had come too late. Moreover, it was one thing to increase efficiency at the top, it was another to ensure the effective implementation of policy.

Of necessity, the police and military were central to the policy of restoring order. For political reasons, the cabinet was reluctant to impose martial law and turn the country over to the military. The police, who were increasingly forced to withdraw from outlying areas, were unable to cope with the situation. It was for this reason that in May 1920 it was decided to recruit special armed police (the Black and Tans and Auxiliaries) from the ranks of ex-servicemen in England.[6] This only served to exacerbate the problem. Implicit in the government's policy was the belief that moderate opinion could be won over to supporting the Government of Ireland bill, once the extremists had been rooted out. In fact the indiscipline of the Black and Tans and their harsh use of reprisals only served to further alienate moderate opinion in Ireland and to turn opinion in England and internationally against the government's policy. The mounting litany of reprisals and outrages by the Black and Tans and Auxiliaries, such as the burning of creameries, the sacking of Balbriggan and the burning of part of Cork city, helped discredit the government's policy and brought protests from, among others, the archbishop of Canterbury. The unwillingness or inability of the government to condemn such incidents and prevent their recurrence added to the problem. The decision at the end of 1920 to introduce martial law in parts of the south of Ireland, was a recognition both of the fact that the situation was continuing to deteriorate and of the need for the military authorities to reassert control over the Auxiliaries.

What finally sealed the failure of the policy of restoring order as a prelude to any settlement was the election for the proposed new southern Irish parliament. Sinn Féin refused to recognise the new assembly but used the elections as elections to the Dáil. With the exception of the Trinity College seats, which returned four unionists, Sinn Féin members were returned unopposed in all southern constituencies. It was no longer possible to pretend that the Government of Ireland Act represented a possible solution, except to the Ulster question. Nor, given the reaction in Britain and abroad against the government's harsh policy, was further coercion a realistic option. By now martial law had been extended throughout most of Ireland and an official policy of reprisals had been instigated. But despite Lloyd George's claims to have 'murder by the throat' and optimistic reports from Hamar Greenwood claiming that they were finally getting the upper hand, it was clear to most observers that little progress was being made. An escalation of the repression would have brought an even greater public outcry and little compensating military gain. [7]

Only in one respect was the government's policy a success. It had become increasingly clear that sooner or later the government would have to come to terms with Sinn Féin. Lloyd George's refusal to accept this until the Government of Ireland Act was passed and the new northern parliament had met for the first time allowed him to deal with the northern question first before turning to deal with the rest of Ireland. Significantly the first crack in his no concessions policy came when he agreed to the urgings of General Smuts and of the king himself, that the latter's speech at the opening of the new parliament in Belfast should strike a conciliatory note.[8] At the same time it was agreed to invite de Valera to London for negotiations. While Sinn Féin might argue otherwise, partition was an accomplished fact before the government sought to come to terms with nationalist Ireland.

The Truce

Lloyd George had previously rejected a truce with Sinn Féin. Lord French had raised the idea early in 1920 and Macready had suggested it more than once. In December 1920, Archbishop Clune of Western Australia acted as a go-between in an attempt to get talks going. A truce of some sort would, he thought, be a *sine qua non* of any such negotiations. At the same time, Fr Michael O'Flanagan, vice-president of Sinn Féin, apparently on his own initiative, made a similar attempt. Both initiatives foundered when Lloyd George insisted that the IRA would have to surrender arms before talks could begin although it is doubtful whether either side was seriously interested in negotiations at this stage.[9]

In the first half of 1921 informal attempts to organise talks failed before Lloyd George's invitation to de Valera. One very practical problem in the way of negotiations was that it was not clear who they should be with. In December 1920, Clune had initially proposed to meet Griffith and Eoin MacNeill. Having visited Ireland, and met Collins, he concluded that he was the key figure. While Lloyd George shared this assessment, it posed a problem for him. Collins, insofar as he was known at all, was closely associated in the public mind with the 'murder gang' which Lloyd George had repeatedly stigmatised as evil incarnate and with which he refused to have any truck. The return of de Valera from America where he had been since June 1920, facilitated the advent of peace negotiations. De Valera, despite his role in the 1916 rising, was seen as a more independent political figure. Indeed the only doubt was whether he could in fact control the militants. [10]

Lloyd George's initiative was almost stifled before it began when de Valera was arrested by the military in Dublin. Following hurried consultations behind the scenes, he was quickly released in time to receive the invitation to a conference in London. De Valera consulted his cabinet colleagues and, in an attempt to emphasise that he spoke for Ireland as a whole and not just the nationalist community, summoned a meeting with the leaders of unionist opinion. Not surprisingly Craig declined his invitation to attend. Only then did de Valera formally accept Lloyd George's invitation. A truce was hastily agreed which came into effect on 11 July. It provided for the suspension of operations by both sides while negotiations continued. By 14 July, de Valera was in London.[11]

If the speed with which events had begun to move prompted hopes that a quick settlement might be reached, such optimism proved to be misplaced. Four meetings took place between de Valera and Lloyd George between 14 and 21 July but they were largely in the nature of preliminary skirmishing. Lloyd George sought to play the role of the elder statesman and to overawe the younger man. De Valera, for his part, said little and stuck to his basic position. His main tactic was to extract an offer from Lloyd George which could then be considered by the Dáil. Eventually Lloyd George presented such a proposal: he offered Ireland the status of a dominion but with specified limitations particularly in the area of trade. The document expressed support for Irish unity but the proposal was not to apply to Northern Ireland except with the consent of the northern parliament. This proposal, although a long way short of what was demanded by Sinn Féin, was a major advance on what was contained in the Government of Ireland Act and represented the final abandonment of Gladstonian Home Rule.

At their final meeting, de Valera dismissed Lloyd George's offer and pointedly left without the document. Later, however, he did send a messenger for it so that a detailed response could be formulated with his colleagues in Dublin. He returned to Ireland reasonably satisfied: as his official biographers concluded: 'It is doubtful whether he gained anything; certain that he had given nothing away.' Lloyd George, who described negotiating with de Valera as being like riding a merry-go-round always one horse behind, would probably have agreed. [12]

Although no agreement had been reached, neither side wished to break off the negotiations. It suited the Irish side particularly to allow the truce to continue until the autumn when conditions would be more favourable for a renewal of the guerrilla campaign. There ensued a protracted correspondence between de Valera and Lloyd George which lasted until late September, seeking to establish a basis for another conference. The letters from both sides were repetitive and wandered through the realms of history and abstract political theory but they did allow the Irish side the opportunity, perhaps for the first time, to formulate their demands more precisely. It is at this time that de Valera's idea of external association as an alternative to dominion status began to develop. His main objection to the latter was that in practice Ireland could never really have dominion status because of her closeness to Britain. He had told Lloyd George in London that he would accept the status enjoyed by the dominions in practice – a status which he judged sprang from their distance from Britain rather than any legal entitlement. That status could be acquired for Ireland through external association as an independent country with the British Commonwealth. This would apparently have meant independence for Ireland in domestic affairs and dominion status otherwise but it was a complicated arrangement never fully worked out and clearly understood only by de Valera. It lacked the simple clarity and appeal of 'the republic'.

The key point at issue in the correspondence was de Valera's repeated insistence that the Irish delegates would be representatives of a sovereign independent state and Lloyd George's equally emphatic insistence that no British government could accept that. Finally it was agreed that there would be no preconditions. As de Valera put it, it was 'precisely because neither side accepts the position of the other that there is a dispute at all, and that a conference is necessary to search for and discuss such adjustments as might compose it'.[13] Lloyd George's fresh invitation to a conference in London to discuss 'how the association of Ireland with the community of nations known as the British empire may be reconciled with Irish national aspirations' was formally accepted by de Valera on 30 September and the conference met for the first time on 11 October. [14]

The Treaty

It was clear from de Valera's visit to London and his subsequent correspondence with Lloyd George that the prospects for a settlement were not good.[15] No doubt this contributed to the unwillingness of many of the Irish leaders, most notably de Valera, to join the delegation to London. De Valera proposed to the Dáil cabinet that Griffith should lead the delegation, with Collins as his deputy. They in turn suggested that he should go. The cabinet split evenly in a vote on the matter which was settled by de Valera's own casting vote. Collins agreed to go only after considerable persuasion and Cathal Brugha and Austin Stack refused to go. Robert Barton and two lawyers, George Gavan Duffy and Éamon Duggan completed the delegation. [16]

De Valera's decision not to lead the delegation proved contentious. One historian has commented that he was in America when he should have been in Ireland and in Ireland when he should have been in London.[17] When the names of the delegation came before the Dáil for ratification, W T Cosgrave, then minister for local government, took the unprecedented step of proposing an amendment to the cabinet's motion to the effect that de Valera should head the delegation. They were, he said, sending over a team but leaving their ablest player in reserve.[18] De Valera's view was that by holding himself in reserve he would give the Irish delegates a fall back position. He would be all the better placed to defend the Dáil's position in the event of a breakdown if he was not implicated in unsatisfactory proposals. He could see the possibility for division and wished to keep himself open to preserve national unity. This tactic made sense as long as the delegates were well briefed on it and had clear guidelines on what their minimum demands should be. Although de Valera told the Dáil that they went 'with a cabinet policy', it was not clear precisely what that policy was. It should have been clear from his correspondence with Lloyd George what the likely areas of disagreement were and how far the British side were likely to go. The lack of clear guidelines on the Irish side was a serious mistake.

The conference opened in London on 11 October and continued until 6 December when the *Articles of agreement for a treaty between Great Britain and Ireland* were signed. The British representatives were Lloyd George, Winston Churchill, Lord Birkenhead, Austen Chamberlain, Worthington-Evans, Hamar Greenwood and Gordon Hewart. While the discussions began and ended with plenary sessions, much of the detailed negotiation was done in informal side-sessions particularly between the delegation leaders. While such sessions were probably necessary, they did militate further against a clear consistent approach on the Irish side and added to the disunity which had existed in the delegation from the outset. Collins felt he could rely only on Griffith. He distrusted Barton, who felt excluded from much of the negotiation, and Erskine Childers, the delegation secretary, whom he correctly judged had been appointed by de Valera to keep an eye on things.[19] The isolation of Childers was unfortunate as he probably knew more about constitutional law and the government of the commonwealth than anyone on either delegation.

Though considerable time and energy were devoted to the fiscal and economic matters, the two crucial issues were Ireland's constitutional status and the position of Ulster. Regarding the latter, with a northern Irish parliament in existence Lloyd George could play the honest broker and argue that, whatever he himself might like, nothing could be done without its consent. He did affect to pressure Craig to accept Irish unity and when this failed encouraged the belief that the proposed Boundary Commission would be likely to reduce the size of Northern Ireland and make it less viable, but that was as far as he could or would go.

Regarding Ireland's status, he was unwilling and, given his own weakness within the coalition, probably unable to go beyond dominion status. He rejected the concept of external association which was proposed on several occasions by the Irish side. Collins, in particular, had presented a document which anticipated developments in the status of the dominions which were to take place a decade later. [20]

The Irish side attached considerable importance to the position of the crown and the oath of allegiance because they were seen as symbolising in a public way the sovereignty issue. Griffith displayed an early willingness to compromise on the oath if other issues could be settled. This provoked objections from Dublin and counter-objections that the powers of the delegation were being undermined.[21] Although the difference was smoothed over for the moment, it was clear that there was potential for serious trouble here.

A draft treaty was taken back to Dublin by the delegation and discussed on 3 December. From subsequent accounts, it is clear that it was not a very satisfactory discussion. The members of the delegation were exhausted after a twelve-hour night crossing from Holyhead. Following an acrimonious seven-hour meeting, the outcome was inconclusive. The majority of the cabinet were unhappy with the proposed oath but it was less clear what the general attitude was to other aspects of the draft and the delegates were left unclear as to exactly how they were to proceed. A moment for decisive guidance had been missed.[22]

On their return to London, external association was suggested once more at the insistence of Barton and Duffy but to no avail. Sensing a breakthrough, the British side accepted some small changes in the oath and repeated their willingness to accept Irish unity if the northern parliament would agree. At the outset, the Irish tactic had been to break on Ulster if a break seemed inevitable. This outcome was feared by Lloyd George who felt that this was where the British case was most vulnerable to criticism involving as it did the exclusion of majority populations in Fermanagh and Tyrone. He was relieved when, early in the conference, Griffith, unknown to the other Irish delegates, promised not to break on Ulster if Britain proposed an all-Ireland parliament and, if Northern Ireland opted out, established a boundary commission.

Lloyd George now invoked that promise and Griffith agreed to sign. Following a slightly melodramatic presentation of a choice of war or peace by Lloyd George, Collins and Duggan did likewise and finally, with great reluctance, Barton and Duffy. Hours after the document had been signed, Collins, who sensed that while one conflict may have been ending, a new one was beginning, penned a poignant and prophetic letter to a friend:

> When you have sweated, toiled, had mad dreams, hopeless nightmares, you find yourself in London's streets, cold and dank in the night air.
> Think – what have I got for Ireland? Something which she wanted these past seven hundred years. Will anyone be satisfied with the bargain? Will anyone? I tell you this – early this morning I signed my death warrant. I thought at the time how ridiculous – a bullet might just as well have done the job five years ago...
> These signatures are the first real step for Ireland. If people will only remember that, the first real step. [23]

The terms of the treaty signed in London gave Ireland dominion status i.e. the same constitutional status as Canada, Australia, New Zealand and South Africa. Its parliament was to have responsibility for the 'peace, order and good government' of the Free State, as it was styled. It was given full control over customs, tariffs and economic policy generally but would assume liability for the service of a proportion of the public debt of the United Kingdom. The crown was to be represented by a governor general appointed in the same way as the governor general of Canada. Members of the Free State parliament were to take an oath swearing allegiance to the constitution of the Free State and to the crown by virtue of 'the common citizenship of Ireland with Great Britain and her adherence to and membership of the group of nations forming the British Commonwealth of Nations'. The government of the Free State was to afford to the British navy and airforce the use of specified naval facilities at Berehaven, Queenstown, Cobh and Lough Swilly and in time of war such harbour and other facilities 'as the British government may require'.

As far as Northern Ireland was concerned, the treaty was defined as applying to all of Ireland but the northern parliament could by an address of both houses to the king opt out within one month. In the likely event of that happening, a commission of three persons, one appointed by the government of the Free State, one by the government of Northern Ireland and the third, the chairman, to be appointed by the British government, was to determine the boundaries between Northern Ireland and the rest of Ireland 'in accordance with the wishes of the inhabitants, so far as may be compatible with economic and geographic conditions'. The provisions in the Government of Ireland Act regarding the establishment of a Council of Ireland were to continue. Both the Northern Ireland and Free State parliaments were explicitly barred from making any laws which would directly or indirectly endow any religion or which would in any way restrict religious freedom. [24]

Settlements and divisions

The treaty of course had to be ratified by the British parliament and the Dáil. At Westminster, it was approved without significant opposition on 16 December. Ratification by the Dáil was less certain so the focus of attention, for three months firmly on London, turned back again to Ireland. What followed reveals much about the nature of the nationalist movement and helped set the agenda for a new generation.

News of the signing of the treaty came as a shock to de Valera. He initially assumed that a breakthrough had been made but when the actual terms began to filter through the mood changed. He considered asking for the resignations of the ministers on the delegation but was persuaded to summon them to a cabinet meeting instead. At that meeting, Griffith, Collins, Barton and Cosgrave supported the treaty while de Valera, Brugha and Stack opposed it. Outnumbered in the cabinet, de Valera turned to the Dáil, which assembled on 14 December to consider ratification. The debate continued in a series of public and private meetings until 7 January when the treaty was ratified by 64 votes to 57. By then the nationalist movement was irreversibly split. The establishment of the new state was to be accompanied by a bloody and bitter civil war.

The major criticisms of the treaty arising in the Dáil debates centred on the question of sovereignty. Objections to dominion status, the position of the crown, the role of the governor general and the oath were all rooted in the belief that sovereignty had not been achieved. In some respects, the division which emerged was one between principle and pragmatism, between those who having declared and fought for a republic would not settle for less and those who felt that the treaty was the best bargain that was achievable in the circumstances. Brugha, Stack, and Mary MacSwiney typified the former while Collins, Barton and Cosgrave typified the latter. It was the sort of division which is not unusual in a situation where an attempt is made to translate a long-term ideal into practice. Had O'Connell or Parnell succeeded then similar problems might have arisen over Repeal or Home Rule. In this case the process was all the more traumatic because it followed a military campaign involving suffering and sacrifice.

Of necessity during the years of struggle and hardship, independence and particularly the republic occupied an almost mystical position. It was a utopian goal which motivated and sustained the movement. The predominance of the military over the political campaign meant that there was little time available for defining that goal. The difficulties implicit in the attempt to transform the dream into reality were increased – some would say made insurmountable – by the realities of the military situation and of party politics, both in England and in Ireland.

Collins told the Dáil very forcibly that military victory was not possible. It was a question then of persisting in 'an impossible fight' or accepting the treaty which provided 'not the ultimate freedom that all nations aspire to and develop to, but the freedom to achieve it'. He had no time for 'melodramatic defiance or self-sacrifice for something falsely said to exist, or for mere words and formalities which are empty... What we fought for at any particular time was the greatest measure of freedom obtainable at that time'.[25] For some, however, this smacked of expediency. Mary McSwiney voiced the distaste of the hard-line republicans for such pragmatism: 'The issue', she said,

> was not between peace and war; it is between right and wrong, and no man could salve his conscience talking about what is necessary for the peace of the country. I have said I stand here in the name of the dead...Principle is immortal and cannot die, and therefore those of us who stand on principle are among immortals not die-hards'. [26]

However it was not simply a split between principle and pragmatism. De Valera, for example, was not a die-hard; he did not oppose compromise. Much of his manoeuvering in the months before the treaty was signed was based on the assumption that some compromise was possible. In his correspondence with Lloyd George he had barely mentioned the republic. Earlier, before allowing his name to go forward for re-election as president, he expressly warned that he did not consider that the republican oath bound him to that form of government. It was only a commitment to do what he thought best for the Irish people. He would not be deterred from any proposal which he considered in the best interests of the people. He accepted office only on the understanding that no road was barred and that every method could be considered. He went so far as to say that those who could not agree might resign.[27] He was concerned to prepare the way for a settlement and to avoid a split with the die-hards. That was part of his thinking in not going to London.

De Valera, as Ronan Fanning puts it, opposed the treaty 'not because it was a compromise but because it was not *his* compromise'.[28] His compromise was external association. He had made some efforts to sell this option to Brugha and Stack in the expectation that it might be accepted by the British but might not be by die-hard republicans. It was only rather belatedly and half-heartedly put before the Dáil after the treaty had been signed, in the shape of the so called 'Document Number 2'. His main objection to the treaty was the oath which symbolised the continuance of British authority. As the division grew and the sides became polarised, the subtleties of his position were forgotten and he tended to take his stance on the high ground of 'the Republic'.

The treaty debates brought into the open divisions within the Sinn Féin movement which already existed but which were not so evident. These had begun to emerge almost as soon as negotiations began. As an umbrella organisation, it sheltered a range of outlooks, not all republican. These differences had been glossed over in the face of a shared enemy. For example, it came as no surprise that Arthur Griffith did not hold out for a republic. Nor were all of the differences ideological. Brugha and Collins had long since been on poor terms, partly because of Brugha's suspicion of the IRB and partly because of personal jealousy. Similarly, Stack had reason to dislike Collins and Mulcahy. Most importantly, relations between de Valera and Collins had not been good for some time, at least since de Valera suggested during the War of Independence that Collins should go to America. Collins had apparently been interested in going to London for the original negotiations with Lloyd George but had been overruled. When de Valera pushed him into going in October he suspected that he was being 'set up'. [29]

Such suspicions and rivalries can be exaggerated in retrospect but they did play a part in events. The personal disputes within the Irish delegation soured the atmosphere from the start and militated against them being an efficient negotiating team. They negotiated as much as individuals as members of a team and they confronted the dilemma of what to settle for in a similar fashion. Equally, de Valera's attitude to the treaty was not helped by his sense of exclusion. Although the delegates did have power to sign, it had been agreed that any proposed settlement would be referred back first. He felt personally hurt that the treaty was signed without reference to him and that he only learned its details belatedly. In similar circumstances but with a more united leadership, this problem might not have arisen.

There were also divisions between the politicians and the army. For obvious reasons, Collins carried huge weight in the army while de Valera, who was not closely involved in the military campaign, did not. He was seen as a figure-head by some, as a politician by others. When, during the truce, he attempted to assert Dáil control over the army his efforts created considerable resentment especially among those close to Collins who was in London at the time. De Valera's scheme would have placed the control of the army in the hands of Brugha, minister of defence, and in the process considerably reduced the independence of the army and the power of Collins. The treaty split put paid to the scheme.[30]

Another example of the rivalries which existed was the suspicion between those who were and those who were not members of the IRB. After 1916, the IRB was much less significant but, as we have seen, it did continue to exist and to exercise influence. It was to some extent an army within an army, run by Collins who owed much of his power to the IRB. Many of the key positions in the army were occupied by IRB men. There was no IRB conspiracy as is shown by the fact that it changed its constitution to facilitate recognition of the Dáil as the government of the republic rather than the IRB. But there was some ill feeling and suspicion among those on the outside. Collins saw the IRB as the real custodian of the republican tradition. Significantly it helped him to draw up a draft oath for presentation to Lloyd George. However, while there were accusations that the acceptance of the treaty was orchestrated by the IRB by putting pressure on TDs, the IRB itself was by no means unanimous about the Treaty. A majority on the supreme council supported it, but the organisation as a whole split. [31]

All these factors helped shape attitudes but they did not alone determine how people divided on the treaty. While the popularity of Collins may have ensured a more decisive majority in favour of the treaty in the Army and the IRB than in the Dáil, they did split. The only real pattern emerging in an analysis of the split in the army is that support for the treaty was highest at the top and opposition was highest at the bottom. [32]

This raises two other possible patterns, social and geographical. It has been suggested that opposition to the treaty was highest among the 'men of no property' while support came mainly from the middle class. There is some truth in this. It should hardly be surprising that those with a stake in the country should be more attracted by peace and stability than those who had little to lose. The business community, the farmers and professional bodies all supported the treaty. Likewise the catholic hierarchy welcomed the treaty while the lower ranks of the clergy were more evenly divided. Support was strongest in the east of the country and opposition strongest in the west. Significantly the opposition to the treaty was stronger among the small farmers and landless men of the west than among the farming community of the south where much of the Anglo-Irish war had centred. [33]

It would, however, be misleading to push this line of argument too far. Landless men were to be found on both sides as were professionals and businessmen. In the Dáil there was no clear pattern along class or occupational lines. A large majority of the professionals went pro-treaty while a large majority of the businessmen went anti-treaty. The financial clauses which had caused such difficulty when the various Home Rule bills were being drafted, and which were arguably of great significance for the new state, attracted little attention. Neither in the Dáil nor in the country was there any debate on the social and economic implications of the treaty and the labour movement remained officially neutral. Indeed the failure of the republican leadership to harness the social and economic dimension has often been commented on. [34]

It is clear that the treaty was popular in the country generally. De Valera accepted that the return of the TDs to their constituencies during the Christmas recess had helped swing the vote against the treaty as they came under strong pressure from their constituents to support the treaty.[35] Virtually every nationalist newspaper in the country welcomed it. Similarly the response from county councils and local bodies of all descriptions was overwhelmingly in favour.[36] It is more difficult however to gauge the reaction of those without a voice.

Perhaps the most striking feature of the debate on the treaty is the absence of any significant reference to partition. Anti-partitionism was later to become the major badge of republicanism but it is clear that at this time the northern issue was not a point of division between the parties. That is not to say that neither side was concerned with it. It was seen as another day's work. The northern question had long been ignored by Sinn Féin. The expulsion of catholic workers from the shipyards and the outbreak of sectarian rioting in the summer and autumn of 1920 provoked a boycott of Belfast goods which only added to northern unionist distrust. The establishment of a parliament in Belfast passed without any effective response from the south which was preoccupied with the Anglo-Irish war.

There is evidence that at least some of the nationalist leaders were by 1921 beginning to work out a more considered policy on the north. De Valera, for example, met Craig for talks in May. Although little was achieved, the fact that the meeting took place was itself significant. In August, he told the Dáil that the first priority was to establish contact. If Britain would recognise an Irish republic he would be willing to allow counties to vote themselves out. In other words he had arrived at the position espoused by Redmond at the Buckingham Palace conference, with the difference that the demand was now a republic, not Home Rule. De Valera argued that the only other alternative was to use force to coerce Ulster. This he thought would not work and would be to make the same mistake on Ulster as the British were making with Ireland.[37] While some of the northern deputies were not very happy with the Treaty's provisions for Ulster, de Valera specifically stated that this was not the source of the difficulty. As if to emphasise this, in Document Number 2, his alternative to the treaty, he accepted its terms in this area.

The settlements of 1920-22 could not have been predicted in 1886 or 1912. Dominion status was a major advance on Gladstonian Home Rule and really only became a viable alternative after the first world war and the rise of Sinn Féin. Paradoxically, however, the more successful Sinn Féin was in achieving its goal of 'ourselves alone', the more likely was partition. It has been argued that Sinn Féin in 1921 would have been better advised to push for unity rather than the republic.[38] Both Griffith and de Valera expressed a willingness to compromise to some extent on sovereignty for the sake of a united Ireland but ultimately the emphasis was on sovereignty rather than unity. Griffith accepted dominion status without unity while de Valera's complaint was that the treaty gave neither sovereignty nor unity. [39]

The aftermath of the treaty, the establishment of a provisional government and the slide into civil war are discussed in the next volumes of this series.[40] The dramatic events of 1921-2 saw the closing of one chapter in Irish history and Anglo-Irish relations and the opening of another. They mark the climax of one period and set the context for an independent and partitioned Ireland. In an era laden with tragic ironies, perhaps the greatest irony was that when the civil war, predicted by many as far back as 1912, finally came, it was between nationalist and nationalist rather than between nationalist and unionist. And the greatest tragedy was that its effect was, not to inaugurate a new era when attention would turn to other pressing issues, but to enshrine the national question on the agenda of Irish politics for at least another generation. In that sense, whatever their merits, the settlements of 1920-22 helped perpetuate division.

Notes

Chapter 1

1   G M Trevelyan, *English social history* (London, 1962), vii.

2   *Report of the royal commission appointed to inquire into the financial relations of Great Britain and Ireland*, pp 47-9, [Cd 8261], 1896, xxxiii; *Report of the committee on Irish finance*, pp 3-5, [Cd 6153], H.C. 1912-13, xxxiv; *Return relating to imperial revenue for the year ending 31st day of March 1913*, H.C. 1913 (199), xli. For a development of these points, see P Travers, 'The last years of Dublin Castle: the administration of Ireland 1890-1921', Australian National university Ph.D. thesis, 1981, pp 279-331.

3   R Barry O'Brien, *Dublin castle and the Irish people* (London, 1909), pp 25-6.

4   Ibid.

5   M Finnane, *Insanity and the insane in post-famine Ireland* (London, 1981), p.14.

6   Ibid., Appendix A.

7   M Daly, *Social and economic history of Ireland since 1800* (Dublin, 1981), p.104.

8   After 1920, emigration began to grow again but the rate remained under 10 per thousand until the early 1950s when it returned to levels close to the 1880s. W E Vaughan and A J Fitzpatrick, *Irish historical statistics: population 1821-1971* (Dublin, 1978), p 226.

9   Conflated from *Irish historical statistics: population* pp 261-3.

10   *Ireland and the Irish question: a collection of writings by K Marx and F Engels* (New York, 1972), quoted in D Fitzpatrick, 'Irish emigration in the later nineteenth century', *Irish historical studies*, xxii, no. 86 (Sept. 1980), 133.

11   Fitzpatrick, 'Irish emigration in the later nineteenth century', pp 127 and 137.

12   D Fitzpatrick, *Irish emigration 1801-1921* (Dublin, 1984), p.1.

13   *Irish historical statistics: population,* p.27.

14   L Kennedy, 'Farmers, traders and agricultural politics in pre-independence Ireland', in S Clark and J Donnelly Jr (eds), *Irish peasants* (Manchester, 1983; pbk 1987), p.342.

15   See W F Mandle, 'The Gaelic Athletic Association and popular culture 1884-1924', in O MacDonagh, W F Mandle and P Travers (eds) *Culture and nationalism 1750-1950* (London, 1983), pp 104-21 and 'Sport as politics: the Gaelic Athletic Association 1884-1916', in R Cashman and M McKernan (eds), *Sport in history* (Brisbane, 1980), pp 92-112.

16   See for example, B Coldrey, *Faith and fatherland: the Christian Brothers and Irish nationalism 1838-1921* (Dublin, 1988), pp 87-112 and 223-70.

17   *Irish historical statistics: population*, p.49.

18   J H Whyte, '1916: revolution and religion', in F X Martin (ed.), *Leaders and men of the easter rising: Dublin 1916* (London, 1967), p.221.

19   P Travers, 'The priest in politics: the case of conscription' in MacDonagh et al., *Culture and nationalism*, pp 161-81.

20   Quoted in *Irish Times*, 4 Feb. 1978.

21   J D Clarkson, *Labour and nationalism in Ireland* (New York, 1925), p.97.
22   Ibid., pp 192 and 201.
23   A Mitchell, *Labour in Irish politics 1890-1930* (London, 1974), p.21.
24   O MacDonagh, *Early victorian government* (London, 1976), p.196.

Chapter 2
1   See for example C Tennant, *Ireland and England, or the Irish land and church question* (London, 1868), pp 12-14.
2   *Irish historical statistics: population*, p.27; T W Moody, *Davitt and the Irish revolution 1846-82* (Oxford, 1981), p 560; J Macaulay, *Ireland in 1872* (London 1873), p.284; W E Vaughan, *Landlords and tenants 1848-1904* (Dublin, 1984), pp 3-5; P Buckland, *Irish unionism I: the Anglo-Irish and the new Ireland 1885-1902* (Dublin, 1972), xvi-xvii.
3   J H Morgan (ed.), *The new Irish constitution* (London, 1912), pp 174-8.
4   Vaughan, *Landlords and tenants* , p.14; M Daly, *Social and economic history of Ireland since 1800* (Dublin, 1981), p.39;   T Garvin, *The evolution of Irish nationalist politics* (Dublin, 1981), p.75.
5   Ibid.; D Fitzpatrick, 'Class, family and rural unrest in nineteenth century Ireland', in P J Drudy (ed.), *Ireland: land, politics and people* (Cambridge, 1982), pp 11-36.
6   M Davitt, *The fall of feudalism in Ireland* (London, 1904), p.77.
7   J S Donnelly, *The land and people of nineteenth century Cork* (London, 1975), pp 250-8; Vaughan, *Landlords and tenants*, pp 27-35; P Bew, *Land and the national question in Ireland, 1858-1882* (Dublin, 1978) pp 30-1; S Clark, *Social origins of the Irish land war* (Princeton, 1979), pp 246-303.
8   Clark, *Social origins*, pp 262-76.
9   Davitt, *Feudalism*, pp 125-6.
10   Ibid., pp 116-37; Moody, *Davitt*, pp 250-8; Lyons, *Parnell*, pp 80-1.
11   Moody, *Davitt*, p.289.
12   Ibid., p.291.
13   Davitt, *Feudalism*, pp 147-54; *Freeman's Journal*, 9 June 1879.
14   Morgan, *New Irish constitution*, pp 182-3; Davitt, *Feudalism*, pp 321-8.
15   Ibid., pp 358-64; T Corfe, *The Phoenix Park murders* (London, 1968), p,142; P J Tynan, *The Irish national invincibles and their times* (New York,1894), pp 271-3.
16   Morgan, *New Irish constitution*, pp 186-7.
17   L Geary, *The plan of campaign 1886-91* (Cork, 1986),pp 7-13; Davitt, *Feudalism*, p.516.
18   Ibid., pp 521-2; Geary, *Plan of campaign*, pp 128-9, 140-1, and 180; F S L Lyons, *John Dillon: A biography* (London, 1968), p.108.
19   Ibid., pp 226-8.
20   *Irish Times*, 3 Sept. 1902.
21   An act to amend the law relating to the occupation and ownership of land in Ireland...., *Public General Acts, 1903,* pp 187-225.
22   'Blue notes', 1920-21, Civil services, class iii, 17 (Irish Land Commission, pp 9-10, PRO, T 165/47; H C Debs, 4th Series, vol. 172, 1285; H L Debs, 4th Series, vol. 177, 272-86.
23   M Winstanley, *Ireland and the land question 1800-1922* (London, 1984), p.39.

24 'Unrest in Ireland', Memorandum, 18 June 1907, PRO, Cab 37/89/70. See also P Bew, *Conflict and conciliation in Ireland 1890-1910* (Oxford, 1987), pp 122-202.
25 L Ginnell, *The land question* (Dublin, 1917); *Irish Times*, 3 May 1920.
26 J W Boyle, 'A marginal figure: the Irish rural labourer', in S Clark and J S Donnelly Jr, *Irish peasants* (Manchester, 1983), pp 331-5; *Kildare Observer* 12 July and 23 Aug. 1920; D Fitzpatrick, 'The disappearance of the Irish agricultural labourer, 1841-1912', *Irish economic and social history*, vii (1969), pp 75, 81 and 88.
27 See, for example, B Solow, *The land question and the Irish economy 1870-1903* (Cambridge, Mass., 1971).

Chapter 3

1 M MacDonagh, *The home rule movement* (Dublin, 1920), pp 6-10; D Thornley, *Isaac Butt and home rule* (London, 1964), pp 92-3.
2 Ibid., p.91.
3 Butt, *Irish federalism* p 39. See also L McCaffrey, *Isaac Butt and the beginnings of home rule* (Philadelphia, 1962), p.11.
4 MacDonagh, *Home rule* p.13.
5 J Swift MacNeill (ed.), *Proceedings of the home rule conference* (Dublin,1873); Thornley, *Butt,* p 170.
6 McCaffrey, *Irish federalism*, p.19.
7 MacDonagh, *Home rule*, p.56.
8 Thornley, *Butt*, pp 219-21; McCaffrey, *Irish federalism*, pp 26-7.
9 *Nation*, 8 and 15 July 1876.
10 McCaffrey, *Irish federalism*, pp 31 and 37-8.
11 Ibid., pp 40-42.
12 *Nation,* 22 Feb. 1879.
13 Davitt, *Feudalism*, p.110; Lyons, *Parnell,* pp 15-41.
14 P Bew, *C S Parnell* (Dublin, 1980), p.36.
15 C C O'Brien, *Parnell and his party* (London, 1969), pp 119-33.
16 Ibid.
17 Ibid., p 143.
18 B Walker, 'The Irish electorate, 1868-1915', *IHS*, xviii, no.71 (March, 1973), 386-91; Lyons, *Parnell*, pp 266-8.
19 C C O'Brien, *Parnell*, pp16-17 and 152-3.
20 J Loughlin, *Gladstone, home rule and the Ulster question 1882-93* (London, 1986), pp 35-52.
21 Ibid.
22 Ibid.
23 *Nation*, 31 Jan.1885.
24 Quoted in G Morton, *Home rule and the Irish question* (London, 1980), pp 87-8.
25 *Freeman's Journal*, 6 Oct. 1885.
26 Loughlin, *Gladstone*, p.54.
27 For nationalist reaction to the Home Rule bill, see Loughlin, *Gladstone*, pp 293-4.
28 Lyons, *Parnell*, pp 452-64.
29 Davitt, *Feudalism*, pp 635-8.
30 Ibid; E W Hamilton, Diary, 1 Jan. 1890, B.L. Add. MS 48652.

31 Bew, *Parnell*, p.126; Davitt, *Feudalism*, pp 636-7.
32 R Barry O'Brien, *The life of Charles Stewart Parnell*, (London, 1899) ii, pp 158-9.; Davitt, *Feudalism*, p.636.
33 A bill to amend the provision for the future government of Ireland, 1-2, H.C. 1893-4 (209), iii, 255-71.
34 J McCarthy and Mrs Campbell Praed, *Our book of memories* (London, 1912), pp 325-7.

Chapter 4

1 The standard work on the subject is L P Curtis, *Coercion and conciliation in Ireland 1800-1892* (New Jersey,1963). For a recent reassessment, see A Gailey, *Ireland and the death of kindness* (Cork, 1987).
2 G Balfour, 'Unionist policy in relation to rural development in Ireland', in S Rosenbaum (ed.), *Against home rule: the case for union* (London, 1912), p.226.
3 *The Times*, 9 Mar. 1887.
4 For an elaboration of this argument, see Gailey, *Death of kindness,* pp 295-322.
5 'Blue notes', 1910-11, Class ii, 85 (Department of Agriculture), p 25, PROT165/36; R B McDowell, *The Irish administration*, p.220; W L Micks, *An account of the constitution, administration and dissolution of the congested districts board for Ireland from 1891 to 1923* (Dublin, 1925), p.18.
6 *Royal commission on the financial relations of Great Britain and Ireland, first report, evidence*, p.129, [Cd 7720-1], H.C. 1895, xxxvi.
7 See for example, G H Murray to under secretary, 8 Aug. 1905, 28 Feb. 1906, 21 Oct. and 13 Dec. 1907, 5 and 18 Mar. 1908, PRO, T 14/85/318, 1110-23, T 14/88/332-4, 545-6, 950-1 and 1014-5; Micks, *Congested districts board*, pp 162-3.
8 Ibid., p 150; 'Blue notes', 1920-21, Class ii, 37, pp 2-3.
9 Zetland to Balfour, 27 Oct.1890, Balfour Papers, B.L., Add.MS 49802, f.127.
10 Rosenbaum, *Against home rule*, pp 227-8; Davitt, *Feudalism*, p.663; H Plunkett, *Ireland in the new century,* (London, 1904), p.244; Wyndham to Balfour, 20 Sept. 1901, Balfour papers, B.L., Add. MS 49803, ff. 211-19.
11 'Blue notes', 1920-21, Class ii, 37 (Congested districts board), pp 2-5; Micks, *Congested districts board*, p.13; 'The Dudley report on congestion in Ireland', memorandum by Birrell, 2 June 1908, p.4, PRO, Cab.37/93/71.
12 Plunkett, *New century*, pp 244-5.
13 Ibid., p.220. For a detailed account of the establishment of the department, see ibid., pp 210-56.
14 Ibid., pp 220-24; Rosenbaum, *The case*, pp 234-5.
15 'Blue notes', 1920-21, Class ii, 35 (Department of agriculture and technical instruction) pp 1-2, PRO, T 165/46. Technical Instruction was defined as instruction in the principles of science and art applicable to industry. The department's powers in the area of fisheries were operable only outside the Congested Districts.
16 Ibid.; Plunkett, *New century*, pp 234-5. For the internal organisation of the department, see *Department of agriculture and technical instruction (Ireland), report of the committee of inquiry*, [Cd 3572], H.C. 1907, xxii.
17 Plunkett to Balfour, 23 June 1904, Balfour Papers, B.L., Add. MS 49792, ff 60-3; Plunkett, *New century*, pp 61-121 and 214-71.

18 McDowell, *Irish administration*, pp 226-7; Bryce to Campbell Bannerman, 15 and 17 Dec. 1905, Campbell-Bannerman papers, B.L., Add. MS 41240, ff 322-6; H.C. Debs, 4th series, clxxiii, 161 and 171-2.

19 R B O'Brien, *Dublin castle and the Irish people* (Dublin, 1909), pp 305-6; Plunkett, *New century*, pp 244-5; Micks, *Congested districts board*, pp 120-9.

20 Plunkett, *New century*, pp 175-209; Rosenbaum, *The case*, pp 230-34. For a first hand account of the growth of the IAOS see R A Anderson, *With Plunkett in Ireland* (London, 1935).

21 Plunkett, *New century*, p 190.

22 H C Debs, 4th series, clxxix, 160-83; McDowell, *Irish administration*, p. 229; Anderson, *With Plunkett*, pp 105-35.

23 Catherine Shannon, 'Arthur Balfour and the Irish question, 1874-1921', University of Massachusetts Ph.D. thesis, 1976, pp 57-65 and 'The Ulster liberal unionists and local government reform 1885-98', *IHS*, xviii, no. 73 (March 1973), pp 407-23; H.C. Debs, 4th series, vol. i, 726-95.

24 Gailey, *Death of kindness*, pp 40-50.

25 Local government act, elections. Returns, 1899, PRO, CO 904/184/1.

26 Ibid.

27 MacDonnell to Ripon, 17 and 27 Sept.1902, Ripon Papers, B.L., Add. MS 49804, ff 26-7 and 89-93; Dunraven, *The outlook in Ireland* (London, 1907), pp 288-90; 'Sir A.P MacDonnell, under-secretary for Ireland', memorandum by Long, 31 March 1905, PRO, Cab. 37/77/55.

28 *The Times*, 26 Sept. 1904.

29 *The Times*, 27 Sept. 1904; J W Mackail and G Wyndham, *The life and letters of George Wyndham* (London, 1925), pp 754-62; Memorandum by Long, 31 March 1905, PRO, Cab. 37/75/55; P B Allison, 'George Wyndham, romantic conservative 1863-1913', p.182, Ph.D. thesis, university of Rochester, 1974,.

30 MacDonnell to Ripon, 27 Feb. and 3 March 1905, Ripon Papers, B.L., Add. MS 43542, ff 127-9 and 132-5.

31 Long to Sandars, 15 March 1905, Balfour papers, B.L., Add. MS 49776.

32 P Buckland, *Irish unionism*, pp 15-28.

33 Ibid., pp 83-127.

34 E Bowen, *Bowen's Court and seven winters* (London, 1984), pp 435-7.

Chapter 5

1 T M Healy, *Letters and leaders of my day* (London, 1928), ii, p.423.

2 *Report of the royal commission appointed to inquire into the financial relations of Great Britain and Ireland*, [Cd 8262], 1896, xxxiii.

3 O'Brien, *An olive branch*, pp 110-11; Memorandum by Lord Cadogan, 26 July 1901, PRO, Cab. 37/57/72.

4 'Relief of distress in Ireland', memorandum by Gerald Balfour, 2 Nov. 1897, PRO, Cab. 37/45/41.

5 O'Brien, *An olive branch*, p.105.

6 Memorandum by Lord Cadogan, 26 July 1901, PRO, Cab 37/57/72. The figures for 1901 are for the seven month period to July only.

7 O'Brien, *An olive branch*, p.104.

8 Ibid., pp 101-25.

9 Ibid., pp xxii-xxxix.

10   H C Debs, 4th Series, clii, 19 Feb. 1906, 180-81
11   Ibid., 23, 28, and 180-93; D R Gwynn, *The life of John Redmond* (London, 1932), p.115.
12   'Note of an interview with Sir A. MacD.', n.d., Redmond papers, NLI, MS 15203; MacDonnell to Bryce, 9 Aug. 1906, Bryce papers, NLI, MS 11013; Bryce to MacDonnell, 13 Aug. 1906, MacDonnell papers, Bodl.,MS Eng. hist, f. 27; Dillon to Redmond, 17 Jan and O'Connor to Redmond, 27 Jan 1907, Redmond papers, NLI, MSS 15182 and 15215; Memoranda by MacDonnell and Birrell, 28 Feb, 5 Mar., and 27 Apr. 1907, PRO, Cab. 37/87/23, 36 and 54.
13   A C Hepburn, 'The Irish council bill and the fall of Antony MacDonnell', *IHS*, xvii, no. 68 (Sept. 1971), pp 486-7.
14   Ibid., p 478-9; MacDonnell to Ripon, 18 Apr. 1907, Ripon papers, B.L., Add. MS 43542, f.16.
15   Dillon to Morley, 19 Dec. 1906. Copy in Bryce papers, NLI, MS 11014; Memorandum by Birrell, 5 Mar. 1907, PRO, Cab. 37/87/26.
16   Birrell to Bryce, 17 June 1907, Bodl., Uncatalogued Bryce, U.B. 46.
17   Bryce to Alice Stopford Green, 23 May 1907, Bryce papers, NLI, MS 15070.
18   Morley to Campbell-Bannerman, 27 Dec. 1906, Campbell-Bannerman papers, B.L. Add. MS 41223, f.204.
19   'Unrest in Ireland', memorandum by MacDonnell, 18 June 1907, PRO, Cab. 37/89/70; Birrell to MacDonnell, 29 Aug. and 2 Sept. 1907, MacDonnell papers, Bodl., MS Eng. hist. c. 350, ff 15-6.
20   H C Debs, 4th series, clvii, 28 May 1906, 108-16.
21   H C Debs, 4th series, clii, 518-28; 782-86, 1525-54.
22   H C Debs, 4th series, clxxii, 369; clxxvii, 1265-79; clxxviii, 1232-56; clxxxi, 635; clxxxii, 181-5.
23   Memorandum by Bryce, 17 Dec. 1906, PRO, Cab. 37/85/99
24   Memoranda by Birrell, 19 Nov. 1907 and 2 June 1908, PRO, Cab. 37/85/99 and 93/71; MacDonnell to Birrell, Sept. 1907. Copy in Ripon papers, B.L., Add MS 43542, ff 203-7; Archbishop Walsh to MacDonnell, 20 Oct. 1906 and 4 Feb. 1907, MacDonnell papers Bodl., MS Eng. hist. c 351, ff 151-7.
25   Asquith to King, 10 Feb. and 13 Apr. 1910, PRO, Cab.41/32/45 and 40/9.
26   Ibid., 16 March 1910, PRO, Cab. 41/40/8.
27   P Jalland, *The liberals and Ireland* (London, 1980), pp 26-7.
28   Asquith to King, 25 October 1911, Cab. 41/33/27; Jalland, *The liberals*, p.30.
29   Asquith to King, 15 Dec. 1911, PRO, Cab. 41/33/33.
30   *Government of Ireland Act* in E Curtis and R B McDowell, *Irish historical documents 1172-1922* (London, 1943), pp 292-7.; Jalland, *The liberals,* pp 42-3.
31   Ibid., pp 44-8.
32   J Redmond, *Ireland and the war* (Dublin, 1915), pp 6-12; *The Times*, 4 and 16 Sept. 1914.
33   Rev. D O'Hara to Dillon, 30 Sept. 1914 TCD, Dillon papers; M MacDonagh, *The Irish at the front* (London, 1916) p.4; Memorandum by Eoin MacNeill on a meeting between Dillon and Kitchener, Bulmer Hobson papers, NLI, MS 13174/13; Lyons, *Dillon*, pp 360-1.
34   D Miller, *Church, state and nation in Ireland 1898-1921* (Dublin,1973), p.311.
35   Fogarty to Redmond, 3 June 1915, Redmond papers, NLI MS 15188.
36   *Royal commission on the rebellion in Ireland, evidence*, p.3, [Cd 8311], H.C. 1916, XI.

37   S Gwynn, *John Redmond's last years*, pp 158-218; D Gwynn, *John Redmond,* pp 411-5; Lyons, *John Dillon*, pp 362-3; Redmond to Birrell, 19 Apr. 1915, Redmond papers, NLI, MS 15,169.

38   MacDonagh, *Irish at the front*, pp 15-6.

39   Donovan (joint secretary of the volunteers) to Redmond, 7 Feb. 1917, Redmond papers, NLI, MS 15185.

40   Police reports on the volunteers, 1916, PRO, C.O. 904/23/5, p.73. Redmond to Donovan and Kettle (Joint Secretaries), 31 Oct. 1916; Donovan to Redmond 15 Nov. 1916, Redmond papers, MS 15185.

41   Donovan to Redmond, 7 Feb. 1917, Redmond papers, NLI, MS 15185; Moore to *Freeman's Journal*, 27 July 1917.

42   Kettle to *Freeman's Journal*, 27 Sept. 1916; Police reports 1916, C.O. 904/23/5, p 26.

43   Ibid, pp 4, 11-12, 21 and 26; C.O. 903/29/2; *Freeman's Journal* 27 July and 6 Aug. 1917.

44   Dillon to O'Connor, 19 Aug 1916, TCD, Dillon papers, 335.

45   Dillon to O'Connor, 21 Jan. 1918, TCD, Dillon papers, 435.

46   Ibid., 23 Apr. 1918, 468.

47   H C Debs, 5th Series, 11 Apr. 1918; 16 Apr. 1918, 321-4

48   F S L Lyons, *The Irish parliamentary party* (London, 1951), pp 158-76; J L Mc Cracken, *Representative government in Ireland* (London, 1958), pp 32-3.

Chapter 6

1   Quoted in P S O'Hegarty, *A history of Ireland under the union* (London, 1952), p 612.

2   Gavan Duffy, Dr Sigerson and D Hyde, *The revival of Irish literature* (Dublin, 1894), pp 117-19.

3   D P Moran, *The philosophy of Irish-Ireland* (Dublin, 1905), pp 30-1.

4   *United Irishman* , 15 March 1900.

5   O'Hegarty, *Ireland under the union,* p.641.

6   R Davis, *Arthur Griffith and non-violent Sinn Féin* (Dublin, 1974), pp 81-2.

7   L O'Broin, *Revolutionary underground: the story of the Irish republican brotherhood 1858-1924* (Dublin, 1976), pp 2-6.

8   Ibid., pp 20-21; Moody, *Davitt*, pp 250-66 and 325-6.

9   This account is based largely on Mandle, 'Sport as politics: the Gaelic Athletic Association 1884-1916' in Cashman and McKernan, *Sport in history,* pp 99-123.

10   Davis, *Sinn Féin*, p.54.

11   B Hobson, *History of the Irish volunteers* (Dublin, 1918), pp 108-28; O'Broin, *Revolutionary underground*, p.153.

12   Ibid.; *Royal commission on the rebellion, evidence*, p.5 [Cd 8279], H.C. 1916, xi.

13   O'Hegarty, *Ireland under the union*, p.687; Hobson, *Ireland yesterday and tomorrow* (Tralee, 1968), p.71.

14   R Dudley Edwards, *Patrick Pearse: the triumph of failure* (London, 1977), pp 173-84.

15   O'Broin, *Revolutionary underground*, p.167.

16   *Royal commission on the rebellion, evidence*, p.3.

17   Lord Longford and T P O'Neill, *Éamon de Valera* (London, 1970), pp 17-18.

18   Quoted in J D Clarkson, *Labour and nationalism in Ireland* (New York, 1925), p.307.
19   'Notes of an interview with Lord Midleton', 29 Feb. 1916, Ms. Nathan 369; Nathan to Birrell, 25 March 1916, Ms Nathan 466; Nathan Notebook, Ms Nathan, 475; L O'Broin, *Dublin castle and the 1916 rising* (London, 1966), pp 72-3.
20   Birrell to Nathan, 3 May 1916, MS Nathan 477; *Royal commission on the rebellion, evidence*, pp 6-10.
21   F X Martin, 'Eoin MacNeill and the easter rising', *IHS*, no. 47 (March,1961), 230 ff; O'Broin, *Revolutionary underground*, pp 169, 173.
22   G A Hayes-McCoy, 'A military history of the 1916 rising', in K B Nowlan (ed.), *The making of 1916: studies in the history of the rising* (Dublin, 1969), pp 266-7, 293 and 303.
23   PRO, CO 904/23/5, p.5.
24   PRO, C.O. 903/19, pp 52-5 and 903/105.
25   PRO, C.O. 904/23/3, pp 44 and 104.
26   P Beaslai, *Michael Collins and the making of a new Ireland* (London, 1926), p.166.
27   O'Broin, *Revolutionary underground*, p.180.
28   Darrell Figgis, *Recollections of the Irish war* (Dublin,1927), p.192; Liam Deasy, *Towards Ireland free* (Dublin,1973), p.18.
29   'Intelligence Notes', 1918.
30   PRO, C O 904/19, p.48, 904/107.
31   D Macardle, *The Irish republic* (Dublin, 1937), p.250.
32   P Travers, 'The priest in politics: the case of conscription', in MacDonagh et. al. *Culture and nationalism* pp 161-81.
33   Figgis, *Recollections*, pp 198-9; R Taylor, *Michael Collins* (London, 1958), p.96; Sinn Féin standing committee minute book, 10 Apr. 17 May,1918; Macardle, *The Irish republic*, p.273; Memorandum by Edward Shortt, 6 May 1918, PRO, Cab.24/50, G.T. 4452; Report of inspector general of the RIC, April 1918, PRO, C O 904/105.
34   Figgis, *Recollections*, p.193.
35   PRO, Cab. 23/4, W.C. 414A, 22 May 1918; *Documents relative to the Sinn Féin movement*, Cd. 1108, xxix, 429, 1921.
36   *Kerryman*, 19 Oct. 1918; *Nationality*, 23 Nov. 1918; Macardle, *Irish republic*, pp 842-5.
37   *Spectator*, 11 Jan. 1919; *Globe,* quoted in *Nationality*, 18 Jan. 1919; *Manchester Guardian*, 30 Dec. 1918.
38   McCracken, *Representative government in Ireland*, pp 32-3.
39   Democratic programme, First Dáil 1919.
40   *Kerryman*, 19 Oct. 1918; A. Griffith, Preface to L M Fogarty, *Fintan Lalor: patriot and political essayist*, p.ix.
41   D Breen, *My fight for Irish freedom* (Dublin, 1924), p.32; C Townshend, *The British campaign in Ireland 1919-21* (Oxford, 1975), p.16.

Chapter 7
1   Conflated from *Irish historical statistics : population*, pp 56, 66.
2   P Buckland, *Irish unionism two: Ulster unionism* (Dublin,1973), pp 22-5.
3   Ibid., pp 28-9.

4   P Bew and F Wright, 'The agrarian opposition in Ulster politics', Clark and Donnelly, *Irish peasants*, pp 211-27; B. Walker, 'The land question and elections in Ulster 1868-86', in ibid,, pp 243-53; Loughlin, *Gladstone*, p.31.
5   'The case of the Ulster protestants', memo. by Bryce, 12 Mar 1886, Gladstone Papers, BL Add.Ms 56447, ff 1-10.
6   W S Churchill, *Lord Randolph Churchill* (London, 1906), p.59.
7   R F Foster, *Lord Randolph Churchill* (Oxford, 1981), p.256.
8   H M Hyde, *Carson* (London, 1953), p.60.
9   Foster, *Churchill,* pp 253-6.
10   Loughlin, *Gladstone*, p.296
11   Ibid., pp 167-71.
12   J Bardon, *Belfast,an illustrated history* (Belfast, 1982) p. 150.
13   M W Dewar, *Orangeism* (Belfast, 1967), p.152.
14   Buckland, *Ulster unionism*, pp 15-17.
15   *Northern Whig*, 18 June 1892; Dewar, *Orangeism*, p.153; Loughlin, *Gladstone*, pp 280-1.
16   *Northern Whig*, 18 June 1893.
17   *Irish historical statistics: population*, p.35; Bardon, *Belfast*, pp 156-7.
18   Draft note from Balfour to Sandars, Balfour Papers, BL Add.MS 49763; memo. by Long, 28 Apr. 1905, Balfour Papers, BL Add.MS 49776, ff 56-7; *The Times*, 31 March 1905.
19   F S L Lyons,'The Irish unionist party and the devolution crisis of 1904-5', *IHS*, vi (1948/9), p.13.
20   Printed for Cabinet, Feb.1912. PRO, Cab.37/109/23.
21   Hyde, *Carson*, p.291.
22   Ibid.; Buckland, *Ulster unionism*, p.53.
23   Dewar, *Orangeism*, p 158; A T Q Stewart, *The Ulster crisis* (London, 1969), pp 54-7; R Blake, *The unknown prime minister* (London, 1955), p.129.
24   Stewart, *Ulster crisis*, p.62.
25   PRO, Cab.37/109/23, 30.
26   Jalland, *Liberals and Ireland*, pp.76, 207.
27   Ibid., p.213.
28   Ibid., pp 212-3; Asquith to George v; 27 Apr. and 2 May 1914. PRO Cab. 41/35/7and12.
29   Asquith to King, 12 March 1914, PRO, Cab. 41/35/7; Jalland, *Liberals and Ireland*, pp 222-4.
30   K Jeffery (ed.), *The military correspondence of Field Marshall Sir Henry Wilson* (London, 1985), pp 9-10.
31   Asquith to King, 15 Dec.1911, PRO, Cab. 41/33/33.
32   H Samuel, 'A Suggestion for the solution of the Ulster question', 18 Dec. 1913, PRO Cab.37/117/95; Asquith to King, 14 Nov.1913, PRO, Cab.41/34/34.
33   Asquith to King, 14 Nov. 1913 and 23 Jan. 1914, PRO, Cab. 41/34/36 and 36/6.
34   Asquith to King, 5 Mar.1914, PRO Cab.41/35/6.
35   H Nicholson, *George V* (London, 1952), Ch.xv. The following account of the conference is based on notes written by John Redmond. See D Gwynn, *The history of partition* (Dublin, 1950), pp 117-31.
36   See, for example, Jalland, *Liberals and Ireland*, p.254.
37   Asquith to King, 25 July 1914, PRO, Cab.41/35/20.

38   M Laffan, *The partition of Ireland* (Dublin, 1983), p.1.
39   H E D Harris, *The Irish regiments in the first world war* (Cork, 1968) pp 82-3, 221.
40   Devlin to Dillon, 15 May 1916, TCD, Dillon Papers.
41   Asquith to King 27 June, 5 July 1916, PRO Cab. 41/37/24 and 25; Memos by Landsdowne and Long, 21, 23 June, PRO Cab. 37/150/11and15.
42   Hyde, *Carson*, p.403.
43   Dillon to O'Connor, 334, 26 Sept. 1916, TCD, Dillon Papers.
44   Laffan, *Partition*, p.55.
45   For a detailed account of the Convention, see R B McDowell, *The Irish convention 1917-18* (London, 1970).
46   W.C.383, 5 Apr.1918, PRO, Cab. 23/6.
47   W.C.385,9, 6 and 11 Apr. 1918, PRO, Cab.23/5,6.
48   Carson to Lloyd George, 14 Feb. 1918, HLRO LG F/6/3/6; I Colvin, *The life of Lord Carson* (London, 1936) iii, 326. For a detailed discussion of federalism at this time, see J Kendle, 'Federalism and the Irish Question in 1918', *History*, lvi (1971), pp 207-30.
49   Colvin, *Carson*, pp 329-30.
50   T Jones, *Whitehall diary*, i, (London, 1969). p.61.
51   'Federalism': Memo. by Long, 9 May 1918, HLRO, L.G. F/32/5/35; Kendle, 'Federalism and the Irish question', p.225.
52   ibid., pp 215, 218-9; F Guest to Lloyd George, 3 Apr.1918, HLRO, L.G. F/21/2/20.
53   Committee on Home Rule, 16 Apr. and 9 May 1918, HLRO, L.G. F/68/22.
54   Memo. for cabinet,4 Nov.1919, PRO, Cab.27/68, CP 56.
55   Buckland, *Ulster unionism*, pp 115-19; Laffan, *Partition,* p.67.
56   Hyde, *Carson*, pp 445-6; Buckland, *Ulster unionism,* p.127.

Chapter 8

1   Punch 29 June 1921.
2   See, for example, Bonar Law to Stamfordham, 14 and 17 Sept.1919, HLRO, B.L.101/3/146and148.
3   Wilson to Milne, 14 May, 2 June 1920; Churchill to Wilson,25 June 1920, in Jeffery, *Henry Wilson,* pp 170,177,181.
4   Discussion on Ireland, 30 Apr.1920, PRO, Cab.23/21; Macready to Lloyd George, 1 May 1920, HLRO, L.G. F/36/2/13.
5   Reports by Fisher, 12,15 May 1920, HLRO L.G. F/31/1/32,33.
6   Cabinet, 21 May 1920, PRO, Cab.23/21.
7   Lord Longford, *Peace by ordeal* (London,.1935; pbk 1972), p.57; Greenwood to Lloyd George, 26 Jan.1921, HLRO, L.G. F/19/3/2.
8   Jones, *Whitehall diary,* pp 74-5; Cabinet, 24 June 1921, PRO, Cab. 23/26.
9   Cabinet, 9,13,24,29 Dec.1920, PRO, Cab.23/23.
10   Mark Sturgis diary, 13 June 1921, PRO 39/50/4; Jones, *Whitehall diary,* p. 60.
11   Lord Longford and T. O'Neill, *Éamon de Valera* (London, 1974), pp 124-30.
12   Ibid., *De Valera*, p 138; T Ryle Dwyer, *Éamon de Valera* (Dublin, 1980), p.43.
13   De Valera to Lloyd George, 19 Sept.1921, *Dáil Éireann, Official correspondence relating to the peace negotiations* (Dublin,1921).

14   Lloyd George to de Valera, 29 Sept. 1920; de Valera to Lloyd George, 30 Sept.1920, ibid.
15   See, for example, De Valera to J.McGarrity, 27 Dec.1921, NLI, McGarrity Papers, Ms 17440.
16   Longford and O'Neill, *De Valera*, pp 145-6; Ryle Dwyer, *De Valera*, p.46.
17   O MacDonagh, *Ireland, the union and its aftermath* (London, 1977), p. 106.
18   *Dáil Éireann (private sessions)*, 14 Sept.1921, pp 94-5.
19   De Valera to McGarrity, 27 Dec. 1921, NLI, McGarrity papers, MS 17440 L O'Broin, *Michael Collins* (Dublin, 1980), pp 90-92.
20   Lord Birkenhead, *F E Smith* (London, 1959), pp 382-3.
21   Longford and O'Neill, *De Valera*, pp 152-4.
22   Ibid., pp 160-2; Ryle Dwyer, *De Valera*, p.53; O'Broin, *Collins*, pp 104-5.
23   Quoted in O'Broin, *Collins*, p.113.
24   For the full text of the treaty, see E Curtis and R B McDowell, *Irish historical documents* (London, 1943).
25   P Beaslai, *Collins*, ii, 321 and 426-7. *Dáil Éireann,treaty debates*, 19 Dec. 1921 and 7 Jan.1922, pp 30-6 and 303-4.
26   *Dáil Éireann 1921-2 (private sessions)*, p.248.
27   Ibid.,pp 57-9.
28   R Fanning, *Independent Ireland* (Dublin, 1983), p.3.
29   Beaslai, *Collins*, p.276; Notes on the differences between Cathal Brugha and Stack and other members of the Volunteer Executive and Cabinet, UCDA, Mulcahy Papers, P 7/D/96;Longford and O'Neill, *De Valera*, pp 147-8; O'Broin, *Collins*, p.89.
30   Dáil Cabinet, 15 Sept., 25 Nov. 1921, SPO, DE1/3.
31   De Valera to McGarrity, 27 Dec.1921, NLI, McGarrity Papers, Ms 17440; Mulcahy note, 29 Oct.1963, UCDA, Mulcahy Papers P7/D/3. O'Broin, *Revolutionary underground,* pp 195-205.
32   E Rumpf and A C Hepburn, *Nationalism and socialism in twentieth century Ireland* (Liverpool, 1977), p.35
33   Ibid., pp 28-68.
34   E Strauss, *Irish nationalism and British democracy* (London,.1951) pp 265-71.
35   De Valera to McGarrity 27 Dec. 1987, NLI, McGarrity Papers, Ms.17440.
36   Clarkson, *Labour and nationalism*, p.450.
37   *Dáil Éireann (private sessions)* p.39; see also J. Bowman, *De Valera and the Ulster question* (Oxford,1982) pp 47,55.
38   J A Murphy, *Ireland in the twentieth century* (Dublin,.1975) p.38.
39   H Nicholson, *George V* (1952) p.357; Longford and O'Neill, *De Valera*, p.152.
40   Fanning, *Independent Ireland*, pp 1-39; D Harkness, *Northern Ireland since 1920* (Dublin,.1983), pp 1-21.

Bibliographical note

General surveys:

The most comprehensive general survey of the period is F S L Lyons, *Ireland since the famine* (London, 1971). Briefer but more stimulating are O MacDonagh, *Ireland: the union and its aftermath* (rev. ed. London, 1977); J Lee, *The modernisation of Irish society 1848-1918* (Dublin, 1973).

Government and society:

For an introduction to the social and economic history of the period, see M E Daly, *Social and economic history of Ireland since 1800* (Dublin, 1981); L M Cullen, *Life in Ireland* (London, 1968); L M Cullen, *An economic history of Ireland since 1660* (London, 1972). For the administration of Ireland, see R B McDowell, *The Irish administration 1801-1914* (London, 1964); E O' Halpin, *The decline of the union* (Dublin, 1987). On insanity, see M Finnane, *Insanity and the insane in post famine Ireland* (London, 1981). The best recent summary of Irish emigration is D Fitzpatrick, *Irish emigration 1801-1921* (Dublin, 1984). On religion see S J Connolly, *Religion and society in nineteenth century Ireland* (Dublin, 1985); R B McDowell, *The church of Ireland 1869-1979* (London, 1975); D Keenan, *The church in nineteenth century Ireland* (Dublin, 1983); D W Miller, *Church, state and nation in Ireland, 1898-1921* (Dublin, 1973). The best recent survey of Irish education is J Coolahan, *Irish education: its history and structure* (Dublin, 1981). see also D H Akenson, *The Irish educational experiment* (London, 1970); N Atkinson, *Irish education: a history of educational institutions* (Dublin, 1969). The best modern treatment of the importance of the GAA is W F Mandle, *The Gaelic Athletic Association and Irish nationalist politics 1884-1924* (London, 1984). On Irish labour, see A Mitchell, *Labour in Irish politics 1890-1930* (London, 1974); E Larkin, *James Larkin, Irish labour leader, 1876-1947* (London, 1961); R Dudley Edwards, *James Connolly* (Dublin, 1981); A Morgan, *James Connolly: a political biography* (Manchester, 1988).

Land:

This area has undergone a process of 'relentless revisionism' in the last twenty years. For an up to date summary see W E Vaughan, *Landlords and tenants in Ireland 1848-1904* (Dublin, 1984); M J Winstanley, *Ireland and the land question 1848-1922* (London, 1984). In depth studies include J S Donnelly, *The land and people of nineteenth century Cork* (London, 1975); P Bew, *Land and the national question in Ireland 1858-1882* (Dublin, 1978); S Clark, *Social origins of the Irish land war* (Princeton, 1979); B Solow, *The land question and the Irish economy 1870-1903* (Cambridge, Mass, 1971); E D Steele, *Irish land and British politics* (Cambridge, 1974); S Clark and J S Donnelly Jr, *Irish peasants* (London, 1983); L Geary, *The plan of campaign 1886-1891* (Cork, 1986). For Davitt, see T W Moody, *Davitt and the Irish revolution 1846-1882* (Oxford, 1981). Davitt's own account of the period,

The fall of feudalism in Ireland (London, 1904), is still well worth reading.

Home Rule:

There is a need for a good, modern account of Home Rule. The best approach is through the various biographies: D Thornley, *Isaac Butt and Home Rule* (London, 1964); F S L Lyons, *Charles Stewart Parnell* (London, 1974); P Bew, *C S Parnell* (Dublin, 1980); R Foster, *Charles Stewart Parnell: the man and his family*; M Hurst, *Parnell and Irish nationalism* (London, 1968). C C O'Brien, *Parnell and his party* (London, 1969); G Morton, *Home rule and the Irish question* (London, 1980); J. Loughlin, *Gladstone, home rule and the Ulster question 1882-1893* (Dublin, 1986); J L Hammond, *Gladstone and the Irish nation* (London, 1938); L McCaffrey, *Isaac Butt and the beginnings of home rule* (Philadelphia, 1962).

New conservatism and the Anglo-Irish twilight:

For the new conservatism in Europe, see J Weiss, *Conservatism in Europe 1770-1945* (London, 1977). The standard work on constructive unionism is L P Curtis, *Coercion and conciliation in Ireland 1800-1892* (New Jersey, 1963). The most recent treatment is A. Gailey, *Ireland and the death of kindness* (Cork, 1987). Plunkett's *Ireland in the new century* (London, 1904, reissued in 1970 by Kennikat Press) is the best summary of his philosophy. P Buckland's *Irish unionism: the Anglo-Irish and the new Ireland 1885-1922* (Dublin, 1972) is the best account of the Anglo-Irish in decline.

The Irish party after Parnell:

The standard work is F S L Lyons, *The Irish parliamentary party 1890-1910* (London, 1951). See also his *John Dillon* (London, 1968). William O'Brien's *An olive branch in Ireland and its history* (London, 1910) provides a first hand account of many of the events dealt with here. A modern biography of Redmond is long overdue, but see D.R. Gwynn, *The Life of John Redmond* (London, 1932). P. Bew's *Conflict and conciliation in Ireland 1890-1910* (Oxford, 1987) is an innovative and somewhat contentious account of constitutional nationalism in the period. For the Home Rule crisis 1912-14 see P Jalland, *The Liberals and Ireland* (London, 1980).

New Nationalism:

On Irish nationalism generally see D G Boyce, *Nationalism in Ireland* (London, 1982); T. Garvin, *The evolution of Irish nationalist politics* (Dublin, 1981) and *Nationalist revolutionaries in Ireland* (Oxford, 1987). P S O'Hegarty's *A history of Ireland under the union* (London, 1952) remains an invaluable source. On Sinn Féin, see R Davis, *Arthur Griffith and non-violent Sinn Féin* (Dublin, 1974). The best account of the IRB is L O'Broin, *Revolutionary underground: the story of the Irish republican brotherhood 1858-1924* (Dublin, 1976). On 1916, see L O'Broin, *Dublin castle and the 1916 rising* (London, 1970); K B Nowlan (ed.), *The making of 1916: studies in the history of the rising* (Dublin, 1969); F X Martin (ed.), *Leaders and men of the easter rising: Dublin 1916* (Dublin, 1967). In addition there are several useful biographies, notably R Dudley Edwards, *Patrick Pearse: the triumph of failure* (London, 1977) ; Lord Longford and T P O'Neill, *Éamon de Valera* (London, 1970); L O'Broin, *Michael Collins* (Dublin, 1980). For the Anglo-Irish War see C Townshend, *The British campaign in Ireland* (Oxford, 1973); G Dangerfield, *The damnable question* (London, 1979); D G Boyce,

Englishmen and Irish troubles: British public opinion and the making of Irish policy 1918-1922 (London, 1972); D Macardle, *The Irish republic* (Dublin, 1937). For the impact on the localities, see D Fitzpatrick, *Politics and Irish life 1913-1921* (Dublin, 1977).

Ulster:

P Buckland's *Irish unionism two: Ulster unionism* (Dublin, 1973) is a good survey. See also Loughlin's *Gladstone*; A T Q Stewart, *The Ulster crisis* (London, 1969); M Laffan, *The partition of Ireland* (Dublin, 1983); and the various biographies, notably R F Foster, *Lord Randolph Churchill* (Oxford, 1981); H M Hyde, *Carson* (London, 1953); P Buckland, *James Craig* (Dublin, 1980).

The Treaty:

The standard work remains Lord Longford, *Peace by ordeal* (London, 1935; pbk 1972). See also R Fanning, *Independent Ireland* (Dublin, 1983); O'Broin, *Collins*; J Bowman, *De Valera and the Ulster question 1917-1973* (Oxford, 1982); Macardle, *The Irish republic* (Dublin, 1937).

Index